D0045167

# BEGINNER'S GRAMMAR OF THE GREEK NEW TESTAMENT

WILLIAM HERSEY DAVIS, M.A., Th.D.

# BEGINNER'S GRAMMAR
## OF THE
# GREEK NEW TESTAMENT

BY

## WILLIAM HERSEY DAVIS, M.A., Th.D.

ASSOCIATE PROFESSOR OF NEW TESTAMENT INTERPRETATION
IN THE SOUTHERN BAPTIST THEOLOGICAL SEMINARY
LOUISVILLE, KENTUCKY

HarperSanFrancisco

*A Division of* HarperCollins*Publishers*

ISBN: 0-06-061710-1

94 95 96 HAD 56 55 54 53 52 51 50

# INTRODUCTION

It gives me the greatest pleasure to write some words of an introductory nature to the *Beginner's Grammar of the Greek New Testament* by my beloved colleague, Dr. W. H. Davis. The need of this book is urgent. Hardly a week goes by that I am not asked to recommend such a book to young ministers, to pastors, to laymen, to women, many of whom wish to learn how to read the Greek New Testament without the advantage of a teacher. There are a number of grammars that undertake to do this thing, but they all start in the wrong way, except Moulton's *Introduction*, which is not well suited to American schools.

It is a curious thing how traditionalism in linguistic teaching has held in slavery so many men who teach Greek today precisely as it was done a hundred years ago. The revolutionary progress made by Brugmann and Delbrück in comparative philology is left to one side for technical scholars. Professor Davis starts the student right. The standpoint of Thumb's revision of Brugmann's *Griechische Grammatik* is presented with clearness and precision. The student who starts with Davis's *Beginner's Grammar* can go right on to my *Short Grammar of the Greek New Testament* without a break or jolt. Then he will be ready for my *Grammar of the Greek New*

*Testament in the Light of Historical Research*. It is
only a step further to the Brugmann-Thumb *Griechische Grammatik* and in the same direction. In
my experience of thirty-five years as a teacher of
the Greek New Testament I have always had numbers of men who floundered over the cases, the prepositions, the tenses, the voices, the modes, because
they had learned these basal things in the old un-
scientific way. It is like pulling eye-teeth for such
a one to learn that the genitive is not the whence-
case, but only the case of kind or genus, and that
the ablative is the whence-case. If one gets it into
his head that the root idea of tense is time, he may
never get it out and he will therefore never understand the beauty of the Greek tense, the most won-
derful development in the history of language.
Professor Davis is absolutely at home in the new
science of language and, I may add, is the most
brilliant student of Greek that I have ever had. One
should, if possible, take the college course in ancient
Greek. He needs this background and this contact
with the glorious period of the Greek language. But
the New Testament is the chief glory of the Greek
tongue, and one can begin it in the right way under
Professor Davis's tutelage.

Professor Davis is a master of the papyri and so
of the Koiné in which the New Testament books
are written. He is not giving the grammar of the
literary Attic, but the grammar of the Koiné of the
first century A.D. This fact is the second linguistic
discovery that has revolutionized the study of the
Greek New Testament. Comparative philology and

the papyri discoveries have put the old grammars out of date and all the new ones that ignore the tremendous progress thus made. It is now known that the Greek of the New Testament is not literary Attic nor is it a peculiar Hebrew jargon or sacred Greek dialect. At bottom it is simply straight Koiné of the first century A.D. like that found in the inscriptions of Asia Minor and in the papyri of Egypt. The papyri give us many thousands of examples of the language of the life of the first century A.D. in Egypt. There are business contracts, bills, deeds, marriage contracts, wills, decrees, love letters, business correspondence, anything and everything that made up the life of the people of the time. These relics preserve the language of people of all degrees of culture. The Koiné means the language common to people everywhere, not merely the language of the common people. It was the means of communication all over the Roman Empire. The most of the papyri examples give the vernacular form of the Koiné, but there are specimens of the literary Koiné also. The New Testament is mainly in the vernacular Koiné, but it is the vernacular of men of great ability and some of them have a decided literary flavor, as we see in the writings of Luke, the Epistles of Paul, the Epistle to the Hebrews.

Language changes with the years if it is alive. Changes occur in the meaning of words, and here the papyri give very great help in showing what the words of the New Testament meant in everyday life. Dr. Davis himself has found over two thousand words in the papyri not given in any of the

Greek lexicons. But the forms of the Koiné show numerous changes from those in the Attic. Dr. Davis's *Grammar* gives the forms of the Koiné, not of the Attic Greek. Syntax shows some changes also, and these are given rightly.

There are Hebraisms and Aramaisms in the Greek New Testament, but the number is nothing like so great as was once thought to be the case. It is natural that Jews who spoke and wrote the Koiné should reveal here and there familiarity with Hebrew and Aramaic. Even Luke, probably a Greek, has the ear-marks of Aramaic sources and of knowledge of the Septuagint. But, in the main, the New Testament is written in the current Koiné, as one would expect.

It should be added that Dr. Davis confines himself to a Beginner's Grammar. He does not try to teach the ancient Attic on the one hand nor to go over the ground of my *Short Grammar* on the other. He definitely undertakes to prepare students for the *Short Grammar*, and he does it with consummate skill. He supplies in masterly fashion the book that was needed. He will smooth the path for the beginner in the Greek New Testament. He will make it so easy that one will wonder why he was so long starting on the road that leads one into the heart of the greatest of all the books of earth, the Greek New Testament.

A. T. ROBERTSON

*Louisville, Ky.*

# NOTE TO FIFTH EDITION

In the present edition various corrections and a few additions have been incorporated. A revised and enlarged edition is planned to appear when circumstances warrant it. I thank my colleague, Dr. E. A. McDowell, Jr., for corrections and valuable suggestions. He is at work on a Koine reader which may be used in conjunction with the Grammar.

W. HERSEY DAVIS

*Louisville, Kentucky,*
*1942*

# PREFACE

Dr. A. T. Robertson wrote in the Preface to his *Short Grammar of the Greek New Testament*: "Three types of New Testament grammars are needed: a beginner's grammar for men who have had no Greek training, an advanced and complete grammar for scholars and more critical seminary work, an intermediate handy working grammar for men familiar with the elements of Greek both in school and in the pastorate." This book is designed to meet the need for the first type. It is intended for those who are beginning the study of the Greek New Testament or have an imperfect knowledge of the essentials of the Greek of the New Testament, and to serve as a preparation for *A Short Grammar of the Greek New Testament* (A. T. Robertson).

The book is a beginner's book. It is the result of class-room experience of many years. The need and preparation of a beginner's class in Greek has determined the method and order of presentation. The Greek of the New Testament is the Koiné of the first century A.D. It is presented as such in this book. The historical development of the Greek language has been kept in mind.

No forms or words are given which do not occur in the Greek New Testament. All illustrations and sentences for translation have been taken from the

New Testament. Those words which are of the most frequent occurrence are presented first.

In this book especial stress has been laid upon the meaning of the cases, the prepositions, and the tenses, wherein most beginner's books have been faulty. The author wishes to record his great indebtedness to his teacher, Professor A. T. Robertson, D.D., LL.D., of the Southern Baptist Theological Seminary, for instruction and for invaluable assistance. Without his encouragement the work would not have been begun nor would it have been brought to completion. Whatever of worth this book may have, it owes much (if not all) to his rare scholarship and experience of many years as a teacher of the Greek New Testament. In fact his monumental work *A Grammar of the Greek New Testament in the Light of Historical Research* is the authority from which this book drew at all points. Of course he is not at all responsible for any faults or errors which this book may contain.

The names of many writers whose works were consulted, the author cannot here recount, except Brugmann-Thumb (*Griechische Grammatik*).

In conclusion the author wishes here to express his thanks to his colleague, Professor F. M. Powell, A.M., Th.D., for valuable criticisms of a great part of the book in manuscript, to his friend, Dr. A. R. Bond, for expert criticism and preparation of the Index, and to his father, Rev. Q. C. Davis, Albemarle, N.C., for his sympathy and guidance.

W. HERSEY DAVIS

*Louisville, Ky.*

# CONTENTS

# CONTENTS

## PART II: SUPPLEMENT TO PART I

# PART I: LESSONS

# BEGINNER'S GRAMMAR OF THE GREEK NEW TESTAMENT

## LESSON I

### The Alphabet

**1.** The Greek alphabet had in the Koiné or Hellenistic period twenty-four letters.

| Form of capital letters | Name | Form of small letters | Sounded as [1] |
|---|---|---|---|
| A | alpha | α | a in *fa*ther |
| B | beta | β | b in *boy* |
| Γ | gamma | γ | g in *go* |
| Δ | delta | δ | d in *d*ay |
| E | epsilon | ε | e (short) in m*e*t |
| Z | zeta | ζ | z in da*z*e |
| H | eta | η | { e in f*ê*te / a in m*a*te |
| Θ | theta | θ | th in *th*in |
| I | iota | ι | { i in pol*i*ce / i in f*i*t |

[1] The sounds adopted as equivalent to the vowels in Greek are given for the sake of a consistent method of pronunciation. Already in the first century A.D. some of the vowels and diphthongs were sometimes pronounced alike, as in Modern Greek, and consequently were confused: thus ει, ι, η, ῃ, υ, υι, οι (being pronounced alike) were sometimes written one for another; so with ε and αι, and ο and ω. The confusion of vowels and diphthongs of *ē* sound is called *itacism*.

There is clear evidence that in the first century A.D., β had the twofold pronunciation of *b* and *v* (labiodental), as in Modern Greek, and γ had begun to have the value of *y* (the *j* value of *i* before *e* and *i* sounds).

19

| Form of capital letters | Name | Form of small letters | Sounded as |
|---|---|---|---|
| K | kappa | κ | k in *k*eep |
| Λ | lambda | λ | l in *l*ed |
| M | mu | μ | m in *m*an |
| N | nu | ν | n in *n*et |
| Ξ | xi | ξ | x in la*x* |
| O | omicron | ο | o (short) in *o*mit |
| Π | pi | π | p in *p*eg |
| P | rho | ρ | r in *r*un |
| Σ | sigma | σ ς | s in *s*it |
| T | tau | τ | t in *t*en |
| Υ | upsilon | υ | u in Fr. t*u*, Ger. T*ü*r |
| Φ | phi | φ | ph in gra*ph*ic |
| X | chi | χ | ch in Ger. i*ch*, Scotch lo*ch* *ch*asm |
| Ψ | psi | ψ | ps in to*ps* |
| Ω | omega | ω | ō (long) in n*o*te |

*a.* At the end of a word sigma is written ς, elsewhere σ; as in σεισμός.

At first learn the form of the small letters only. Write each letter many, many times, pronouncing its name each time, until the whole alphabet can from memory be uttered and written without hesitation.

**2.** Every Greek word has as many syllables as it has separate vowels or diphthongs.

Learn the sound of each letter.

Pronounce aloud the following words:

| | | | |
|---|---|---|---|
| θε-λω, | the-lō | γρα-φη, | gra-phē |
| νο-μος, | no-mos | λε-γω, | le-gō |

| βλε-πω, | ble-pō | σω-ζω, | sō-zō |
| φι-λος, | phi-los | κοσ-μος. | kos-mos |
| νυξ, | nux | ε-χω, | e-chō |
| α-δελ-φος, | a-del-phos | ψυ-χη, | psu-chē |
| αν-θρω-πος, | an-thrō-pos | θε-λη-μα | the-lē-ma |

## LESSON II

### Vowels, Diphthongs, Breathing

**3.** There are seven vowels: α, ε, η, ι, ο, υ, ω. η is the long form of ε, and ω is the long form of ο; ε and ο are always short, η and ω always long. This list, then, corresponds in a way to the English a, e, i, o, u. α, ι, υ are sometimes long and sometimes short; the long and short forms are not distinguished by separate characters.

**4.** A diphthong is two vowel sounds fused into one. The diphthongs are:

αι = ai in *ai*sle      ου = ou in gr*ou*p

αυ $\begin{cases} = \text{au in Ger. h}au\text{s} \\ = \text{ou in h}ou\text{se} \end{cases}$      ευ = eu in f*eu*d

ει = ei in h*ei*ght      ηυ = approximately the same sound as ευ.

οι = oi in *oi*l      υι = we

Also there are ᾳ, ῃ, ῳ; but the ι (iota written underneath a vowel is called 'iota-subscript') does not affect the sound of the vowel.

**5.** Many Greek words begin with a sound equivalent to the English *h*. This sound is indicated by writing a sign (῾) called the rough breathing over a vowel or

diphthong at the beginning of a word (over the
second vowel of a diphthong). Thus ὁδος=hodos;
εὑρισκω=heurisko. If an initial vowel or diphthong
is not pronounced with an *h*, the sign ('), called the
smooth breathing, is written over it. Thus ἀκουω=
akouo; οὐρανος=ouranos. Initial υ always has the
rough breathing.

**6.** Write the following in English (Roman) letters in
accordance with the equivalents given in 1 and 4.

βαλετε εἰς τα δεξια μερη του πλοιου το δικτυον και
εὑρησετε. τις ἀρα οὑτος ἐστιν; ἡ ψυχη αὑτου ἐφοβηθη. οἱ
ἀνθρωποι ἐξηλθον ἐκ του οἰκου.

Write the following words in Greek characters:
kai palin ērxato didaskein para tēn thalassan. kai
sunagetai pros auton ochlos pleistos, hōste auton eis
ploion embanta kathēsthai. periblepsamenos autous
legei ide hē mētēr mou kai hoi adelphoi mou.

## LESSON III

### Accent

**7.** Most Greek words are written with accents.
The accents are the acute ('), the grave (`), and the
circumflex (˜). Thus, λαμβάνει τὸν δοῦλον; ἀκούω τῆς
φωνῆς. On inspection it will be noticed that the
accent stands over the vowel of the accented syllable,
and in a diphthong over the second vowel.

**8.** To us in English accent means a stress of the
voice. Also to the native Greeks of today it means
simply stress of voice. Originally, however, accents
indicated the tone or pitch of the voice in pronouncing syllables.

In pronunciation we make no distinction between the accents.

**9.** The last syllable of a word is called the ultima; the next to the last, the penult; and the one before the penult, the antepenult.

**10.** Learn the following verbs:

| | | | |
|---|---|---|---|
| ἄγω, | I lead, bring, go | θέλω, | I wish, will |
| ἀκούω, | I hear | λαμβάνω, | I take, receive |
| βλέπω, | I see, look at | λέγω, | I say |
| γινώσκω, | I know | πέμπω, | I send |
| γράφω, | I write | πιστεύω, | I believe |
| εὑρίσκω, | I find | ἔχω, | I have, hold |

Write and pronounce aloud each of these words (with the proper breathing and accent) fifteen to twenty times, associating with each word its meaning, as

ἄγω, á-gō, *I lead*.   Notice how the breathing and accent are written together when they occur on the same syllable.

ἀκούω, a-koú-ō, *I hear*.   Observe that the accent is written over the second vowel of the diphthong ου.  See 7.[1]

**11.** Observe that: 1. Every initial vowel or diphthong has a breathing. 2. The acute accent stands on the penult. The accent of verbs is generally thrown as far back as possible from the last syllable. This is known as *recessive* accent. Here the position of the accent is determined by the last syllable:

[1] Sections in the Lesson Part are referred to by the simple number (as 7). Sections in the Part dealing with Etymology are referred to by a section sign (§) before the number (as § 6).

(1) If the last syllable is long, the accent falls on the penult. (2) If the last syllable is short, the accent falls on the antepenult. (3) A syllable is long if it contains a long vowel or diphthong; otherwise it is short. 3. The ending -ω in each of these words has the force of the personal pronoun *I* in English.

**12.** 1. In Greek the endings of verbs generally express the different persons, as *I, thou (you), he, we, ye (you), they.* What is the ending of each verb in 10? The endings of verbs denoting person are called *personal endings;* they are fragments of old pronouns and are inseparable from the verb. But in English the personal pronouns are separate from the verb and are generally written before it.

In the case of most verbs the original personal endings in the singular of the present indicative are no longer apparent in the forms of the -ω-verbs.

2. The verb affirms action (including "state"). A Greek verb has tense, mode, and voice. Tense expresses the state of the action of the verb; mode gives the manner of affirmation of the verb, how it is made; voice tells how the action of the verb is related to the subject. Verbs indicate affirmation by the personal endings.

The student should now begin to make a Greek-English and an English-Greek vocabulary arranged according to the alphabet. A good note book of convenient size should be used.

## LESSON IV

**13.** Present Indicative Active

1. λέγ-ω, *I am saying,* λέγ-ο-μεν, *we are saying,*
   *I say* *say*
2. λέγ-εις, *you are say-* λέγ-ε-τε, *ye are saying,*
   *ing, say* *say*
3. λέγ-ει, *he, she, or it* λέγ-ουσι, *they are say-*
   *is saying, says* *ing, say*
   Infinitive, λέγ-ειν, *to be saying, to say*

**14.** Only in the indicative mode in Greek do the tenses show time absolutely. The main idea of tense is the *"kind of action,"* the state of action. Even in the indicative time is a secondary idea. Continued action, or a state of incompletion, is denoted by the present tense,—this kind of action is called *durative* or *linear*. The action of the verb is shown in progress, as *going on*. Observe that the indicative mode in Greek has practically the same declarative force as it has in English. In 13 the subject is represented as acting.

**15.** To conjugate a verb is to give all the variations in its terminations in the proper order. As given in 13, λέγω is said to be conjugated in the present indicative active and present infinitive active.

**16.** Observe in the conjugation of λέγω: 1. The stem λεγ- remains unchanged throughout. 2. A vowel follows this stem. 3. The vowel is o before endings that begin with μ or ν, and ε before other letters. This vowel (sometimes designated º/ₑ) is called the *thematic* vowel. 4. The thematic vowel is followed by an ending (the personal ending, see 12) clearly seen in -μεν and -τε of the first and second persons plural.

Thus, λέγ-ε-τε is composed of the stem λεγ-, the thematic vowel -ε-, and the personal ending -τε.

**17.** The personal endings of the active voice, primary tenses,[1] in their primitive form were these:

| Singular | | Plural | |
|---|---|---|---|
| 1. -μι, | *I* | -μεν, | *we* |
| 2. -ς (for -σι), | *thou* | -τε, | *ye* |
| 3. -σι (for -τι), | *he, she, it* | -νσι (for -ντι), | *they* |

The personal endings are remnants of personal pronouns.

**18.** The thematic vowel with the personal ending may be exhibited thus:

| | |
|---|---|
| 1. ο-μι | ο-μεν |
| 2. ε-ς (for ε-σι) | ε-τε |
| 3. ε-σι (for ετι) | ο-νσι (for ο-ντι) |

*a.* The first person singular -ω is probably the result of dropping the personal ending -μι and the consequent lengthening of the thematic vowel ο to ω. *b.* -εσι and -ετι of the second and third persons singular result in -εις and -ει respectively. *c.* In -ονσι of the third person plural ν is expelled and ο is lengthened to ου (such vowel change is called *compensatory lengthening*).

**19.** The resultant endings from combination of the thematic vowel and the personal ending are

---

[1] The primary tenses are the present, the future, and the perfect; the secondary tenses are the imperfect, the aorist, and the pluperfect.

1. -ω, *I*                       -ομεν, *we*
2. -εις, *thou*                  -ετε, *ye*
3. -ει, *he, she, it*            -ουσι, *they*

*These forms must be mastered.* Nothing short of absolute mastery of forms will answer the purpose.

**20.** The infinitive does not have personal endings. It is a verbal substantive in a fixed case form. -ειν is the result of contraction of the thematic vowel ε and the old locative ending -εν (-ενι).

**21.** Exercises for pronunciation and translation.

I. Translate into English:

1. βλέπει, ἀκούομεν, γινώσκετε.   2. λαμβάνουσι, γράφεις, ἔχει, πιστεύομεν.   3. πέμπειν, εὑρίσκει, ἄγετε, γινώσκουσι.   4. θέλομεν βλέπειν, ἔχομεν, γινώσκετε.   5. ἄγουσι, λαμβάνει, ἔχουσι.

II. Translate into Greek:

1. We know, I see, he finds.   2. You send, they know, ye lead.   3. We wish to know, he hears.   4. They write, he has, you believe.

## LESSON V

### The Second Declension or Declension of o-Stems

**22.**                    VOCABULARY

ἄρτος, *bread*              νόμος, *law*
θρόνος, *throne*            ὄχλος, *crowd*
κόσμος, *world*             τόπος, *place*
λίθος, *stone*             χρόνος, *time*
λόγος, *word*              φίλος, *friend*

The student should take up the words of the vocabulary, one at a time, writing and pronouncing (aloud) each word with its proper accent and breathing until it can be spoken or written without hesitation. Learn thoroughly the meaning of each word. Do not take up a new word until the preceding word has been thoroughly mastered.

**23.** Observe: 1. All the words in the vocabulary end in -ος. 2. All these substantives belong to the o-declension. 3. They all have an acute accent on the penult.

**24.** In Greek all nouns (substantive and adjectives) are declined in one of three declensions. Substantives of the second declension have stems in -o-. The *stem* of a word is that part of it which remains virtually unchanged in all its forms.

**25.** The declension of λόγος, of the second declension, is:

STEM λογο-

|  | *Singular* | *Plural* |
|---|---|---|
| Nom. | λόγος, *a word* | λόγοι, *words* |
| Gen. | λόγου, *of a word* | λόγων, *of words* |
| Abl. | λόγου, *from a word* | λόγων, *from words* |
| Loc. | λόγῳ, *in*, or *at, a word* | λόγοις, *in* or *at words* |
| Ins. | λόγῳ, *with* or *by a word* | λόγοις, *with* or *by words* |
| Dat. | λόγῳ, *to* or *for a word* | λόγοις, *to* or *for words* |
| Acc. | λόγον, *a word* | λόγους, *words* |
| Voc. | λόγε, *O word* | λόγοι, *O words* |

*a.* In the dat. sing. the ending -ῳ is for -ο + αι (dat. case-ending) = ωι = ῳ. In the loc. sing. the ending -ῳ is for -ο + ι (loc. case-ending) = οι = ωι = ῳ. In the ins. sing. the ending -ῳ is for -ο + α (ins. case-ending) = ω. Because the forms of these cases were pronounced alike, they early came to be written alike. *b.* The genitive and ablative cases early came to have their forms alike. *c.* The loc., ins., and dat. plural have the ending of the instrumental case -οις. *d.* So far as the form goes the vocative is strictly not a case. *The endings of* λόγος *must be absolutely mastered.*

**26.** 1. Note that the accent on λόγος remains on the same syllable throughout the declension. *In the declension of a substantive the accent is kept, if possible, on the same syllable on which it rests in the nominative case.*

2. The accent of the nominative case must be learned by observation of each word.

**27.** It is to be observed, from 25, that in Greek there are eight cases (appearing under five case-forms): Nominative, Genitive, Ablative, Locative, Instrumental, Dative, Accusative, and Vocative. The *nominative* is the case of the subject, corresponding roughly to the English nominative. The *genitive* is the *specifying* case, expressed in English by the possessive or the objective with *of*. The ablative is the *whence* case (origin or separation), expressed in English by *off*, *out*, *from*, *away*, etc. The *locative* is the *in* case, corresponding to the English *in*, *on*, *among*, *at*, *by*. The *instrumental* is the case of *means* or association, expressed in English by *with*, *by*, etc. The *dative* is the case of personal interest (denoting advantage or disadvantage), corresponding to the English *to* or *for*, or indirect object. The *accusative* is the case of *extension* (whether of thought or verbal action), corresponding roughly to the English direct object. The vocative is the case of address.

**28.** In Greek the case-endings of nouns express the relation of words to each other, and to other parts of the sentence. In English this relation is generally expressed by prepositions (such as *of, for, at, on, in, by*, etc.) and position of words.

**29.**                    EXERCISES

I.  1. λίθῳ, κόσμου, θρόνων.  2. λόγοι νόμου.  3. λέγει ὄχλῳ.  4. λαμβάνομεν ἄρτον.  5. ὄχλος ἀκούει λόγον νόμου.

II.  1. In a place, of a world.  2. For a friend, laws of thrones.  3. He takes a stone.  4. We have bread for a world.  5. Ye speak words to crowds.


### LESSON VI

#### Declension of o-Stems (Continued)

**30.**                    VOCABULARY

| | | | |
|---|---|---|---|
| ἄγγελος, | *angel, messenger* | διδάσκαλος, | *teacher* |
| ἄνθρωπος, | *man* | θάνατος, | *death* |
| ἀπόστολος, | *apostle* | κύριος, | *Lord* |

In ἄγγελος the first γ is pronounced like *ng*. γ is always pronounced *ng* when it comes before κ, γ, χ, or ξ. Some words of the vocabularies so far given occur 1000 times in the New Testament.

**31.** Nouns of the o-declension whose nominatives end in -ος are generally masculine in gender (rarely feminine).

**32.** Declension of the masculine article ὁ *the*, and ἄνθρωπος:

STEM ἀνθρωπο-

| | *Singular* | | *Plural* | |
|---|---|---|---|---|
| Nom. | ὁ ἄνθρωπος, | *the man* | οἱ ἄνθρωποι, | *the men* |
| Gen. | τοῦ ἀνθρώπου, | *of the man* | τῶν ἀνθρώπων, | *of the men* |
| Abl. | τοῦ ἀνθρώπου, | *from the man* | τῶν ἀνθρώπων, | *from the men* |
| Loc. | τῷ ἀνθρώπῳ, | *in* or *at the man* | τοῖς ἀνθρώποις, | *in* or *at the men* |
| Ins. | τῷ ἀνθρώπῳ, | *with* or *by the man* | τοῖς ἀνθρώποις, | *with* or *by the men* |
| Dat. | τῷ ἀνθρώπῳ, | *to* or *for the man* | τοῖς ἀνθρώποις, | *to* or *for the men* |
| Acc. | τὸν ἄνθρωπον, | *the man* | τοὺς ἀνθρώπους, | *the men* |
| Voc. | ἄνθρωπε, | *O man* | ἄνθρωποι, | *O men* |

**33.** Observe: In the declension of ἄνθρωπος: 1. The acute accent stands on the antepenult in the nominative case, and the ending -ος is short. 2. When the ultima becomes long, as in the endings -ου, -ῳ, -ων, -οις, -ους (3, 4, and 11, (3)) the accent moves to the penult. Cf. 23, 2. 3. Final -οι, although a diphthong, is considered short in determining the place of accent in the o- declension.

**34.** The acute accent may stand on the ultima, penult, or antepenult.

1. The acute accent cannot stand on the antepenult when the ultima is long, but may stand on the penult.

2. The acute accent (´) on a final syllable is changed to the grave (`) when another word immediately follows without any intervening mark of punctuation.

**35.** Note: 1. The article in the nominative case has no accent,—it is to be pronounced with the following word. 2. The circumflex accent is written over the gen., abl., loc., inst., dat. cases of the article; and the syllable on which it stands is long. 3. The grave accent in the acc. case of the article. 4. The rough breathing over the nom. case of the article.

**36.** The definite article ὁ, *the*, is an adjective, and, like all adjectives in Greek, it is declined and agrees in gender, number, and case with the word it modifies.

**37.**    Exercises

I. 1. τῷ διδασκάλῳ, ἀνθρώπων, τοῖς ἀποστόλοις. 2. ἄγγελοι τοῦ κυρίου, τῷ θρόνῳ τοῦ κόσμου. 3. ὁ φίλος γράφει. 4. ὁ κύριος λέγει. 5. ὁ διδάσκαλος γινώσκει τοὺς νόμους. 6. οἱ φίλοι πέμπουσι ἄρτον τοῖς ἀποστόλοις.

II. 1. With a stone, at the place, of the world. 2. He sees the crowd. 3. The man wishes to find bread for the apostles. 4. We see the friends of the Lord.

## LESSON VII

### Declension of o-Stems (Continued)

**38.**          Vocabulary

| | | | |
|---|---|---|---|
| ἀδελφός, | *brother* | ἔργον, | *work* |
| θεός, | *God* | ἱερόν, | *temple* |
| λαός, | *people* | ἱμάτιον, | *garment* |
| οὐρανός, | *heaven* | παιδίον, | *little child* |
| υἱός, | *son* | τέκνον, | *child* |

The diphthong in υἱ with the rough breathing, as in υἱός, is pronounced like *hwee*.

**39.** Declension of οὐρανός.

Stem οὐρανο-

| *Singular* | | *Plural* |
|---|---|---|
| Nom. | οὐρανός | οὐρανοί |
| Gen. | οὐρανοῦ | οὐρανῶν |
| Abl. | οὐρανοῦ | οὐρανῶν |
| Loc. | οὐρανῷ | οὐρανοῖς |
| Ins. | οὐρανῷ | οὐρανοῖς |
| Dat. | οὐρανῷ | οὐρανοῖς |
| Acc. | οὐρανόν | οὐρανούς |
| Voc. | οὐρανέ | οὐρανοί |

**40.** Note that: 1. In every gen., abl., loc., ins., and dat. the acute (´) is changed to the circumflex (˜). 2. In the diphthongs -οῦ and -οῖς the circumflex is written over the second vowel. See 7.

**41.** A long ultima in the gen., abl., loc., ins., and dat. cases, if accented, receives the circumflex accent.

**42.** Learn the declension of the neuter substantive ἔργον with the neuter article τό *the*. Neuter substantives of the o- declension have their nominatives sing. in -ον.

STEM ἐργο-

| Singular | Plural |
|---|---|
| Nom. τὸ ἔργον | τὰ ἔργα |
| Gen. τοῦ ἔργου | τῶν ἔργων |
| Abl. τοῦ ἔργου | τῶν ἔργων |
| Loc. τῷ ἔργῳ | τοῖς ἔργοις |
| Ins. τῷ ἔργῳ | τοῖς ἔργοις |
| Dat. τῷ ἔργῳ | τοῖς ἔργοις |
| Acc. τὸ ἔργον | τὰ ἔργα |
| Voc. ἔργον | ἔργα |

**43.** It is to be observed in the declension of ἔργον:
1. The nom., acc., and voc. cases in the singular
have the same ending, -ον; and the same cases in
the plural have the ending -α. 2. The inflection of
the other cases is the same as that of masculine
substantives.

**44.** The neuter article, τό *the*, differs in its inflection
from the masculine article only in the nom. and
acc. cases.

**45.** EXERCISES

I. 1. τῷ υἱῷ τοῦ Θεοῦ. 2. εὑρίσκουσι τὸν υἱὸν ἐν¹ τῷ
ἱερῷ. 3. ὁ διδάσκαλος θέλει λέγειν τοῖς τέκνοις. 4. ὁ
Θεὸς οὐρανοῦ πέμπει τοὺς ἀγγέλους τοῖς ἀνθρώποις. 5. οἱ
ἀδελφοὶ ἔχουσι ἄρτον καὶ² ἱμάτια τοῖς παιδίοις.

II. 1. For the brothers and of the brothers.
2. The friend finds the garments of the children.
3. We see the son in the temple. 4. The teacher
wishes to speak to the little child.

¹ ἐν, *in*, is used with the locative case.
² καί, *and*, used more times than any other conjunction in the
New Testament.

## LESSON VIII

### Declension of o-Stems (Concluded)

**46.**                          VOCABULARY

| | | | | |
|---|---|---|---|---|
| δοῦλος, ὁ, | *servant* | δῶρον, τό, | *gift* |
| μισθός, ὁ, | *pay, wages,* | πλοῖον, τό, | *boat* |
| | *reward* | | |
| οἶκος, ὁ, | *house* | ποτήριον, τό, | *cup* |
| οἶνος, ὁ, | *wine* | πρόσωπον, τό, | *face* |
| ὀφθαλμός, ὁ, | *eye* | σάββατον, τό, | *Sabbath* |

ἀπό, prep., *from, off,* used only with the ablative case in the New Testament.

Notice that when the breathing and circumflex accent belong to the same vowel, the circumflex is written directly over the breathing, as in οἶκος, etc.

**47.** The following are the declensions of δοῦλος and δῶρον:

|  | STEM δουλο- | | | STEM δωρο- | |
|---|---|---|---|---|---|
| *Singular* | *Plural* | | *Singular* | *Plural* |
| Nom. δοῦλος | δοῦλοι | | Nom. δῶρον | δῶρα |
| Gen. δούλου | δούλων | | Gen. δώρου | δώρων |
| Abl. δούλου | δούλων | | Abl. δώρου | δώρων |
| Loc. δούλῳ | δούλοις | | Loc. δώρῳ | δώροις |
| Ins. δούλῳ | δούλοις | | Ins. δώρῳ | δώροις |
| Dat. δούλῳ | δούλοις | | Dat. δώρῳ | δώροις |
| Acc. δοῦλον | δούλους | | Acc. δῶρον | δῶρα |
| Voc. δοῦλε· | δοῦλοι | | Voc. δῶρον | δῶρα |

**48.** Observe that: 1. The circumflex accent(´) occurs on a long syllable only. 2. When the circumflex accent is written on the penult, the last syllable

is short.  3. When the last syllable becomes long,
the circumflex accent is changed to the acute.
Cf. 26, 1.

**49.** The circumflex accent may stand on the ultima
or the penult.  It cannot stand on the antepenult.
The circumflex accent cannot stand on the penult
when the ultima is long.  When the ultima is short
and the penult is long, the penult takes the circumflex accent, if it is to be accented.

**50.**              EXERCISES

I.   1. ἐν τοῖς ἔργοις τοῦ νόμου.  2.  ὁ κύριος τοῦ οὐρανοῦ ἔχει τὰ δῶρα τοῖς δούλοις.  3. ἀπὸ τοῦ νόμου καὶ ἀπὸ
τῶν ἀποστόλων.  4. τοῖς ὀφθαλμοῖς βλέπομεν τὸν οἶνον ἐν
τῷ ποτηρίῳ.  5. τὸ παιδίον γινώσκει τὸν ἀδελφόν.

II.  1. In the world and in the temple.  2. From
the temple and from heaven.  3. The apostles
receive bread for the servants.  4. We know the law
and believe.  5. The son wishes to speak to the
children.

## LESSON IX

### Present Indicative Middle

**51.** The Greek verb has three voices: active, middle, and passive.  The active and passive voices are
used as in English; the active voice represents the
subject as acting; the passive voice represents the
subject as acted upon.

**52.** The middle voice represents the subject as
acting with reference to himself.  Thus:  1. As

acting directly on himself (direct middle): λούω, *I wash;* λούομαι, *I wash myself.* 2. As acting for himself or for his own interest in some way: ἀγοράζω, *I buy;* ἀγοράζομαι, *I buy for myself.*

*a.* Precisely how the subject acts with reference to himself, the middle voice *per se* does not tell. This precise relation is determined by the meaning of the verb itself and the context. *b.* Often it is impossible to translate the shade of meaning given by the middle. Yet in some verbs there is a bold change in meaning.

**53.** The conjugation of the present indicative middle of λούω, *I wash,* is

|          | *Singular* |          | *Plural* |
|----------|-----------|----------|----------|
| 1. λού-ο-μαι, | *I wash myself* | λου-ό-μεθα, | *we wash ourselves* |
| 2. λού-ῃ, | *you wash yourself* | λού-ε-σθε, | *ye wash yourselves* |
| 3. λού-ε-ται, | *he washes himself* | λού-ο-νται, | *they wash themselves* |

Present infinitive middle λού-ε-σθαι, *to wash oneself.*

Observe that the appended translation is the direct middle. If ἀγοράζομαι *I buy for myself,* etc., were given, the indirect middle would be seen.

**54.** The primary middle personal endings are:

|          | *Singular* |          | *Plural* |
|----------|-----------|----------|----------|
| 1. -μαι, | *I* | -μεθα, | *we* |
| 2. -σαι, | *thou (you)* | -σθε, | *ye* |
| 3. -ται, | *he, she, it* | -νται, | *they* |

The thematic vowel (°/ε) and personal endings:

|   |          |          |
|---|----------|----------|
| 1.| -ομαι    | -ομεθα   |
| 2.| -εσαι    | -εσθε    |
| 3.| -εται    | -ονται   |

Observe in the conjugation of λούω that:

1. The second person sing. λούη is for λούεσαι.
-η arose from the dropping of σ and the contraction
of ε and αι=ηι=η. Rarely is ει found instead of
η.

2. αι in these personal endings is considered
short, hence the accent on the antepenult. The
same principle of accent is to be observed as in 11
and 13.

3. The thematic vowel (°/ε) is found as in the
active voice.

4. The present middle infinitive ending is -σθαι.
The αι is considered short.

**55.**    Vocabulary

| | | | |
|---|---|---|---|
| ἀγοράζω, | I buy | ἀγοράζομαι, | I buy for myself |
| ἅπτω, | I fasten to | ἅπτομαι, | I fasten myself to, touch |
| λούω, | I wash | λούομαι, | I wash myself |
| νίπτω, | I wash | νίπτομαι, | I wash myself |
| παύω, | I stop | παύομαι, | I stop myself, cease |
| φυλάσσω | I guard, keep | φυλάσσομαι, | I guard myself, keep myself |

This vocabulary is given as a simple illustration
of the middle.  Any verb may be used in the middle
voice.

**56.**                    EXERCISES

I.  1. ἀγοράζεται, φυλάσσῃ, παύομαι.  2. νίπτομαι τὸ
πρόσωπον.  3. φυλάσσεται ἀπὸ τοῦ κόσμου.  4. ὁ δοῦλος
ἀγοράζεται τὸ πλοῖον.  5. ἁπτόμεθα καὶ λουόμεθα.  6.
παύεσθε καὶ λέγουσι.

II. 1. He ceases, they wash themselves.  2. You
buy bread for yourself.  3. The apostle washes his
(the) face.  4. The child guards himself from the
man.


## LESSON X

### Present Indicative Passive

**57.**                    VOCABULARY

| | |
|---|---|
| βάλλω, *I throw* | κρίνω, *I judge* |
| διδάσκω, *I teach* | στέλλω, *I send* |
| ἐγείρω, *I raise up* | σώζω, *I save* |
| κηρύσσω, *I announce, proclaim* | |

εἰς,      prep., *into*, used with the accusative only.
ὑπό,     prep., used with the ablative (see 86), *by;*
          with the accusative, *under*.

**58.** The passive voice is later than the active and
middle and did not develop distinctive personal
endings.  The middle and passive are the same in
form, except in the *future* and *aorist*.  For the meaning of passive see 51.

**59.** The following is the present indicative passive
of λύω *I loose.*

| *Singular* | | *Plural* | |
|---|---|---|---|
| 1. λύ-ο-μαι, | *I am (being) loosed* | λυ-ό-μεθα, | *we are (being) loosed* |
| 2. λύ-ῃ, | *you are (being) loosed* | λύ-ε-σθε, | *ye are (being) loosed* |
| 3. λύ-ε-ται, | *he is (being) loosed* | λύ-ο-νται | *they are (being) loosed* |

Present passive infinitive λύ-ε-σθαι, *to be loosed.*

**60.** It is to be observed that the present passive voice uses the present middle endings. The present middle and passive voices have the same form.

**61.** Generally the context will make clear whether the middle or passive voice is meant.

**62.**    EXERCISES

I.   1. βλέπονται, πέμπεται, ἀκούεις, ἀκούῃ.   2. σῴζει, σωζόμεθα, κρίνομαι, ἄγεται.   3. διδάσκω, διδάσκονται, βάλλει, βάλλεται.   4. ἐγείρεσθε ἀπὸ τῶν νεκρῶν.[1]   5. ὁ λόγος διδάσκεται ἐν τῷ ἱερῷ.   6. οἱ δοῦλοι στέλλονται εἰς τὸν οἶκον.   7. γράφεται ἐν τῷ νόμῳ.   8. πιστεύουσι εἰς τὸν κύριον καὶ σῴζονται.   9. κρινόμεθα ὑπὸ τοῦ κυρίου.

II.   1. He sends and is sent.   2. He believes and is saved.   3. The word is proclaimed in the temple. 4. The son of man is judged.   5. The stone is thrown into the house.   6. The bread is taken from the apostle.   7. You are judged by the son of man.

---

[1] νεκρός, *dead.*

## LESSON XI

### Imperfect Indicative Active

**63.** VOCABULARY

αἴρω, *I take up, bear*     μέλλω, *I am about* (or *go-*
βαπτίζω, *I baptize*          *ing*) *to do some-*
ἐσθίω, *I eat*               *thing*
κράζω, *I cry out*        μένω, *I remain*

**64.** The imperfect tense is made on the present stem. Thus pres. λέγ-ω; imp. ἔ-λεγ-ον.

**65.** The imperfect indicative represents an action as *going on* in past time (*durative* or *linear* action in past time),—this action may be simultaneous, prolonged, descriptive, repeated, customary, interrupted, attempted, or begun, according to the context and the meaning of the verb itself.

**66.** The personal endings of the secondary [1] active tenses are:

|  | *Singular* | *Plural* |
|---|---|---|
| I. | -ν | -μεν |
| 2. | -ς | -τε |
| 3. | none | -ν or -σαν. |

**67.** The imperfect indicative active of λούω, *I wash:*

| | *Singular* | | *Plural* |
|---|---|---|---|
| I. | ἔ-λου-ο-ν, *I was wash-ing* | ἐ-λού-ο-μεν, | *we were wash-ing* |
| 2. | ἔ-λου-ε-ς, *you were washing* | ἐ-λού-ε-τε, | *ye were wash-ing* |
| 3. | ἔ-λου-ε, *he was wash-ing* | ἔ-λου-ο-ν, | *they were washing* |

[1] See 17, footnote I.

*a.* In the third pers. plu. the form ἐ-λού-ο-σαν is sometimes found. *b.* In the plural forms like ἐλούαμεν, ἐλούατε, ἔλουαν sporadically appear.

**68.** Observe that: 1. The thematic vowel is °/ε as in the present indicative. 2. The third person sing. has no personal ending. 3. Before the stem λου- is ε. This ε is called the *augment.*

**69.** The augment is probably an old adverb for "then." The augment in the imperfect places linear action in past time. At times it is difficult to translate this Greek tense into English, because of the absence of a true imperfect in English.

**70.** The indicative of the secondary (or historical) tenses, besides having different personal endings, has also an augment. This augment is of two forms: 1. If the stem begins with a consonant, the vowel ε is commonly prefixed—called *syllabic* augment. 2. But if the stem begins with a vowel, that vowel is lengthened—called *temporal* augment. Thus:

α becomes η   (ᾳ becomes ῃ)
ε becomes η   (αι becomes ῃ) [except in 2 Ti. i:16,
ο becomes ω   (αυ becomes ηυ)   where it remains αι]
ι becomes ῑ
υ becomes ῡ
ει may become η, but remains ει in New Testament.
ευ may become ηυ, but usually remains ευ in New
       Testament.
οι generally becomes ῳ, but sometimes remains οι in
       New Testament.

E.g., ἄγω, *lead;* ἦγον, *I was leading;* ἀκούω, *hear;*

ἤκουον, *I was hearing;* ἐγείρω, *raise up;* ἤγειρον, *I was raising up;* αἴρω, *take up;* ἦρον, *I was taking up.*

θέλω has η in the imperfect, ἤθελον. Sometimes μέλλω has η, thus ἤμελλον.

**71.** EXERCISES

I. 1. ἐμένετε, ἔκραζε, ἔβαλλες. 2. ηὑρίσκομεν, ἐπίστευον, ἤκουε. 3. ἔμενον ἐν τῷ οἴκῳ. 4. τὸ τέκνον ἔβαλλε λίθους. 5. ὁ κύριος ἔσωζε τοὺς ἀνθρώπους. 6. οἱ ἀπόστολοι ἐκήρυσσον τὸν λόγον.

II. 1. You were saying. 2. They were eating the bread. 3. The teacher was sending garments for the children. 4. He was taking up the child from the boat. 5. The men were leading the servants into the house.

## LESSON XII

### Prepositions

**72.** VOCABULARY

ἀπό, prep., *from, off, away from,* used with the ablative only.

εἰς, prep., *into,* used with the accusative only.

ἐκ (ἐξ), prep., *out, out of, from within,* used with the ablative only. ἐξ before words beginning with a vowel.

ἐν, prep., *in,* used with the locative only. The resultant meaning of ἐν and the locative is sometimes instrumental.

παρά, prep., *beside,* used with the locative, ablative, and accusative.

σύν, prep., *with*, used with the instrumental only.

ἀποστέλλω, *send forth*
εἰσάγω, *bring in*
ἐκβάλλω, *throw out, cast out*
παραλαμβάνω, *take, receive*
συνάγω, *gather together*

Some prepositions do not have an accent. Words which do not have an accent are called proclitics and are to be pronounced with the following words.

**73.** Prepositions are adverbs specialized to define more clearly the meanings of cases, many of which come to be used in composition with verbs.

Prepositions were originally free adverbs. These adverbs were brought gradually into closer relation with nouns, and many of them into a closer connection with verbs.

**74.** Prepositions are used to bring out more clearly the idea of case. They help the cases; the case calls in the preposition to aid in expressing more sharply the meaning of the case. "It is the *case* which indicates the meaning of the preposition, and not the preposition which gives the meaning to the case." Then, strictly speaking, prepositions (in Greek) do not "govern" cases. Take παρά, meaning *beside*, for example: with locative, παρὰ τῷ δούλῳ, *by* or *at the side of the servant;* with the ablative, παρὰ τοῦ δούλου, *from the side of the servant;* with the accusative, παρὰ τὸν δοῦλον, *along side of the servant.*

*a.* The cases used with prepositions are the ablative, genitive, locative, instrumental, and accusative.

*b.* The dative is not used with any of the prepositions in the New Testament, except probably ἐγγύς (Acts ix:38) and ἐπί.

**75.** In composition with verbs the preposition has commonly two uses.

1. The preposition is merely local: e.g., ἐκ-βάλλω, *I throw out, cast out;* καταβαίνω, *I am going down.*

2. The preposition intensifies or completes the idea of the verb: e.g., ἐσθίω, *I eat;* κατεσθίω, *I eat up* (*down*). This is called the "perfective" force of the preposition.

*a.* Sometimes prepositions change the meaning of the verb and blend with it.

**76.** When a preposition ends in a vowel, as ἀπό, παρά, the final vowel is dropped before a verb that begins with a vowel: e.g., παρέχω is for παρα + εχω, *I provide, supply.* When compound verbs receive the augment, the final vowel of the preposition is dropped: e.g., παραλαμβάνω, *I receive;* παρελάμβανον, *I was receiving;* ἀποστέλλω, *I send forth,* ἀπέστελλον, *I was sending forth;* κατάγω, κατῆγον.

*a.* The prepositions περί and πρό do not drop their final vowel; e.g., προάγω, *I go before;* περιάγω, *I go about.*

**77.** EXERCISES

I. 1. οἱ ἀπόστολοι ἔμενον ἐν τῷ οἴκῳ. 2. ὁ κύριος ἀπέστελλε τοὺς υἱοὺς εἰς τὸν κόσμον. 3. ὁ θεὸς ἐγείρει τοὺς νεκροὺς ἐκ θανάτου. 4. παρελαμβάνομεν τὸν λόγον τοῦ θεοῦ ἀπὸ τοῦ κυρίου. 5. ὁ ἄνθρωπος πέμπεται παρὰ τοῦ θεοῦ. 6. οἱ δοῦλοι ἔμενον σὺν τοῖς ἀνθρώποις.

II. 1. He was sending the child out of the boat.
2. The child was throwing stones into the house.
3. The servants were eating up the bread. 4. The
Lord was sending forth the apostles. 5. The teacher
is about to receive the bread from the child.


## LESSON XIII

### The Imperfect Indicative Middle and Passive

**78.**                    VOCABULARY

ἀναβλέπω,  *I look up, re-*   δοξάζω, *I glorify*
             *cover sight*    πείθω, *I persuade*
ἀπέχω,    *I keep off, have*  φέρω, *I bear, carry*
           *in full* (of re-  ἀνά,  prep., *on, upon,*
           ceipts); Midd.           *along;* used with
           *I keep myself*          accusative only
           *from, abstain.*         in New Testa-
ἀποθνήσκω, *I die*                   ment.
διώκω,    *I follow after, pursue, persecute*

**79.** The personal endings in the secondary [1] tenses
of the indicative middle and passive are:

|  | *Singular* |  | *Plural* |
|---|---|---|---|
| 1. | -μην, *I* | -μεθα, *we* |
| 2. | -σο, *thou (you)* | -σθε, *ye (you)* |
| 3. | -το, *he, etc.* | -ντο, *they* |

[1] The terms "primary" and "secondary" apply to the indicative
mode only.

**80.** The conjugation of λύω in the imperfect indicative middle is:

| Singular | Plural |
|---|---|
| 1. ἐλυόμην, *I was loosing (for) myself* | ἐλυόμεθα, *we were loosing (for) ourselves* |
| 2. ἐλύου, *you were loosing (for) yourself* | ἐλύεσθε, *ye were loosing (for) yourselves* |
| 3. ἐλύετο, *he was loosing (for) himself* | ἐλύοντο, *they were loosing (for) themselves* |

*a.* In the second pers. sing., ἐλύου, -ου is for -εσο; intersonantic σ drops out and εο contract to ου.

**81.** Observe: 1. The thematic vowel °/ε. 2. The augment. 3. The accent in first pers. sing.

**82.** As in the present tense, so also in the imperfect, the middle and passive voices are alike in form.

**83.** The conjugation of λύω in the imperfect indicative passive is:

| Singular | Plural |
|---|---|
| 1. ἐλυόμην, *I was being loosed* | ἐλυόμεθα, *we were being loosed* |
| 2. ἐλύου, *you were being loosed* | ἐλύεσθε, *you were being loosed* |
| 3. ἐλύετο, *he was being loosed* | ἐλύοντο, *they were being loosed* |

**84.** Review the present indicative active (13), middle (53), and passive (59), and the imperfect indicative active (67).

**85.** The personal endings of the verb have to express

1. The *person* of the verb.

2. The *number* of the verb.

3. The *voice* of the verb.

In fact they express everything that has to do with the subject.

4. In the indicative they tell whether primary or secondary.

*The personal endings of the verb must be mastered.* The importance of the forms of the verb cannot be overstressed. If the verb-forms thus far given are thoroughly learned, the student has overcome the greater part of the difficulty in the regular verb.

**86.** ὑπό (prep.) is used with the ablative case to denote the *agent*, *by*, especially with the passive voice; e.g., ἐβαπτίζοντο ὑπὸ 'Ιωάνου, *they were being baptized by John.*

**87.**              EXERCISES

I.  1. ἐπαυόμην, ἐλούετο, φυλάσσεται.  2. οἱ ἀπόστολοι ἀπείχοντο¹ ἀπὸ τοῦ κόσμου.  3. ἐν τῷ οἴκῳ ἐδοξάζετο ὁ κύριος.  4. τὸ τέκνον ἤγετο ὑπὸ τοῦ ἀνθρώπου.  5. ἐσώζου καὶ ἀνέβλεπες.

II.  1. The word was being preached by the apostles.  2. The children were washing themselves. 3. I was being judged by men.  4. The angel of the Lord was being heard.  5. The law was being taught in the temple.  6. The servants were looking up into the heavens.

¹ The augment in the imperfect of ἔχω is εἶχον, for ἔεχον is ἔσεχον.

## LESSON XIV

### The First Declension or Declension of α- Stems

**88.** VOCABULARY

| | | | |
|---|---|---|---|
| ἀρχή, | beginning | ἀγάπη, | love |
| γραφή, | writing, scripture | διαθήκη, | covenant, testa- |
| ἐντολή, | commandment | | ment |
| ζωή, | life | δικαιοσύνη, | righteousness |
| φωνή, | voice | εἰρήνη, | peace |
| ψυχή, | soul | κώμη, | village |

**89.** All substantives of the first declension whose nominatives end in α or η are feminine in gender.

**90.** The feminine article (ἡ) and nominatives in -η are declined as follows:

φωνή, voice          κώμη, village

STEM φωνα-          STEM κωμα-

| | Singular | Plural | Singular | Plural |
|---|---|---|---|---|
| Nom. | ἡ φωνή | αἱ φωναί | κώμη | κῶμαι |
| Gen. | τῆς φωνῆς | τῶν φωνῶν | κώμης | κωμῶν |
| Abl. | τῆς φωνῆς | τῶν φωνῶν | κώμης | κωμῶν |
| Loc. | τῇ φωνῇ | ταῖς φωναῖς | κώμῃ | κώμαις |
| Ins. | τῇ φωνῇ | ταῖς φωναῖς | κώμῃ | κώμαις |
| Dat. | τῇ φωνῇ | ταῖς φωναῖς | κώμῃ | κώμαις |
| Acc. | τὴν φωνήν | τὰς φωνάς | κώμην | κώμας |
| Voc. | φωνή | φωναί | κώμη | κῶμαι |

**91.** Observe: 1. The stem ends in α, and is therefore called the α-declension. 2. Iota-subscript is always written in the loc., ins., and dat. singular (see 25 a).

3. When the nominative sing. ends in -η the η is retained throughout the singular. 4. In the nominative plural -αι is considered short in determining place and kind of accent.

**92.** The ending -αις in the loc., ins., and dat. plural is a new formation on the analogy of -οις in ο-stems. See 25 c.

**93.** Nouns that have an acute accent on the last syllable (ultima) are called *oxytones* (sharp tones); e.g., φωνή, ζωή. Learn that *all* oxytones of the first and second declension have the circumflex accent over the ultima in all the genitives, ablatives, locatives, instrumentals, and datives,   See 40.

**94.** The gen. and abl. plu. of substantives of the first or α- declension always have the circumflex accent on the ultima, no matter where the accent is in the nominative singular, since -ῶν is contracted from -έων derived from -άων.   Thus κώμη, but κωμῶν.

**95.** Compare the feminine article (ἡ) with the endings of φωνή. Notice that, as in the case of the forms ὁ and οἱ of the masculine article, the forms ἡ and αἱ do not have an accent. These forms of the article are called proclitic: they are to be pronounced as a part of the following word.

**96.**              EXERCISES

I.   1. αἱ ψυχαὶ τῶν ἀνθρώπων σώζονται.   2. ἐν ἀρχῇ ὁ λόγος ἠκούετο.   3. ἡ ἐντολὴ τῆς ζωῆς ἐλέγετο ὑπὸ τοῦ κυρίου.   4. αἱ γραφαὶ ἐδιδάσκοντο ἐν τῷ ἱερῷ.   5. ἐξεβάλλοντο ἐκ τῶν κωμῶν.   6. ἡ διαθήκη ἐγράφετο τοῖς ἀνθρώποις.

II.  1. From the beginning, in the village.  2. He is teaching the scriptures.  3. We have peace in the soul.  4. The sons were receiving the testament.  5. The apostles heard the commandment from the Lord.  6. The soul is being saved and finds peace and righteousness.


## LESSON XV

### First Declension (Continued)

**97.**          VOCABULARY

ἁμαρτία, ἡ, *sin*                    καρδία, ἡ, *heart*
βασιλεία, ἡ, *kingdom*        σοφία, ἡ,   *wisdom*
ἐκκλησία, ἡ, *assembly, (church)*  ἀλήθεια, ἡ, *truth*
ἐξουσία, ἡ,   *authority, power*   ἀσθένεια, ἡ, *weakness*
ἡμέρα, ἡ,   *day*                    μάχαιρα, ἡ, *sword*

**98.**  1. As we have seen, a substantive in Greek has *case, number*, and *gender*.

2. There are three genders: *masculine, feminine* and *neuter*.

**99.** Nearly all substantives of the second declension with nominatives in -ος are masculine;[1] and all substantives of the second declension with nominatives in -ον are neuter.

**100.** All substantives of the first declension with nominatives in -η or -α are feminine.  Those with

---

[1] ὁδός, *way, road*, and ἔρημος, *wilderness, desert*, are feminine in gender.

nominatives in -ης or -ας are masculine. See Lesson XVI.

But the gender of substantives must often be learned by observation. Hereafter in this book the gender will be indicated in the vocabulary by the article placed after the substantive. (This method is used by most lexicons.) The masculine article, ὁ, indicates masculine gender; the feminine article, ἡ, feminine gender; the neuter article, τό, neuter gender.

**101.** Substantives of the first declension with nominatives in -α (preceded by ε, ι, or ρ) are declined as follows:

καρδία, *heart*      ἀλήθεια, *truth*

STEM καρδια-      STEM ἀληθεια-

|      | *Singular* | *Plural* | *Singular* | *Plural* |
|------|-----------|----------|-----------|----------|
| Nom. | καρδία | καρδίαι | ἀλήθεια | ἀλήθειαι |
| Gen. | καρδίας | καρδιῶν | ἀληθείας | ἀληθειῶν |
| Abl. | καρδίας | καρδιῶν | ἀληθείας | ἀληθειῶν |
| Loc. | καρδίᾳ | καρδίαις | ἀληθείᾳ | ἀληθείαις |
| Ins. | καρδίᾳ | καρδίαις | ἀληθείᾳ | ἀληθείαις |
| Dat. | καρδίᾳ | καρδίαις | ἀληθείᾳ | ἀληθείαις |
| Acc. | καρδίαν | καρδίας | ἀλήθειαν | ἀληθείας |
| Voc. | καρδία | καρδίαι | ἀλήθεια | ἀλήθειαι |

**102.** Observe: 1. When ε, ι, or ρ precedes -α in the nominative singular, the α is retained throughout the singular.[1] 2. The -α after ε, ι, or ρ may be long as in καρδία or short as in ἀλήθεια. 3 When the -α is short (in the first declension) in the nominative singular,

---

[1] Sometimes -ης is found in the gen. and abl. sing. after ε, ι, or ρ.

it is also short in the accusative singular. But in the accusative plural the -α is long in the first declension. 4. In the gen., abl., loc., ins., and dat. singular of ἀλήθεια the accent is brought forward to the penult because the ultima is long. Cf. 33, 2, and 26, 1.

**103.**    Exercises

I. 1. ἡ βασιλεία τοῦ θεοῦ. 2. ἡ ἐκκλησία ἔχει ἐξουσίαν. 3. ἡ δικαιοσύνη καὶ ἡ ἀλήθεια ἐν τῷ κόσμῳ ἔμενον. 4. ὁ διδάσκαλος ἔχει τὴν μάχαιραν τῆς ἀληθείας. 5. ἔβλεπον τὴν ἡμέραν τοῦ κυρίου καὶ ἐδόξαζον τὸν θεόν.

II. 1. In the hearts of men. 2. Wisdom was being taught in the church. 3. It is being written in truth. 4. The sword of truth pursues sin. 5. The Lord has power to save men.

## LESSON XVI

### First Declension (Continued)

**104.**    Vocabulary

| | | | | |
|---|---|---|---|---|
| γλῶσσα, ἡ, | tongue | | κεφαλή, ἡ, | head |
| δόξα, ἡ, | glory | | οἰκία, ἡ, | house |
| θάλασσα, ἡ, | sea | | παραβολή, ἡ, | parable |
| μαθητής, ὁ, | disciple | | συναγωγή, ἡ, | synagogue |
| προφήτης, ὁ, | prophet | | χαρά, ἡ, | joy |
| ἐπαγγελία, ἡ, | promise | | ὥρα, ἡ, | hour |

**105.** Substantives of the first declension with nominatives in -α, not after ε, ι, or ρ, are declined as follows:

STEM γλωσσα-

|  | *Singular* | *Plural* |
|------|------------|----------|
| Nom. | γλῶσσα | γλῶσσαι |
| Gen. | γλώσσης | γλωσσῶν |
| Abl. | γλώσσης | γλωσσῶν |
| Loc. | γλώσσῃ | γλώσσαις |
| Ins. | γλώσσῃ | γλώσσαις |
| Dat. | γλώσσῃ | γλώσσαις |
| Acc. | γλῶσσαν | γλώσσας |
| Voc. | γλῶσσα | γλῶσσαι |

**106.** Observe: 1. When ε, ι, or ρ does not precede α of the nom. sing., the α is changed to η in the gen., abl., loc., ins., and dat. sing. 2. When the α is short in the nom. sing. it is also short in the acc. sing.

**107.** Contract substantives of the first declension as γῆ, ἡ, *earth*, and μνᾶ, ἡ, *mina* (a weight and sum of money) are declined like φωνή and καρδία respectively, except that they have the circumflex accent on the ultima throughout.

**108.** Substantives of the first declension with nom. sing. in -ης or -ας are masculine in gender. See 100.

**109.** The declension of προφήτης, ὁ, *prophet*, is

## THE FIRST DECLENSION

STEM προφητα-

| | Singular | Plural |
|---|---|---|
| Nom. | προφήτης | προφῆται |
| Gen. | προφήτου | προφητῶν |
| Abl. | προφήτου | προφητῶν |
| Loc. | προφήτῃ | προφήταις |
| Ins. | προφήτῃ | προφήταις |
| Dat. | προφήτῃ | προφήταις |
| Acc. | προφήτην | προφήτας |
| Voc. | προφῆτα | προφῆται |

**110.** Observe: 1. The gen. and abl. sing. -ου is the same as in the ο- declension. 2. The voc. sing. is -α. Masculine substantives of the first declension in -της have -α in the vocative sing. 3. The plurals of all substantives of the α- declension are alike.

**111.** The singular of νεανίας, ὁ, *youth*, is

Nom. νεανίας,  Gen. νεανίου,  Abl. νεανίου,
Loc. νεανίᾳ,  Ins. νεανίᾳ,  Dat. νεανίᾳ,
Acc. νεανίαν,  Voc. νεανία.

**112.**  EXERCISES

I. 1. ἔχετε χαρὰν καὶ εἰρήνην ἐν ταῖς καρδίαις. 2. οἱ μαθηταὶ ἔλεγον παραβολὰς ἐν τῇ συναγωγῇ. 3. ἐν τῇ γῇ καὶ ἐν τῇ θαλάσσῃ ἐδοξάζετο ὁ κύριος. 4. ἀπὸ τῆς ἀρχῆς ἠκούομεν τοὺς προφήτας. 5. λαμβάνετε τὰς ἐπαγγελίας ἀπὸ τοῦ κυρίου. 6. ἦγον τὸν νεανίαν ἐκ τῆς οἰκίας.

II. 1. They were remaining in the house. 2. Righteousness and love remain in the world. 3. The hour of the Lord is announced. 4. The prophets are teaching the disciples in parables. 5. The promises were spoken from the beginning.

## LESSON XVII

### Adjectives of the First and Second Declension

**113.**      VOCABULARY

| | | | |
|---|---|---|---|
| ἀγαθός, | good | καλός, | good, beautiful |
| ἀγαπητός, | beloved | πιστός, | faithful |
| ἔσχατος, | last | πρῶτος, | first |
| κακός,, | evil, bad | | |

**114.** Most adjectives of the vowel (first and second) declension have three endings, -ος (masc.), -η or -α (fem.), -ον (neut.). Adjectives are declined in *gender*, *number* and *case*.

**115.** The adjective ἀγαθός is declined as follows:

| | *Singular* | | | *Plural* | | |
|---|---|---|---|---|---|---|
| | *Masc.* | *Fem.* | *Neut.* | *Masc.* | *Fem.* | *Neut.* |
| Nom. | ἀγαθός | ἀγαθή | ἀγαθόν | ἀγαθοί | ἀγαθαί | ἀγαθά |
| Gen. | ἀγαθοῦ | ἀγαθῆς | ἀγαθοῦ | ἀγαθῶν | ἀγαθῶν | ἀγαθῶν |
| Abl. | ἀγαθοῦ | ἀγαθῆς | ἀγαθοῦ | ἀγαθῶν | ἀγαθῶν | ἀγαθῶν |
| Loc. | ἀγαθῷ | ἀγαθῇ | ἀγαθῷ | ἀγαθοῖς | ἀγαθαῖς | ἀγαθοῖς |
| Ins. | ἀγαθῷ | ἀγαθῇ | ἀγαθῷ | ἀγαθοῖς | ἀγαθαῖς | ἀγαθοῖς |
| Dat. | ἀγαθῷ | ἀγαθῇ | ἀγαθῷ | ἀγαθοῖς | ἀγαθαῖς | ἀγαθοῖς |
| Acc. | ἀγαθόν | ἀγαθήν | ἀγαθόν | ἀγαθούς | ἀγαθάς | ἀγαθά |
| Voc. | ἀγαθέ | ἀγαθή | ἀγαθόν | ἀγαθοί | ἀγαθαί | ἀγαθά. |

**116.** Observe: 1. In form the masc. is declined exactly like a masculine substantive of the second declension (see οὐρανός, 39); the neuter like a neuter substantive of the second declension (see ἔργον, 42); and the feminine like a feminine substantive in -η (see φωνή, 90).

*a.* The accent of the feminine genitive and ablative plural does not follow the accent of the feminine substantive of the α- declension (given in 94), but the regular accent of the masculine: thus the genitive and ablative plural feminine form of ἔσχατος is ἐσχάτων.

**117.** Adjectives agree with the substantives which they modify, in gender, number, and case; e.g., τοῦ πιστοῦ δούλου; τῇ πρώτῃ ἡμέρᾳ; καλῇ ὁδῷ. Cf. 36.

**118.** Adjectives are used tc refer to substantives in two ways, either (1) as an attribute or (2) as a predicate.

1. In the phrase ὁ πιστὸς δοῦλος, *the faithful servant*, πιστός, *faithful*, is an attribute adjective; it qualifies the substantive, δοῦλος, *servant*, to describe, without any assertion about it.

2. In the phrase ὁ δοῦλος πιστός, *the servant* (is) *faithful*, the predicate adjective πιστός, *faithful*, makes an assertion about the substantive δοῦλος, *servant*.

It is important to understand this distinction between the attribute and the predicate adjective in Greek. The distinction lies in just this, that the predicate presents an additional statement, while the attribute is an adherent description.

**119.** Examples of the positions of the adjective:

1. Attributive position of the adjective —

$$\left. \begin{array}{l} \text{ὁ·πιστὸς δοῦλος} \\ \text{ὁ δοῦλος ὁ πιστός} \end{array} \right\} = the\ faithful\ servant.$$

Note that the adjective comes immediately after the article.

There is another order of the attributive position,
δοῦλος ὁ πιστός. It is not frequent in the New
Testament.

2. Predicate position of the adjective—

$$\left.\begin{array}{l} \text{ὁ δοῦλος πιστός} \\ \text{πιστὸς ὁ δοῦλος} \end{array}\right\} = \text{the servant (is) faithful}$$

Note that the adjective does not come immediately
after the article but either precedes the article or
follows the substantive.

**120.** When the article is not present, the context
must decide whether an adjective is attributive or
predicate; e.g., the phrase πιστὸς δοῦλος (or δοῦλος
πιστός) may be either attributive, *a faithful servant*,
or predicate, *a servant* (is) *faithful*.

**121.** In the New Testament ὅλος, *whole*, never has
the attributive position.

**122.**    EXERCISES

I.  1. ἡ πρώτη ὥρα.  2. οἱ μαθηταὶ οἱ ἀγαπητοὶ ἐδίδασκον
τὸν καλὸν λόγον.  3. τέκνον τὸ ἀγαπητὸν εὑρίσκει τὴν κακὴν
ὁδόν.  4. ἐν ταῖς ἐσχάταις ἡμέραις προφῆται ἠκούοντο.
5. ὁ ἀγαθὸς λόγος ἐκηρύσσετο ἐν ὅλῳ τῷ κόσμῳ.

II.  1. The evil prophet was not [1] proclaiming the
good promises.  2. On the last day the disciple was
speaking in the synagogue.  3. The whole house
was receiving the word of God.  4. In the first hour
of the day they were glorifying the Lord.

[1] See 130.

## LESSON XVIII

**Adjectives of the First and Second Declension (Continued)**

**123.**                     VOCABULARY

αἰώνιος, *eternal*                μόνος,   *only, alone*
δίκαιος, *righteous*             μικρός, *small, little*
ἕτερος, *another*                πονηρός, *evil*
ἴδιος,   *one's own*

**124.** Learn the declension of ἴδιος, *one's own*, and μικρός, *small*, in § B 13.

Observe: 1. When ε, ι, or ρ precedes the final vowel of the stem, the feminine has -α in the nominative sing.

2. In the nom. and gen. plur. fem. the accent follows the masc.

**125.** Some adjectives (especially compounds) have only two endings, the masc. and fem. having the same form: e.g., ἄδικος, -ον, *unjust, unrighteous*.

**126.** Prepositional phrases or adverbs are often used like adjectives in the attributive position: e.g., οἱ ἐν τῷ οἴκῳ ἄνθρωποι, *the men in the house.* The substantive may be absent: e.g., τὰ ἐν τοῖς οὐρανοῖς, *the things in the heavens.*

**127.** The adjective in any gender without a substantive is often used as a practical substantive, usually with the article, but not always: e.g., οἱ καλοί, *the good* (men or people); τὸ ἀγαθόν, *the good thing;* τῇ τρίτῃ, *on the third* (day),—the feminines are usually examples of ellipsis of ἡμέρα, ὁδός, etc.

**128.** As a complement, the infinitive (mostly in the active voice) is used with adjectives, substantives, and verbs that imply power or ability, fitness, capacity, etc. (and their opposites): e.g., δυνατὸς κωλύειν, *able to hinder;* ἐξουσία ἐκβάλλειν, *power to cast out;* δύναμαι ἀκούειν, *I am able to hear.*

**129.**            Exercises

I.   1. οἱ καλοὶ μόνοι σώζονται.   2. οἱ ἐν τῷ οἴκῳ ἤσθιον τὸν ἄρτον.   3. ἐν τῇ πρώτῃ ἔκρινε τοὺς κακούς.   4. ὁ υἱὸς τοῦ ἀνθρώπου ἔχει ἐξουσίαν σώζειν.   5. οἱ δοῦλοι ἔλεγον κακά.

II.   1. On the first day he was preaching in the synagogue.   2. The first, last; the last, first.   3. The faithful are saved.   4. He has power to cast out the evil.   5. The men in the boat know the sea.

## LESSON XIX

### Personal Pronouns and εἰμί, I am

**130.**            Vocabulary

ἀλλά, adversative conj., *but*

γάρ, co-ordinating conj., *for*

γέ, enclitic postpositive particle giving special prominence to a word, *indeed, at least*

δέ, copulative and adversative (milder than ἀλλά) conj., *in the next place, and; but, on the other hand.*

ἐγώ, *I*

εἰμί, *I am*

σύ, *thou (you)*

οὐ
οὐκ  } *not*
οὐχ

*a.* Words that cannot come first in a sentence are called postpositives. γάρ, γέ, and δέ are postpositives. *b.* οὐ is written before consonants; οὐκ before vowels; οὐχ before the rough breathing.

**131.** Generally speaking, the pronoun is a word that stands in place of a substantive. The idea that is set forth by a pronoun is the relation of a subject or object to the speaker. The reason for the use of the pronoun, then, is to avoid the repetition of the substantive.

**132.** The declension of the first personal pronoun ἐγώ, *I*, is

| *Singular* | | | *Plural* | |
|---|---|---|---|---|
| Nom. | ἐγώ, | *I* | ἡμεῖς, | *we* |
| Gen. | ἐμοῦ, μου, | *of me* | ἡμῶν, | *of us* |
| Abl. | ἐμοῦ, μου | etc. | ἡμῶν, | etc. |
| Loc. | ἐμοί, μοι | | ἡμῖν | |
| Ins. | ἐμοί, μοι | | ἡμῖν | |
| Dat. | ἐμοί, μοι | | ἡμῖν | |
| Acc. | ἐμέ, με | | ἡμᾶς | |

**133.** The declension of the second personal pronoun, σύ, *thou*, is

| *Singular* | | | *Plural* | |
|---|---|---|---|---|
| Nom. | σύ, | *thou* | ὑμεῖς, | *ye (you)* |
| Gen. | σοῦ, σου, | *of thee* | ὑμῶν, | *of you* |
| Abl. | σοῦ, σου | etc. | ὑμῶν | etc. |
| Loc. | σοί, σοι, | | ὑμῖν | |
| Ins. | σοί, σοι | | ὑμῖν | |
| Dat. | σοί, σοι | | ὑμῖν | |
| Acc. | σέ, σε. | | ὑμᾶς | |

**134.** Observe: In the singular of the first and second personal pronouns there are, except in the nominative, two forms for each case, an accented form and an unaccented form (which in the first person is also shorter than the accented form). These forms are called *enclitics* (see 138).

**135.** 1. Commonly the accented or emphatic forms are used when emphasis or contrast is desired. Yet it is not certain that all emphasis is absent when the unaccented or enclitic forms are used.

2. With prepositions the emphatic or accented forms are used generally, except with πρός, which ordinarily has πρός με.

3. In general the personal pronouns were not used in the nominative case unless emphasis or contrast was desired: e.g., τὸν ἄγγελον ἔβλεπον ἐγώ, *I was looking at the angel* (It was *I* who was looking at the angel). This follows from the fact that the verb uses the personal pronouns as personal endings (as explained in 17), and no need was felt for the separate expression of the personal pronoun in the nominative.

**136.** The conjugation of the present indicative of εἰμί, *I am*, is as follows:

| *Singular* | *Plural* |
|---|---|
| 1. εἰμί, *I am* | ἐσμέν, *we are* |
| 2. εἶ, *thou art* | ἐστέ, *ye (you) are* |
| 3. ἐστί, *he, she,* or *it is* | εἰσί, *they are* |

Present infinitive εἶναι, *to be*

*a.* εἰμί is for ἐσ-μι; εἶ is for ἐσσι; εἰσι is for (σ)εντι for (h) εντι; εἶναι is probably for ἐσ-ναι. *b.* All the forms of the present indicative of εἰμί, except εἶ, are enclitic (see 138). *c.* It was noted in 18 that the primary act. end. -μι was dropped, and the preceding ο lengthened to ω. Some verbs retain this -μι and do not have the thematic ᵒ/ε. The former make up what is called the ω- conjugation, the latter the μι- conjugation. To the latter belongs εἰμί.

**137.** When the verb εἰμί is used merely as a connective or copula, it has the predicate nominative: e.g., ὁ μαθητής ἐστιν ἄνθρωπος, *the disciple is a man;* see examples below under 138, 1–5. Note that the subject may be known from the predicate whenever the subject has the article and the predicate does not: e.g., ἀγάπη ἐστὶν ὁ θεός, *God is love.* Here ἀγάπη is the predicate because it does not have the article, while θεός does have the article.

**138.** Enclitics are words attaching themselves so closely to the preceding word as to be pronounced with it. Usually they have no accents of their own.

The word before an enclitic is treated as follows:

1. If the preceding word has an acute accent on the antepenult, it receives an additional accent (acute) on its ultima from any enclitic, whether of one syllable (monosyllabic) or of two syllables (dissyllabic):

ὁ διδάσκαλός μου,          *my teacher*
ὁ διδάσκαλός ἐστιν ἀγαθός, *the teacher is good*

2. If the preceding word has an acute accent on the penult, its accent is not affected in any way:

then a monosyllabic enclitic loses its accent; but a dissyllabic enclitic retains its accent:

ὁ λόγος μου, *my word;* ἡ καρδία σου, *thy heart*
ὁ λόγος ἐστὶν αἰώνιος, *the word is eternal*

3. If the preceding word naturally has an acute accent on the ultima, it keeps its own accent, and any enclitic loses its accent.

 ὁ ἀδελφός σου,   *thy brother*
 οἱ ἀδελφοί εἰσι πιστοί, *the brothers are faithful*

4. If the preceding word has a circumflex accent on the penult, it receives an additional accent (acute) on its ultima from any enclitic:

 ὁ δοῦλός μου,   *my servant*
 ὁ δοῦλός ἐστι δίκαιος, *the servant is just*

5. If the preceding word has a circumflex accent on the ultima, its accent is not affected in any way, and any enclitic loses its accent:

 ὁ υἱὸς τοῦ ἀδελφοῦ μου, *the son of my brother*
 οἱ δοῦλοι τοῦ θεοῦ ἐσμεν, *we are the servants of God*

**139.** Observe: 1. A monosyllabic enclitic regularly loses its accent. 2. A dissyllabic enclitic retains its accent only under the condition named in 2 above.

**140.** An enclitic sometimes retains its accent:

 1. When there is emphasis on the enclitic or when the enclitic begins a sentence.

 2. ἐστί is written ἔστι at the beginning of a sentence, when it means *exist* or *is possible*, and when it immediately follows ἀλλ' (ἀλλά), εἰ, καί, μή, οὐκ, ὅτι, τοῦτ' (τοῦτο), ὡς.

**141.** A proclitic (see note to 72 and 95) or an enclitic followed by an enclitic receives an acute accent: e.g. ὅ γε δοῦλός μού ἐστι.

(But under 138–140 modern critics and editors differ.)

**142.** EXERCISES

I. 1. ὑμεῖς ἐστε τὰ τέκνα τοῦ θεοῦ. 2. ἡμεῖς γὰρ γινώσκομεν τὸν κύριον. 3. ἡ δὲ ἀλήθεια οὐκ ἔστιν¹ ἐν ἡμῖν. 4. ἐγώ εἰμι ἡ ὁδὸς καὶ ἡ ἀλήθεια καὶ ἡ ζωή. 5. τοῦτό² ἐστι τὸ ἔργον τοῦ θεοῦ. 6. ἀλλὰ οὐ λόγοις ὑμεῖς σώζεσθε.

II. 1. My house is in the village. 2. We are the servants of the Lord. 3. The way is bad, but you know me. 4. You are a prophet, for from you are sent forth words of wisdom. 5. We have bread for you (sing.). 6. You are my disciples.

## LESSON XX

Third Personal Pronoun. Imperfect Ind. of εἰμί

**143.** VOCABULARY

ἄλλος,-η,-ο, *other*
αὐτός,-ή,-ό, *self, very, same;*
    *he, she, it*

εἰ, conj., *if*
ὅλος,-η,-ον, *whole*
ὅτι, conj., *because, that*
σκοτία, ἡ, *darkness*

---

¹ Certain words, i.e. words ending in -σι, the third personal sing. of past tenses (in -ε), and ἐστί, may add ν. This is called movable ν. Movable ν in the older Greek was written when it would be followed by a word beginning with a vowel; but later it was written before consonants and vowels. ² τοῦτο, *this* (neuter).

**144.** The declension of αὐτός is as follows:

### Singular

|      | Masc.  | Fem.   | Neut.  |
|------|--------|--------|--------|
| Nom. | αὐτός  | αὐτή   | αὐτό   |
| Gen. | αὐτοῦ  | αὐτῆς  | αὐτοῦ  |
| Abl. | αὐτοῦ  | αὐτῆς  | αὐτοῦ  |
| Loc. | αὐτῷ   | αὐτῇ   | αὐτῷ   |
| Ins. | αὐτῷ   | αὐτῇ   | αὐτῷ   |
| Dat. | αὐτῷ   | αὐτῇ   | αὐτῷ   |
| Acc. | αὐτόν  | αὐτήν  | αὐτό   |

### Plural

|      | Masc.  | Fem.   | Neut.  |
|------|--------|--------|--------|
| Nom. | αὐτοί  | αὐταί  | αὐτά   |
| Gen. | αὐτῶν  | αὐτῶν  | αὐτῶν  |
| Abl. | αὐτῶν  | αὐτῶν  | αὐτῶν  |
| Loc. | αὐτοῖς | αὐταῖς | αὐτοῖς |
| Ins. | αὐτοῖς | αὐταῖς | αὐτοῖς |
| Dat. | αὐτοῖς | αὐταῖς | αὐτοῖς |
| Acc. | αὐτούς | αὐτάς  | αὐτά   |

Observe that αὐτός is declined like ἀγαθός (115) except that αὐτός has no vocative and the neuter nom. and acc. sing. have no -ν.

**145.** Meaning and uses of αὐτός. It is properly a demonstrative.

1. As an intensive pronoun αὐτός means *self;* *himself, herself, itself,* etc.; and is in the predicate position (119, 2):

αὐτὸς ὁ ἄνθρωπος }
ὁ ἄνθρωπος αὐτός } = *the man himself*

2. As an identical pronoun αὐτός means *same,* and is in the attributive position (118, 1):

ὁ αὐτὸς ἄνθρωπος, *the same man*

When the article precedes αὐτός, the meaning is always *the same*.

3. When used alone in the genitive, ablative, locative, instrumental, dative, and accusative cases (the "oblique" cases), this word is the simple personal pronoun of the third person:

βλέπω αὐτόν,     *I see him*
πέμπομεν αὐτούς, *we send them*
ἐν τῷ οἴκῳ αὐτοῦ, *in his house* (in the house of him)
λαμβάνει τὸν ἄρτον ἀπὸ αὐτῆς, *he takes the bread from her*

(With αὐτός in the nominative, sometimes it is not clear whether we have simply an emphatic "he," etc., or an intensive "self.")

**146.** 1. The substantive to which a pronoun refers is called its antecedent:

γινώσκομεν τὸν διδάσκαλον καὶ λέγομεν αὐτῷ, *we know the teacher and speak to him.*
τὸν διδάσκαλον is the antecedent of αὐτῷ

2. A pronoun agrees with its antecedent in gender and number. Cf. διδάσκαλον (masc. gender, sing. number) and αὐτῷ (masc. gender, sing. number).

**147.** 1. ἄλλος is declined (except the accent) like αὐτός. Note -ο in the nom. and acc. neuter singular. ἄλλος is used alone and with the article (but in New Testament never in the senses of "the rest of").

2. ὅλος always has the predicate position in the New Testament. ὅλος ὁ κόσμος, *the whole world.*

**148.** The imperfect indicative of εἰμί, *I am*, is

| *Singular* | | *Plural* | |
|---|---|---|---|
| 1. (ἦν) and ἤμην, | *I was* | ἦμεν and ἤμεθα, | *we were* |
| 2. ἦς and ἦσθα, | *thou wast* | ἦτε, | *ye were* |
| 3. ἦν, | *he was* | ἦσαν, | *they were* |

*a.* The middle form ἤμην has practically thrust out the active form ἦν. *b.* ἦσθα is an old perf. form, found twice in New Testament. *c.* ἤμεθα is found nearly as often as ἦμεν in New Testament.

For the meaning of the imperfect indicative see 65.

**149.** Conditional Sentences.

There are four separate forms for Greek conditions. The first is:

*The condition determined as fulfilled.*

Here any tense of the indicative is used, generally after εἰ, *if*,[1] in the protasis (the if-clause). The apodosis (conclusion) generally has the indicative (any tense), but any mode may be used according to what is wanted, e.g.:

εἰ σώζει τοὺς ἀνθρώπους, τὸν θεὸν δοξάζει, *if he is saving men, he is glorifying God.*

εἰ ἔσωζε τοὺς ἀνθρώπους, τὸν θεὸν ἐδόξαζε, *if he was saving men, he was glorifying God.*

"The indicative *states* the condition as a fact. It may or may not be true in fact. The condition has nothing to do with that, but only with the statement."

The negative of the protasis is generally οὐ, *not.*[2]

---

[1] Infrequently ἐάν, *if*, is used.
[2] A few times μή, *not*, is found.

**150.** EXERCISES

I. 1. βλέπετε αὐτόν. 2. αὐτοὶ ἡμεῖς οὐκ ἐκρινόμεθα, ἀλλὰ αὐτὸν ἐκρίνομεν. 3. ὁ αὐτὸς μαθητὴς ἐλάμβανε τὰ τέκνα καὶ ἐδίδασκεν αὐτά. 4. εἰ μένομεν ἐν αὐτῷ, ζωὴν αἰώνιον ἔχομεν. 5. καὶ λέγει ὁ Ἰησοῦς[1] ὅτι οἱ δοῦλοι αὐτοῦ δοξάζουσι αὐτόν.

II 1. I glorify him. 2. Darkness is not in him. 3. He himself is the life. 4. On (ἐν) the same day he was teaching them. 5. If we receive him, he saves us. 6. We know the truth and proclaim it. 7. He has other servants in the world. 8. He was in the house. 9. They were faithful men.

## LESSON XXI

### Defective ("Deponent") Verbs

### The Demonstrative Pronouns οὗτος and ἐκεῖνος

**151.** VOCABULARY

| | | | |
|---|---|---|---|
| ἀπέρχομαι, | I go away | ἐξέρχομαι, | I go out |
| ἀποκρίνομαι, | I answer | ἔρχομαι, | I go, come |
| βούλομαι, | I wish | πορεύομαι, | I go, proceed |
| γίνομαι, | I become, be | προσέρχομαι | I go to, come to |
| διέρχομαι, | I go through | ἐκεῖνος,-η,-ο, | demons. pron., that (one) |
| δύναμαι, | I am able, can | οὗτος, αὕτη, τοῦτο, | demons. pron. this (one) |
| εἰσέρχομαι, | I enter | | |

[1] Jesus.

διά, prep. (orginally "interval between") with gen. *through, by;* with acc., *because of, for the sake of, on account of.*

πρός, prep. (originally *near, facing*) with loc., *near, by;* with acc., *towards, to;* with abl. (once), *"from the point of view of."*

*a.* Note the many compound[1] verbs in the vocabulary, especially a preposition + ἔρχομαι. Many of these verbs occur hundreds of times in the New Testament. *b.* δύναμαι does not have a thematic vowel; α appears in all persons. In the second pers. sing. two forms are found: δύνασαι and δύνῃ. *c.* γίνομαι is used also as a copula (see 137).

**152.** Defective verbs. Some verbs were used in all the voices in all the tenses, as λύω; some verbs in some tenses were used only in one voice and in other tenses, in another voice, as βαίνω, *I go* (future βήσομαι); some verbs were used in one voice only, as κεῖμαι, *I lie (am laid).*

The term *defective* is applied to those verbs which are used either in the middle voice or in the passive voice and not in the active voice but *seemingly* have a simple active meaning; as αἰσθάνομαι, *I perceive,* in middle voice; βούλομαι, *I wish,* in passive voice.

The verbs in the vocabulary (151) are defective verbs. But some of these verbs have active forms in some tenses, as γίνομαι; second perfect active γέγονα.

These verbs have been called "deponents" (middle or passive) because it was difficult to see the distinctive force of the voice. Yet it is not hard to

[1] See 73–76.

recognize the personal interest of the subject in the verbs in the middle voice.

**153.** The declension of οὗτος is:

*Singular*

|        | *Masc.* | *Fem.* | *Neut.* |
|--------|---------|--------|---------|
| Nom.   | οὗτος   | αὕτη   | τοῦτο   |
| Gen.   | τούτου  | ταύτης | τούτου  |
| Abl.   | τούτου  | ταύτης | τούτου  |
| Loc.   | τούτῳ   | ταύτῃ  | τούτῳ   |
| Ins.   | τούτῳ   | ταύτῃ  | τούτῳ   |
| Dat.   | τούτῳ   | ταύτῃ  | τούτῳ   |
| Acc.   | τοῦτον  | ταύτην | τοῦτο   |

*Plural*

|        | *Masc.* | *Fem.* | *Neut.* |
|--------|---------|--------|---------|
| Nom.   | οὗτοι   | αὗται  | ταῦτα   |
| Gen.   | τούτων  | τούτων | τούτων  |
| Abl.   | τούτων  | τούτων | τούτων  |
| Loc.   | τούτοις | ταύταις| τούτοις |
| Ins.   | τούτοις | ταύταις| τούτοις |
| Dat.   | τούτοις | ταύταις| τούτοις |
| Acc.   | τούτους | ταύτας | ταῦτα   |

**154.** Observe: 1. The rough breathing occurs in the nom. masc. and fem., sing. and plural, but all other forms begin with τ. 2. The diphthong of the penult, ου or αυ, varies as the vowel of the ultima, ο(ω) or α(η). 3. The accent remains on the penult.

**155.** The declension of ἐκεῖνος is like that of αὐτός (except the accent). Note in the neuter sing. nom. and acc. ἐκεῖνο.

**156.** οὗτος and ἐκεῖνος are demonstrative pronouns. In contrast, οὗτος refers, as a rule, to what is near or last mentioned, and ἐκεῖνος to what is remote, or absent.

**157.** Use of οὗτος and ἐκεῖνος. 1. When they are used with a substantive, they commonly have the predicate position: e.g., ὁ λόγος οὗτος or οὗτος ὁ λόγος, *this word;* ἐκείνη ἡ ἡμέρα or ἡ ἡμέρα ἐκείνη, *that day.*

2. When the article does not occur with the substantive, the substantive is in the predicate: e.g., τρίτην ταύτην ἡμέραν, *this a third day (not* this third day).

3. They are often used alone, without substantives: e.g., οὗτος, *this one* (man or person); ἐκείνη, *that woman;* τοῦτο, *this thing;* ταῦτα, *these things;* etc.

**158.**                    EXERCISES

I. 1. ἐκεῖνος δὲ ὁ δοῦλος ἀπέρχεται. 2. τοῦτο τὸ τέκνον εἰσήρχετο εἰς τὸν οἶκον ἐκεῖνον. 3. ἐκεῖνος δίκαιός ἐστιν. 4. αὕτη ἐστὶν ἡ πρώτη ἐντολή. 5. ἐν ἐκείναις ταῖς ἡμέραις κακοὶ προφῆται διήρχοντο τὰς κώμας. 6. ὁ κύριος ἔλεγεν τούτῳ τοὺς λόγους ζωῆς αἰωνίου.

II. 1. This world; that gift. 2. This disciple knows the law and the prophets. 3. This is the work of God. 4. Those children were going to him. 5. This commandment I write to the brethren. 6. On that day he was preaching in the temple.

## LESSON XXII

### Present Subjunctive Active

**159.**  Vocabulary

ἁμαρτάνω, *I sin*

ἀναβαίνω, *I go up, come up, ascend*

ἀνά, prep. (original meaning *on, upon, along*) usually with the accusative in the distributive sense:

ἀνὰ δύο,    *two by two*

ἀνὰ ἑκατόν, *by hundreds*

ἵνα,    conj. generally with subjunctive, *in order that, that*

κατά, prep. (original meaning down) with gen., *down* (upon), *against;* with abl., *down* (from); with acc., *down* (along), *through, according to.*

μετά, prep. (original meaning "midst") with the gen., *with;* with the acc., *after;* μετὰ ταῦτα, *after these things, after this.*

μή,    *not*                    χαίρω, *rejoice*

νῦν,   adv., *now*             πῶς, adv., *how*

**160.** From the previous lessons it has been learned that the Greek verb has *tense, voice,* and *mode,* like verbs in other languages.

**161.** It has been seen (14) that tense has to do with the action of the verb as regards the *state of action.* Voice (51 and 52) has to do with the action of the verb as regards the *subject of the action.* Mode has to do with the *manner of affirmation,* how it is made, and not with action as do voice and tense.

**162.** It has been observed that the indicative is the mode of definite assertion. It is used to affirm positively, definitely, absolutely, undoubtingly. The mode has nothing to do with the actual facts (whether true or untrue), but only with the statement of them. The indicative *states* a thing as true.

**163.** The subjunctive mode is a mode of doubtful statement, of hesitating affirmation, of contingency.

*a.* The subjunctive is usually found in two tenses, the present and the aorist. The perfect subjunctive is very rare.

**164.** The present subjunctive active of λύω is:

| Singular | Plural |
|----------|--------|
| 1. λύω | λύωμεν |
| 2. λύῃς | λύητε |
| 3. λύῃ | λύωσι(ν¹) |

**165.** Observe that: 1. The subjunctive has the primary active personal endings (see 17–19). 2. The long thematic vowel ω/η is the subjunctive mode sign. 3. In the second and third persons sing. η has iota-subscript (ῃ)

**166.** The present subj. of εἰμί is:

| Singular | Plural |
|----------|--------|
| 1. ὦ | ὦμεν |
| 2. ᾖς | ἦτε |
| 3. ᾖ | ὦσι(ν¹) |

Note the circumflex accent.

**167.** The subjunctive is used in clauses of purpose after ἵνα.

¹ See footnote to 142.

Examine closely the following sentences:

ἔρχεται ἵνα βλέπη αὐτόν, *he comes that he may see him.*
ταῦτα λέγομεν ἵνα μὴ ἁμαρτάνωσι, *we say this in order that they may not sin.*

**168.** Note that the negative with the subjunctive is μή.

**169.** There is no time (absolute) element in the subjunctive mode in any tense. The present subjunctive expresses *linear* or *durative* action without reference to time. See 14.

**170.**                            EXERCISES

I. 1. ἐγὼ δὲ ἔρχομαι ἵνα τὸν κόσμον σώζω. 2. κηρύσσομεν ἵνα οἱ ἄνθρωποι ἔχωσι ζωὴν αἰώνιον. 3. πῶς γε δύναται σώζειν;[1] 4. μετὰ ταῦτα ἀπέρχεται εἰς τὴν ἔρημον. 5. ὁ θεὸς λέγει ἡμῖν ἵνα μὴ μένωμεν ἐν τῇ ἁμαρτίᾳ. 6. ὁ 'Ιησοῦς αὐτὸς οὐκ ἐβάπτιζεν, ἀλλ' οἱ μαθηταὶ αὐτοῦ.

II. 1. Now we become the children of God. 2. They baptize in order that they may glorify God. 3. You are not able to hear my word. 4. After these things he goes away in order that they may not see him. 5. How can (is able) he take away our sins?

## LESSON XXIII

### Present Subjunctive Middle and Passive

**171.**                            VOCABULARY

| | | | |
|---|---|---|---|
| ἀσπάζομαι, | *I salute* | καινός,-ή,-όν, | *new* |
| εὐαγγέλιον, τό, | *gospel* | μαρτυρία, ἡ, | *witnessing,* |
| δέχομαι, | *I receive* | | *witness,* |
| καθώς, adv., | *just as, even as* | | *testimony* |

[1] The question mark (;) is the same in form as our semicolon.

οὖν, postpositive adv., *there-*      οὕτως, adv. *thus, in this*
*fore, then, now.*                    *manner, so*

**172.** The present middle and passive subjunctive of
λύω. is:

| Singular | Plural |
|----------|--------|
| 1. λύωμαι | λυώμεθα |
| 2. λύῃ | λύησθε |
| 3. λύηται | λύωνται |

**173.** Observe: 1. The middle and passive forms are
alike (this was seen in the indicative also, 60).

2. The mode sign ω/η is the same as in the active
(see 165, 2).

3. The personal endings are the primary middle
(and passive) endings (see 54 and 60).

*a.* In the second pers. sing. -η is for -ησαι; σ
dropped out, then η and αι contracted to η. Note
iota-subscript under η

**174.** The subjunctive (first person plural) is used
in exhortations: as

χαίρωμεν ἐν τῇ ἀληθείᾳ, *let us rejoice in the truth.*
μὴ λέγωμεν κακά, *let us not speak evil things.*

**175.** Many verbs in Greek are followed by the
genitive case, and many by the dative case, where
the corresponding verbs in English would be followed by the objective case. In each instance the
idea of the case is accented.

ἀκούει τῆς φωνῆς, *he hears the voice.*

(This just tells "kind" of sound.) The accusative

may be used after ἀκούω; then the meaning of the sound is comprehended.

πιστεύομεν αὐτῷ,   *we believe him.*
ἀποκρίνεται τῷ τέκνῳ, *he answers the child.*
δουλεύω αὐτῷ,   *I serve him.*

Note that the dative accents the personal interest.

**176.**   EXERCISES

I. 1. πιστεύωμεν τῷ κυρίῳ. 2. ἀγώμεθα ὑπὸ τῶν ἀποστόλων. 3. καθὼς ἐκεῖνος δίκαιός ἐστιν, ὦμεν δίκαιοι ἡμεῖς. 4. ἐν ἀρχῇ ὁ λόγος ἠκούετο. 5. δεχώμεθα τὴν μαρτυρίαν αὐτοῦ. 6. ἤκουον τῶν φωνῶν τῶν δούλων.

II. 1. Let us not answer him. 2. Let us salute the apostles. 3. Let us receive the truth in order that we may know it. 4. He was preaching the gospel of the new covenant. 5. He is able to take away our sins. 6. Let us be led by the Lord into truth.

## LESSON XXIV

### Second Aorist Indicative Active and Middle

**177.**   VOCABULARY

ἀπέθανον,   *I died;* second aor. of ἀποθνήσκω.

ἔβαλον,   *I threw, cast;* second aor. of βάλλω.

ἐγενόμην,   *I became;* second aor. of γίνομαι.

εἶδον,   *I saw;* second aor.—no present stem in use but ὁράω is used in present tense.

(εἶπον),   *I said;* second aor.—no present stem in

εἶπα,   use, but λέγω is used in the present tense.

ἔλαβον,   *I took;* second aor. of λαμβάνω.

ἔλιπον,     *I left;* second aor. of λείπω.

εὗρον,     *I found;* second aor. of εὑρίσκω.

ἔσχον,     *I got;* second aor. of ἔχω.

ἔφαγον,     *I ate;* second aor.—no present stem in use, but ἐσθίω is used in the present tense.

ἦλθον,     *I went, came;* second aor.—no present stem in use, but ἔρχομαι is used in the present tense.

παρέλαβον, *I received;* second aor. of παραλαμβάνω.

**178.** The *second* aorist is so called in distinction from the *first aorist*, which is to be studied in Lesson XXXVI. They are not two different tenses, but second aorist and first aorist are two forms of the same tense.

**179.** As has already been learned (14), the fundamental idea in tense is the "kind of action." The present tense (and imperfect, 65, 69) expresses durative or linear action. The aorist tense expresses action in its simplest form—undefined; it does not distinguish between complete or incomplete action. The aorist tense treats the action as a point;—this kind of action is called *punctiliar:* ἔχω, *I have, am holding;* ἔσχον, *I got, obtained.*

**180.** This kind of action (punctiliar) is timeless. But time is expressed in the indicative mode by the augment,—punctiliar action in past time, generally.

In narrative the difference between the *aorist indicative* and the imperfect indicative is just this: the aorist indicative expresses *punctiliar action* in past time, while the imperfect indicative expresses *durative* action in past time.

**181.** The second aorist [1] indicative active and middle of λείπω is:

ACTIVE

*Singular*                    *Plural*

1. ἔλιπον                     ἐλίπομεν
2. ἔλιπες                     ἐλίπετε
3. ἔλιπε                      ἔλιπον

Second aorist active infinitive, λιπεῖν.

MIDDLE

1. ἐλιπόμην                   ἐλιπόμεθα
2. ἐλίπου                     ἐλίπεσθε
3. ἐλίπετο                    ἐλίποντο

Second aorist middle infinitive, λιπέσθαι.

**182.** Observe: 1. The difference in form between the second aorist indicative and the imperfect indicative of the same verb is a difference in stem: aorist stem λιπ-; imperfect (having the present stem) λειπ-. 2. The secondary personal endings (66, 79) are used. 3. The augment in the aorist follows the same principles as it did in the imperfect. (70). 4. The accent of the second aorist infinitive is not recessive (11), but in the active is placed on the ultima, and in the midde on the penult.

The endings, -α, -ας, -ε, -αμεν, -ατε, -αν, are found frequently with second aorist stems and almost exclusively with εἶπον.

**183.** Note that the infinitive has no augment. The aorist act. inf. λιπεῖν means simply *to leave*, the action

[1] The second aorist of the thematic vowel °/ε type is introduced here on account of its simplicity and its similarity in inflection to the imperfect, as well as on account of its frequent use.

is punctiliar and timeless; while the present act. infinitive λείπειν means *to be leaving* (or to keep leaving), the action is durative and timeless. So also in the middle.

**184.** The second aorist usually exhibits the simple stem of the verb. The second aorist given here is the thematic type, i.e., uses the thematic vowel $^o/_\epsilon$.

| | Present stem | Present theme | Aorist stem | Aorist theme |
|---|---|---|---|---|
| βάλλω | βαλλ- | βαλλ$^o/_\epsilon$ | βαλ- | βαλ$^o/_\epsilon$ |
| γίνομαι | γιν- | γιν$^o/_\epsilon$ | γεν- | γεν$^o/_\epsilon$ |
| λείπω | λειπ- | λειπ$^o/_\epsilon$ | λιπ- | λιπ$^o/_\epsilon$ |

Note that the second aorist is known by its stem.

**185.** From the forms of the present, imperfect, perfect, etc., it cannot be determined beforehand whether a verb has a first aorist or a second aorist, nor, if it has a second aorist, what the form of the second aorist is. To determine this, the verb must be examined in a lexicon.

**186.** The second aorist act. and middle are formed on the second aorist stem. The aorist passive of all verbs is different from the aorist middle. Review the meaning of the middle (52).

ἐλιπόμην is second aorist indicative middle, *I left for myself*, etc.

**187.** The Greek aorist indicative is not the exact equivalent of any tense in English or in any other language. The Greek aorist and the English preterit do not exactly correspond. The translation given in the vocabulary is just to get the verb idea associated with the verb form. To translate the Greek aorist ind., sometimes the English preterit is used, sometimes the perfect, sometimes the past. The Greek aorist ind. refers the action to the past without any exact specification as to antecedence of action or as to present results of action.

**188.** EXERCISES

I. 1. ἦλθε εἰς τὸν οἶκον. 2. ἐφάγομεν τὸν ἄρτον. 3. ἐν τῷ κόσμῳ ἦν καὶ ὁ κόσμος δι' αὐτοῦ ἐγένετο. 4. εἰς τὰ ἴδια ἦλθεν καὶ οἱ ἴδιοι αὐτὸν οὐ παρέλαβον. 5. ταῦτα εἶπον ὑμῖν ἐν τῷ ἱερῷ. 6. μετὰ ταῦτα ἀπέθανεν τὸ τέκνον.

II. 1. He died on the third day. 2. He took the bread and ate (it). 3. The disciples obtained good promises. 4. They came and saw where (ποῦ) he was abiding. 5. The servant cast a stone into the boat.

## LESSON XXV

### Second Aorist Subjunctive Active and Middle

**189.** VOCABULARY

ἀληθινός, -ή, -όν, *true*     διάβολος, ὁ, *devil*
βίος, ὁ,        *life*     ἐκεῖ, adv., *there*

Learn the capital letters in 1 of Lesson I.

**190.** The second aorist subjunctive active and middle of λείπω is:

ACTIVE

| *Singular* | *Plural* |
|---|---|
| 1. λίπω | λίπωμεν |
| 2. λίπῃς | λίπητε |
| 3. λίπῃ | λίπωσι |

MIDDLE

1. λίπωμαι                    λιπώμεθα
2. λίπῃ                       λίπησθε
3. λίπηται                    λίπωνται

**191.** Observe: 1. There is no augment in the aorist subjunctive. 2. The personal endings are the primary active and middle. 3. The subjunctive mode sign is the long thematic vowel ω/ῃ. 4. The only difference in form between the second aorist subj. (act. and middle) and the present subj. (act. and middle) is in the stem,—present stem λειπ-; aorist stem λιπ-.

**192.** Let it be remembered that the *aorist subjunctive does not denote past time*. But the real time of the subj. is future in relation to the speaker or writer; and this time element is not due to the tense at all.

**193.** The distinction in meaning between the present subjunctive and the aorist subjunctive is only in the *kind of action*. The present subj. expresses *durative action*. The aorist subj. expresses *punctiliar action*.

Example: μὴ ἀποθνήσκωμεν ἐν τῇ ἁμαρτίᾳ, *let us not be dying in sin, let us not continue to die* (or keep on dying) *in sin*. μὴ ἀποθάνωμεν ἐν τῇ ἁμαρτίᾳ, *let us not die in sin*.

In the first example the present (subjunctive) represents the action in progress. In the second example the aorist (subjunctive) just treats the action as a single whole without any reference to progress or completion. It is generally difficult to bring out the difference in an English translation.

**194.** The subjunctive is used in questions of doubt, where the speaker asks what he is to do or say:

πῶς εὕρωμεν αὐτόν; *How are we to find him?*
τί εἴπω; *What am I to say? What shall I say?*
ἐπιμένωμεν τῇ ἁμαρτίᾳ; *Shall we remain in sin?*

**195.** EXERCISES

I. 1. ἐγὼ οὐκ ἦλθον βαλεῖν εἰρήνην ἐπὶ τὴν γῆν. 2. ἄγωμεν καὶ ἡμεῖς ἵνα ἀποθάνωμεν μετ' αὐτοῦ. 3. οὗτος ἦλθεν εἰς μαρτυρίαν ἵνα ἡμεῖς παραλάβωμεν αὐτόν. 4. ἦρον οὖν λίθους ἵνα βάλωσιν ἐπ' αὐτόν. 5. ταῦτα εἶπεν Ἰησοῦς αὐτοῖς ἐν τῷ ἱερῷ.

II. 1. How shall we receive them? 2. Let us not become evil prophets. 3. What shall we eat? 4. The servants came in order that they might find the children. 5. He died that men might have life.

## LESSON XXVI

**Third Declension: Neuter Substantives in -ματ-.**

**196.** VOCABULARY

| | | | |
|---|---|---|---|
| αἷμα, τό, | blood | ῥῆμα, τό, | *word* |
| γράμμα, τό, | *letter* (of alpha- | σπέρμα, τό, | *seed* |
| | bet), *writing* | στόμα, τό, | *mouth* |
| θέλημα, τό, | *will* | σῶμα, τό, | *body* |
| ὄνομα, τό, | *name* | χάρισμα, τό, | *gift, free gift* |
| πνεῦμα, τό, | *spirit* | ἅγιος,-α,-ον, | *holy* |

**197.** The third declension is commonly called the *consonant* declension because most of the nouns have stems ending in a consonant. A few nouns, included in this declension, ended in the vowels ι and υ, which were sometimes semivowels.

**198.** The case endings of the consonant declension are:

|  | *Singular* | | *Plural* | |
|  | *Masc. and Fem.* | *Neut.* | *Masc. and Fem.* | *Neut.* |
|---|---|---|---|---|
| Nom. | -ς or none | None | -ες | -α |
| Gen. | -ος | -ος | -ων | -ων |
| Abl. | -ος | -ος | -ων | -ων |
| Loc. | -ι | -ι | -σι | -σι |
| Ins. | -ι | -ι | -σι | -σι |
| Dat. | -ι | -ι | -σι | -σι |
| Acc. | -ν or -α | none | (-νς), -ας | -α |
| Voc. | none or like nom. or stem | none | -ες | -α |

In the case endings final α is short.

*These forms must be thoroughly mastered.*

Note that the loc., ins., and dat. sing. use the locative ending -ι; and in the plural these cases use the locative ending -σι (see p. 65 n.).

The gen. and abl. plural ending -ων is the same for all the declensions.

The neuter plural nom., acc., and voc. are always alike.

The vocative plural is always the same as the nominative.

**199.** The declension of ὄνομα,[1] *name*, is:

STEM ὀνοματ-

|  | *Singular* | *Plural* |
|---|---|---|
| Nom. | ὄνομα | ὀνόματα |
| Gen. | ὀνόματος | ὀνομάτων |
| Abl. | ὀνόματος | ὀνομάτων |
| Loc. | ὀνόματι | ὀνόμασι |
| Ins. | ὀνόματι | ὀνόμασι |
| Dat. | ὀνόματι | ὀνόμασι |
| Acc. | ὄνομα | ὀνόματα |

**200.** Observe: 1. As in the neuters of the second declension, the nom. acc. and voc. sing. are alike, and the same cases in the plural are alike. 2. The nom. sing. is the mere stem, final τ being dropped.

Note: The consonants that can stand at the close of a word in Greek are ν, ρ, and ς (including ξ and ψ). All other consonants which would occur there are dropped. 3. In the loc., ins., dat., plural, ὀνόμασι, the τ of the stem drops out before σ.

**201.** In declining a substantive of the consonant declension it is necessary to know the *stem*. The *stem* is usually found by dropping the genitive sing. ending -ος. Thus: Nom. στόμα; gen. στόματος; stem στοματ-. The genitive singular, then, must be known before nouns of the consonant declension can be declined.

**202.** The gender of the third declension substantives, except in the case of special classes like the sub-

---

[1] Neuter substantives with nom. in -μα (stem -ματ-) are introduced first on account of their simplicity and importance.

stantives in -ματ-, must be learned with each word
separately.

**203.** *A neuter plural subject* often has its verb in the
singular:

τῶν δώδεκα ἀποστόλων τὰ ὀνόματά ἐστιν ταῦτα, *the names
of the twelve apostles are these.*

**204.**                    EXERCISES

I.  1. τοῦτό ἐστι τὸ σῶμά μου.  2. τὰ ῥήματα  ζωῆς
αἰωνίου ἔχεις.  3. γινώσκομεν τὸ θέλημα τοῦ θεοῦ.  4.
ὄνομα ἦν αὐτῷ 'Ιωάννης.  5. σπέρμα 'Αβραάμ ἐσμεν.  6.
θέλετε ἄγειν ἐφ' (against) ἡμᾶς τὸ αἷμα τοῦ ἀνθρώπου τούτου;

II.  1. This is the will of God.  2. These are the
good seed.  3. The words of the prophet are written
in the scriptures.  4. Let us believe on (εἰς) the
name of the Lord.  5. That one was baptizing them
in the holy spirit.  6. The will of God came through
the mouths of the prophets.


**LESSON XXVII**

**Future Indicative Active and Middle**

**205.**                    VOCABULARY

δαιμόνιον, τό, *demon*

καί, besides the usual connective use, *and*, is used in
the sense of *also*, and *even*.

περί, prep. (original meaning *around* (on all sides))
with gen., *about, concerning;* with abl., *from
around;* with acc., *round about, about, concerning.*

ὑπέρ, prep. (original meaning *over, upper*) with abl.,
*in behalf of, in interest of; instead of; in place of*

*for the sake of; about, concerning;* with acc., *over, above, beyond.*

ὡς, relative, comparative, and temporal adv., *as, when.*

**206.** The future tense is made on aoristic (punctiliar) roots in some verbs and on durative roots in other verbs. The kind of action of the future may be either punctiliar or durative. But in use the future is generally punctiliar.

**207.** The future indicative, as in English, generally denotes what *is going to take place.* It is just the present vividly projected into the future. In English it is done by "shall" in the first person and by "will" in the second and third persons. Yet the future ind. has modal aspects which will be presented later.

**208.** The future indicative active and middle of λύω is:

ACTIVE

| *Singular* | | *Plural* |
|---|---|---|
| 1. λύσω, | *I shall loose* | λύσομεν |
| 2. λύσεις | etc. | λύσετε |
| 3. λύσει | | λύσουσι |

Future active infinitive. λύσειν[1]

MIDDLE

| *Singular* | | *Plural* |
|---|---|---|
| 1. λύσομαι, | *I shall loose myself* | λυσόμεθα |
| 2. λύσῃ | or *for myself,* etc. | λύσεσθε |
| 3. λύσεται | | λύσονται |

Future middle infinitive, λύσεσθαι

---

[1] The future infinitive is found only six times in the New Testament. ἔσεσθαι occurs four of the six times.

*a.* The future passive is quite different from the future middle. *b.* Except in the future and aorist, the middle and passive are alike in form.

**209.** Observe: 1. The primary active and middle personal endings are used. 2. The tense-suffix is σ, added to the root λυ-. 3. The future stem is λυσ-. 4. The thematic vowel is ο/ε. Note that, while the present theme is λυο/ε, the future theme is λυσο/ε.

**210.** Most verbs whose verb stem ends in a single vowel (except the vowels α, ε, and ο) or a diphthong are conjugated in the future like λύσω, λύσομαι.

EXAMPLES: πιστεύω; fut. πιστεύσω. ἀκούω; fut. ἀκούσομαι. κωλύω; fut. κωλύσω.

**211.** Future indicative of εἰμί is:

| *Singular* | | *Plural* |
|---|---|---|
| 1. ἔσομαι, | *I shall be,* | ἐσόμεθα |
| 2. ἔσῃ | etc. | ἔσεσθε |
| 3. ἔσται | | ἔσονται |

Future infinitive, ἔσεσθαι

**212.** Conditional sentences (see 149). The third class conditional sentence is the condition *undetermined*, but *with prospect of determination*. Here the subjunctive after ἐάν (*if*) is used in the condition (if) clause. The conclusion naturally has the future indicative, but may have any tense of the indicative, subjunctive, or imperative.

EXAMPLES:

ἐὰν παραλάβητε ἐμέ, ὑμεῖς ἔσεσθε οἱ μαθηταί μου, *if you will receive me, you shall be my disciples.*

ἐὰν εἴπωμεν ὅτι ἁμαρτίαν οὐκ ἔχομεν, ἡ ἀλήθεια οὐκ ἔστιν
ἐν ἡμῖν, *if we say that we have not sin, the truth is
not in us.*

**213.** EXERCISES

I. 1. Χριστὸς ὑπὲρ ἡμῶν ἀπέθανεν. 2. ἐὰν πιστεύωμεν
τῷ ὀνόματι Ἰησοῦ Χριστοῦ, πιστοί ἐσμεν. 3. ἐὰν παραλά-
βωσι τὰ ῥήματα αὐτοῦ, πιστεύσουσιν αὐτῷ. 4. οὕτως ἔσται
καὶ ἐν ταῖς ἡμέραις τοῦ υἱοῦ τοῦ ἀνθρώπου. 5. περὶ τούτων
μὴ εἴπωμεν. 6. οὕτως δὲ ἔσονται οἱ πρῶτοι ἔσχατοι.

II. 1. The sons of men shall believe on (εἰς) the
word of God. 2. There shall be joy in heaven because (ὅτι) he is saved. 3. Ye shall be with (μετά)
me this day. 4. If he believe me, I shall hear him.
5. Let us go to him.

## LESSON XXVIII

### Future Indicative Active and Middle (Continued)

**214.** VOCABULARY

| | |
|---|---|
| ἀγαπάω, | *I love* |
| αἰτέω, | *I ask for (something)* |
| ἀκολουθέω, | *I follow* |
| γεννάω, | *I beget* |
| ἐρωτάω, | *I ask* (question) |
| ζάω, | *I live* |
| ζητέω, | *I seek* |
| λαλέω, | *I speak* |
| μαρτυρέω, | *I bear witness, testify* |
| παρακαλέω, | *I beseech, exhort, encourage* |
| ποιέω, | *I do, make* |

πληρόω,     *I fill, make full*
τηρέω,      *I keep*
φανερόω,    *make manifest*

Notice that the present stem of these verbs ends in one of three vowels, α, ε, or ο. These are called contract verbs because in the conjugation of the present system these vowels contract with the thematic vowel (and personal ending). These verbs in -άω, -έω, and -όω are contracted only in the present and imperfect, and will be studied in Lessons XLIX, etc. In all other systems these verbs, if regular, are conjugated like the corresponding tenses of λύω.

**215.** The future of

ἀγαπάω    is    ἀγαπήσω;
λαλέω     is    λαλήσω;
φανερόω   is    φανερώσω.

From these forms it is evident that verbs whose stems end in a short vowel (α, ε, ο) generally lengthen that vowel before -$\sigma^o/_\epsilon$ [1] of the future, and then are conjugated like λύσω (see 208).

α is lengthened to η (but α after ε, ι, or ρ is lengthε is lengthened to η    ened to α not η)
ο is lengthened to ω

Thus:      $-\alpha + \sigma^o/_\epsilon = -\eta\sigma^o/_\epsilon$
           $-\varepsilon + \sigma^o/_\epsilon = -\eta\sigma^o/_\epsilon$
           $-o + \sigma^o/_\epsilon = -\omega\sigma^o/_\epsilon$

**216.** 1. The future of

βλέπω (stem βλεπ-) is βλέψω;
νίπτω (stem νιβ-)  is νίψω;
γράφω (stem γραφ-) is γράψω.

---

[1] This is also true of other tense-suffixes.

From this it is seen that stems in π, β, or φ unite with σ, forming ψ; that is π + σ = ψ; β + σ = ψ; φ + σ = ψ.

2. The future of

$$διώκω \text{ (stem διωκ-) is } διώξω;$$
$$ἄγω \quad \text{(stem ἀγ-)} \quad \text{is } ἄξω;$$
$$ἔχω \quad \text{(stem σεχ-)} \quad \text{is } ἕξω.$$

Thus it is seen that stems in κ, γ, or χ unite with σ forming ξ; that is, κ + σ = ξ; γ + σ = ξ; χ + σ = ξ.

3. The future of

$$σώζω \text{ (stem σωδ-) is } σώσω;$$
$$πείθω \text{ (stem πειθ-) is } πείσω.$$

From this it is seen that stems in τ, δ, or θ drop τ, δ, or θ before σ, leaving simple σ; that is, τσ = σ; δσ = σ; θσ = σ.

**217.** Certain consonants are called mutes or stops because in forming them the passage of the breath is for a moment closed.

1. The consonants π, β, φ are called labial mutes or stops, because they are made with the lips.

2. κ, γ, χ are called palatal mutes or stops, because they are made with the soft palate.

3. τ, δ, θ are called lingual (or dental), because they are made with the tongue (or teeth).

**218.** As an aid to memory the changes in mute-stems in forming the future may be exhibited thus:

$$\text{Labials,} \quad π, β, φ + σ = ψ.$$
$$\text{Palatals,} \quad κ, γ, χ + σ = ξ.$$
$$\text{Linguals,} \quad τ, δ, θ + σ = σ.$$

Keep in memory this order of the mutes. They occasion many important changes in formation of words.

**219.** The verb-stem in many verbs is not the same as the present stem: in the case of νίπτω it was observed that the verb-stem is νιβ-; the present stem νιπτ-; and the verb-stem of σώζω is σωδ.[1] The verb-stem of φυλάσσω is φυλακ-; the future is φυλάξω. The future of βαπτίζω (βαπτιδ-) is βαπτίσω.

**220.** The future of any word cannot be certainly determined beforehand. A verb may make its future on a durative root, a punctiliar (aoristic) root, or on a different verb-root. ἔχω has two futures, ἔξω[2] (durative) and σχήσω (punctiliar). The future of ἔρχομαι is ἐλεύσομαι. The future of some verbs occurs only in the middle voice: e.g., γινώσκω, future γνώσομαι. In general a lexicon must be consulted for each verb.

The future of verbs with liquid stems (λ, μ, ν, ρ) will be given in Lesson XLVI.

**221.**              EXERCISES

I.  1. τηρήσομεν τὰς ἐντολὰς αὐτοῦ.  2. ἀκολουθήσω σοι,[3] Κύριε.  3. γνωσόμεθα αὐτόν, ὅτι ὀψόμεθα[4] αὐτὸν καθὼς ἐστιν.  4. ἐν ἐκείνῃ τῇ ἡμέρᾳ αἰτήσεσθε ἐν τῷ ὀνόματί μου καὶ ἐρωτήσω αὐτὸν περὶ ὑμῶν.  5. ἀγαπήσεις κύριον τὸν θεόν σου ἐν ὅλῃ τῇ καρδίᾳ σου καὶ ἐν ὅλῃ τῇ ψυχῇ σου καὶ ἐν ὅλῃ τῇ διανοίᾳ (mind) σου. αὕτη ἐστὶν ἡ πρώτη ἐντολή.  6. τὸ πνεῦμα ἄξει ἡμᾶς εἰς τὴν ἀλήθειαν.

---

[1] ζ is treated as a combination of δ + z (or zδ).

[2] Note the rough breathing on ἔξω.

[3] ἀκολουθέω is followed by the associative-instrumental case.

[4] From ὄπτομαι, I see; stem ὀπ-.

II.  1. We shall know the truth and do it.  2. We shall glorify God.  3. They will bear witness concerning him.  4. We shall persuade our hearts.  5. He will baptize you.  6. The faithful will proclaim the word of God.  7. I shall do the will of God.

## LESSON XXIX

### Third Declension: Lingual Mute Stems

**222.**                    VOCABULARY

> ἄρχων, -οντος, ὁ, *ruler, prince*
> ἐλπίς, -ίδος, ἡ, *hope*
> νύξ, νυκτός, ἡ, *night*
> πούς, ποδός, ὁ, *foot*
> φῶς, φωτός, τό, *light*
> χάρις, -ιτος, ἡ, *grace*
> ἐργασία, ἡ, *work, business*

**223.** Note that the stem of

> ἐλπίς    is    ἐλπιδ-;
> χάρις    is    χαριτ-;
> νύξ      is    νυκτ-.

Observe that the stem in all these substantives end in a lingual mute, and that the nominative is formed by adding ς to the stem.  Thus,

> ἐλπιδς    becomes    ἐλπίς;
> χαριτς    becomes    χάρις;
> νυκτς     becomes    νυκς = νύξ.

For the changes that occur when a mute and ς come together see 216 and 218.

**224.** The declension of ἐλπίς, *hope;* χάρις, *grace;* and νύξ, *night:*

| STEM ἐλπιδ- | STEM χαριτ- | STEM νυχτ- |
|---|---|---|
| *Singular* | | |

| | | | |
|---|---|---|---|
| Nom. | ἐλπίς | χάρις | νύξ |
| Gen. | ἐλπίδος | χάριτος | νυχτός |
| Abl. | ἐλπίδος | χάριτος | νυχτός |
| Loc. | ἐλπίδι | χάριτι | νυχτί |
| Ins. | ἐλπίδι | χάριτι | νυχτί |
| Dat. | ἐλπίδι | χάριτι | νυχτί |
| Acc. | ἐλπίδα | χάριν | νύχτα |

*Plural*

| | | | |
|---|---|---|---|
| Nom. | ἐλπίδες | χάριτες | νύχτες |
| Gen. | ἐλπίδων | χαρίτων | νυχτῶν |
| Abl. | ἐλπίδων | χαρίτων | νυχτῶν |
| Loc. | ἐλπίσι | χάρισι | νυξί |
| Ins. | ἐλπίσι | χάρισι | νυξί |
| Dat. | ἐλπίσι | χάρισι | νυξί |
| Acc. | ἐλπίδας | χάριτας | νύχτας |

*a.* In the accusative singular forms like ἐλπίδαν, νύχταν, are found. *b.* In the acc. singular, the form χάριτα often occurs. *c.* Vocatives in this declension are rare and will be specially mentioned whenever separate forms occur.

**225.** Observe that: 1. In the loc. ins. and dat. plu. a lingual mute drops out before -σι (see 216, 3, 218).

2. In the case of νυξί, χσ changes to ξ after τ dropped out.

**226.** Monosyllables of the third declension generally have the accent on the ultima in the gen., abl.,

loc., ins., and dat. of both numbers. In the gen.
plu. ῶν has the circumflex. But φῶς and παῖς are
accented in gen. plu. thus, φώτων, παίδων.

**227.** When substantives with stems in -ιτ, -ιδ, or -ιθ
are not accented on the ultima, the acc. sing. generally has ν in place of the mute (τ, δ, θ), e.g.,
χάρις (χαριτ-), acc. χάριν (but see 224 b); but when
the accent is on the ultima, the acc. is generally
formed like the acc. of ἐλπίς, ἐλπίδα.

**228.** Declension of ἄρχων, *ruler*, is:

STEM ἀρχοντ-

| | *Singular* | *Plural* |
|---|---|---|
| Nom. | ἄρχων | ἄρχοντες |
| Gen. | ἄρχοντος | ἀρχόντων |
| Abl. | ἄρχοντος | ἀρχόντων |
| Loc. | ἄρχοντι | ἄρχουσι |
| Ins. | ἄρχοντι | ἄρχουσι |
| Dat. | ἄρχοντι | ἄρχουσι |
| Acc. | ἄρχοντα | ἄρχοντας |

**229.** Observe that: 1. The nom. sing. of ἄρχων is
formed from the mere stem without adding anything; final τ of the stem is dropped, for a Greek
word cannot end in τ (see 200, 2 note); then ο of
the stem is lengthened (formative lengthening) to ω.
2. When -ντ- of the stem comes before -σι of the
loc., ins., and dat. plur., both ν and τ are dropped
and the ο of the stem is lengthened to ου (compensatory lengthening). (-ντ- always drops out before
-σι and the preceding vowel lengthened.)

**230.** In expressions of time the locative denotes a point *in which;* the accusative *duration of,* and the genitive time *within which* (kind of time): e.g., νυκτί (or ἐν νυκτί), *in the night,* νύκτα, *during the night;* νυκτός, *at night* (not day).

**231.**                    EXERCISES

I. 1. ὁ Ἰησοῦς ἦλθεν εἰς τὴν οἰκίαν τοῦ ἄρχοντος. 2. τὸ φῶς ἐν τῇ σκοτίᾳ φαίνει.¹ 3. ἐξῆλθεν ἡ ἐλπὶς τῆς ἐργασίας αὐτῶν. 4. καὶ νὺξ οὐκ ἔσται ἔτι.² 5. ἐν ἐκείνῃ τῇ νυκτὶ ἔλαβον αὐτόν. 6. ὑμεῖς ἐστε τὸ φῶς τοῦ κόσμου. 7. τῇ χάριτι δὲ θεοῦ σωζόμεθα ἡμεῖς. 8. ἔνιπτε τοὺς πόδας τῶν μαθητῶν. 9. οὐ γάρ ἐστε ὑπὸ νόμον ἀλλ᾽ ὑπὸ χάριν.

II. 1. They shall bear witness concerning him that (ὅτι) he is the light. 2. We are saved by grace. 3. We are not under law but under grace. 4. We have hope in God. 5. The ruler came to him at night.

### LESSON XXX

**Participles: The Present, Active, Middle, and Passive**

**232.**            VOCABULARY

ἀλλότριος,-α,-ον,  *belonging  to  another*  (another's), *strange*

ἄρτι, adv.,        *now, just now, this moment*

δουλεύω,           *I am a servant, I serve*

ἤ, conj.,          *or*

καρπός, ὁ,         *fruit*

τυφλός, -ή, -όν,   *blind*

φανερός, -ά, -όν,  *manifest*

---

¹ φαίνω, *I shine.*    ² ἔτι, *still, yet;* οὐκ ἔτι, *no longer.*

**233.** The present active participle of λύω:

STEM λυοντ-, *loosing*

Singular

|      | *Masc.* | *Fem.* | *Neut.* |
|------|---------|--------|---------|
| Nom. | λύων | λύουσα | λῦον |
| Gen. | λύοντος | λυούσης | λύοντος |
| Abl. | λύοντος | λυούσης | λύοντος |
| Loc. | λύοντι | λυούσῃ | λύοντι |
| Ins. | λύοντι | λυούσῃ | λύοντι |
| Dat. | λύοντι | λυούσῃ | λύοντι |
| Acc. | λύοντα | λύουσαν | λῦον |

Plural

|      | | | |
|------|---------|--------|---------|
| Nom. | λύοντες | λύουσαι | λύοντα |
| Gen. | λυόντων | λυουσῶν | λυόντων |
| Abl. | λυόντων | λυουσῶν | λυόντων |
| Loc. | λύουσι | λυούσαις | λύουσι |
| Ins. | λύουσι | λυούσαις | λύουσι |
| Dat. | λύουσι | λυούσαις | λύουσι |
| Acc. | λύοντας | λυούσας | λύοντα |

**234.** Observe: 1. The participle is declined in three genders.

2. The stem λυοντ- becomes λύων in the nom. masc. sing., like ἄρχων, and is declined like ἄρχων.

3. The fem. nom. sing. λύουσα is for λυονσα for λυοντια.[1]  The fem. is declined like γλῶσσα (105) of the first declension.

4. The neuter nom. and acc. sing. λῦον is the simple stem, final τ being dropped. (229, 200, 2.)

---

[1] ια is the feminine suffix added to the stem. Apparently τι (ι is a semivowel) became σ, then ν was dropped before σ and o lengthened (compensatory) to ου.

The neuter nom. and acc. plur. ends in -α. Otherwise the neuter forms are like the masculine.

5. The masculine and neut. are declined in the third declension; the fem. in the first.

6. Note that participles are accented like adjectives; but the gen. and abl. fem. plural have the circumflex accent over the ultima like substantives of the first declension The accent is not recessive. The accent of the present active participle of ἀκούω is ἀκούων, ἀκούουσα, ἀκοῦον. Observe the position of the accent in the neuter—not recessive.

**235.** Learn the pres. participle of εἰμί (§ 16).

**236.** The future active participle of λύω, viz., λύσων, λύσουσα, λῦσον, *going to loose*, is declined like the present participle of λύω. It is rare in the New Testament.

**237.** The present middle and passive participle of λύω is:

MIDDLE

| *Masc.* | *Fem.* | *Neuter* | |
|---------|--------|----------|---|
| λυόμενος | λυομένη | λυόμενον, | *loosing (for) oneself.* |

PASSIVE

| | | | |
|---------|--------|----------|---|
| λυόμενος | λυομένη | λυόμενον, | *being loosed* |

Observe that the present middle and passive participles are alike in form.

λυόμενος is declined like ἀγαθός, λυομένη like ἀγαθή, and λυόμενον like ἀγαθόν, except in accent. Thus it is seen that the present, middle, and passive participles are declined like adjectives of the first and second declensions.

**238.** The future middle participle of λύω is λυσόμενος, -η, -ον, *going to loose* (*for*) *oneself;* and is declined like λυόμενος, -η, -ον. This is also rare in the New Testament.

**239.** It is to be observed that the present participles are made on the present stem, and the future act. and middle participles are made on the future stem.

In a mechanical way, the present active, middle, and passive participles of any regular verb may be formed by adding -ων, -ουσα, -ον and -μενος, -μένη, -μενον to the present stem of the verb. Also the future act. and middle participles may be made by adding the same endings to the future stem of a verb. (See 209, 215, 216, 218.)

**240.** The participle is a verbal adjective. It is both verb and adjective at the same time.

1. Being an adjective, the participle is declined in gender, number, and case; it agrees in gender, number and case with the substantive that it modifies; like other adjectives it is either attributive or predicate; and with the article it is used as a substantive.

2. Being a verb also, the participle has voice and tense; governs the cases that the verb takes; and like other verbs it has adverbial modifiers (adjuncts).

**241.** The participle has not time in itself. Time with the participle is purely relative; it gets its time from the verb with which it is used.

**242.** Tense in the participle expresses "kind of action": the present part., *durative action;* the aorist participle, *punctiliar action.*

**243.** The participle has no personal endings and is therefore not limited by a subject. The participle has no subject. It makes no affirmation and is not a mode.

**244.** Note the simple attributive use of the participle with a substantive:

1. ἡ μένουσα ἐλπίς, *the abiding hope*
2. ὁ ἄνθρωπος ὁ λέγων ταῦτα, *the man saying these things*, (the man who says these things).

**245.** Examine carefully the following:

1. ὁ πιστεύων,    *the one believing*, he who believes
2. ὁ γινώσκων,    *the one knowing*, he who knows
3. ὁ ἀκουόμενος,  *the one being heard*, he who is heard
4. ὁ κρινόμενος,  *the one being judged*, he who is judged
5. ὁ δεχόμενος,   *the one receiving*, he who receives
6. τὸ ἐξερχόμενον, *the thing coming out*, that which comes out
7. ὁ λυόμενος,    (Mid.), *the one loosing* (for) *himself*
8. τὰ μὴ βλεπόμενα μένει, *the things not seen abide*

The article and participle in this use are practically equivalent to a relative clause, though not actually equivalent. The article and participle may be in any case: e.g.,

9. ὁ κύριος σώζει τὸν πιστεύοντα ἐν αὐτῷ, *the Lord saves the one believing* (him who believes) *on Him.*
10. πιστεύομεν ἐν τῷ πέμποντι αὐτόν, *we believe in the one sending* (him who sends) *him.*

These examples practically cover the attributive use of the participle.

**246.** The negative used with the participle is generally μή, *not*.

**247.**                    EXERCISES

I.  1. ὁ μένων ἐν αὐτῷ ἔχει ἐλπίδα.  2. οὗτός ἐστιν ὁ βαπτίζων ἐν πνεύματι ἁγίῳ.  3. ὁ γινώσκων τὸν θεὸν ἀκούει ἡμῶν.  4. ὁ θεὸς ἀγάπη ἐστίν, καὶ ὁ μένων ἐν τῇ ἀγάπῃ ἐν τῷ θεῷ μένει καὶ ὁ θεὸς ἐν αὐτῷ μένει.  5. οἱ ἀκούοντες ἐπίστευον ἐν τῷ ἐγείροντι τοὺς νεκρούς.

II.  1. He who receives us receives Him.  2. Let us believe on him who raises the dead.  3. This is he who takes away the sins of the world.  4. He who has grace remains in hope.  5. That day we shall see him who comes in the name of the Lord.


## LESSON XXXI

### Participles: The Second Aorist Active and Middle

**248.**                    VOCABULARY

ἀποθανών, second aorist active participle of ἀποθνήσκω.

βαλών,     second aorist active participle of βάλλω.

γενόμενος, second aorist middle participle of γίνομαι.

εἰπών,     second aorist active participle; no present
            stem; λέγω used in present.

ἐλθών,     second aorist active participle; no present
            stem; ἔρχομαι used in present.

ἰδών,      second aorist active participle; no present
            stem; ὁράω used in present.

λαβών,     second aorist active participle of λαμβάνω.

**249.** It will be seen from the vocabulary that the second aorist active and middle participles of the thematic vowel type have the same endings as the present active and middle participles, -ων and -μενος.

**250.** The declension of λαβών, -οῦσα, -όν, the second aorist active participle of λαμβάνω, is:

STEM λαβοντ-

*Singular*

| | Masc. | Fem. | Neut. |
|---|---|---|---|
| Nom. | λαβών | λαβοῦσα | λαβόν |
| Gen. | λαβόντος | λαβούσης | λαβόντος |
| Abl. | λαβόντος | λαβούσης | λαβόντος |
| Loc. | λαβόντι | λαβούσῃ | λαβόντι |
| Ins. | λαβόντι | λαβούσῃ | λαβόντι |
| Dat. | λαβόντι | λαβούσῃ | λαβόντι |
| Acc. | λαβόντα | λαβοῦσαν | λαβόν |

*Plural*

| | Masc. | Fem. | Neut. |
|---|---|---|---|
| Nom. | λαβόντες | λαβοῦσαι | λαβόντα |
| Gen. | λαβόντων | λαβουσῶν | λαβόντων |
| Abl. | λαβόντων | λαβουσῶν | λαβόντων |
| Loc. | λαβοῦσι | λαβούσαις | λαβοῦσι |
| Ins. | λαβοῦσι | λαβούσαις | λαβοῦσι |
| Dat. | λαβοῦσι | λαβούσαις | λαβοῦσι |
| Acc. | λαβόντας | λαβούσας | λαβόντα |

**251.** Observe: 1. The second aorist active participle of the thematic vowel type is declined like the present active participle in -ων (-οντ), except for the accent. 2. It is formed on the second aorist stem, and has no augment.

**252.** The second aorist middle participle (λαβόμενος, -μένη, -μενον) is declined exactly like the present middle participle. The difference in form lies in the stem: λαβόμενος (stem λαβ-), aorist middle participle; λαμβανόμενος (stem λαμβαν-), present middle participle.

**253.** The aorist participle is used attributively with the article, as is the present participle (244, 245). The difference in meaning is that the present expresses *durative* action and the aorist, *punctiliar* action.

ὁ λαμβάνων, *the one receiving,* he who receives
ὁ λαβών,     *the one having received,* he who received
ὁ γινόμενος, *the one becoming,* he who becomes
ὁ γενόμενος, *the one having become,* he who became

**254.** All participles may be used in the predicate. Study these examples carefully:

1. εἰπὼν ταῦτα ἀπῆλθεν,

    a. *Having said this*
    b. *When he said this*
    c. *After he said this*  ⎫ *he went away*
    d. *He said this and*

2. ἰδὼν ταῦτα ἐδόξαζε τὸν θεόν,

    a. *Seeing this*
    b. *When he saw this*  ⎫ *he was glorifying God*
    c. *Because he saw this*

3. εἰπὼν ταῦτα ἀπέρχεται,

    a. *Having said this*  ⎫ *he goes away*
    b. *After he said this*

4. παρέλαβον αὐτὸν εἰπόντα ταῦτα,

    *They received him* ⎧ *when he said this,*   a.
                       ⎨ *after he said this,*   b.
                       ⎩ *because he said this,* c.

5. τυφλὸς ὢν ἄρτι βλέπω,

   a. *Being blind*        ⎫
   b. *Whereas I was blind* ⎬ *now I see*
                            ⎭

6. ἔρχομαι ζητῶν καρπόν,

   $$I\ come \begin{cases} seeking\ fruit, & a. \\ to\ seek\ fruit, & b. \end{cases}$$

7. πορευόμενοι ἐκήρυσσον,

   a. *Advancing*                    ⎫
   b. *As they were advancing*       ⎬ *they were announcing*
   c. *While they were advancing*    ⎭

8. ἦλθον ζητῶν καρπόν,

   $$I\ came \begin{cases} seeking\ fruit, & a. \\ to\ seek\ fruit, & b. \end{cases}$$

9. ὑπολαβὼν εἶπεν, *answering* (catching up in speech) *he said.*

**255.** From the examples given above it is to be observed that:

1. The action of the present participle may precede (antecedent, Ex. 5), coincide with (simultaneous, Ex. 7), or follow (subsequent, Ex. 8 and 6) the action of the principal verb.

2. The action of the aorist participle may be antecedent to (Ex. 1, 2 *b*, *c*, 3 and 4), or simultaneous with (Ex. 2 *a*, 9), that of the principal verb.

The aorist participle does not express subsequent action, although it may be used proleptically.

Whether the action expressed by a participle is antecedent, simultaneous, or subsequent to that of the principal verb must be determined from the context.

**256.** The participles in the examples under 254 are varieties of what is called the circumstantial participle. The circumstantial participle is practically an additional statement added more or less loosely to the verbal notion of the principal verb. It may agree with the subject or object of the principal verb, or with any other substantive or pronoun in the sentence (see 254, 4). The participle in itself does not express time, manner, cause, purpose, etc., as suggested in the translation of the examples in 254. These ideas are not in the participle, but are suggested by the context.

**257.**                    EXERCISES

I.  1. βλέπει τὸν κύριον ἐρχόμενον πρὸς αὐτὸν καὶ λέγει αὐτῷ Οὗτός ἐστιν ὁ αἴρων τὰς ἁμαρτίας τοῦ κόσμου.  2. οὐ τὸ εἰσερχόμενον εἰς τὸ στόμα κοινοῖ (defiles) ἄνθρωπον ἀλλὰ τὸ ἐξερχόμενον ἐκ τοῦ στόματος τοῦτο κοινοῖ ἄνθρωπον.  3. πορευόμενοι δὲ κηρύσσετε λέγοντες ὅτι ὁ κύριος σώζει τοὺς πιστεύοντας ἐν αὐτῷ.  4. ταῦτα γράφω ὑμῖν περὶ τῶν μὴ δεχομένων ἐμέ.  5. ἐλθὼν οὖν ὁ Ἰησοῦς εὗρεν αὐτόν.

II.  1. He rejoices, saying that he saw the spirit coming upon (ἐπί)[1] him.  2. We saw him while he was teaching in the temple.  3. The Lord said to those who were coming to him that God hears those believing on Him.  4. When he saw the child he went away.  5. Not having received the promises they died.

[1] ἐπί (ἐφ' before rough breathing), prep. (orig. meaning *upon*) with gen., *upon, at, by;* with loc., *upon, on, over;* with acc., *upon, over.*

## LESSON XXXII

**Third Declension (Continued): Mutes and Liquids**

**258.**                     VOCABULARY

| | |
|---|---|
| αἰών, -ῶνος, ὁ, | age (space of time), *world* |
| ἀμπελών, -ῶνος, ὁ, | *vineyard* |
| ἡγεμών, -όνος, ὁ, | *leader, governor* |
| μάστιξ, -ιγος, ἡ, | *whip, scourge, plague* |
| ποιμήν, -ένος, ὁ, | *shepherd* |
| σάρξ, σαρκός, ἡ, | *flesh* |
| σάλπιγξ, -ιγγος, ἡ, | *trumpet* |
| σωτήρ, -ῆρος, ὁ, | *saviour* |
| χείρ, χειρός, ἡ, | *hand* |

**259.** The declension of σάρξ and μάστιξ:

STEM σαρκ-                    STEM μαστιγ-

### Singular

| Nom. | σάρξ | Nom. | μάστιξ |
|------|------|------|--------|
| Gen. | σαρκός | Gen. | μάστιγος |
| Abl. | σαρκός | Abl. | μάστιγος |
| Loc. | σαρκί | Loc. | μάστιγι |
| Ins. | σαρκί | Ins. | μάστιγι |
| Dat. | σαρκί | Dat. | μάστιγι |
| Acc. | σάρκα | Acc. | μάστιγα |

### Plural

| Nom. | σάρκες | Nom. | μάστιγες |
|------|--------|------|----------|
| Gen. | σαρκῶν | Gen. | μαστίγων |
| Abl. | σαρκῶν | Abl. | μαστίγων |
| Loc. | σαρξί | Loc. | μάστιξι |
| Ins. | σαρξί | Ins. | μάστιξι |
| Dat. | σαρξί | Dat. | μάστιξι |
| Acc. | σάρκας | Acc. | μάστιγας |

**260.** Observe: 1. The stems of σάρξ and μάστιξ end in palatal mutes (217, 2). 2. The nominative sing. is formed by adding ς to the stem. For the changes that occur with ς and a palatal mute, see 218. 3. The accent of σάρξ is according to the rule stated in 226.

**261.** A few substantives with stems in a labial mute (π or β) occur in the New Testament. (The nom. is formed by adding ς to the stem and then ends in -ψ, see 218).

EXAMPLES: λίψ, λιβός, ὁ, *the S. W. wind*
σκόλοψ, -οπος, ὁ, *a stake, a thorn*

**262.** The declension of αἰών, ἡγεμών, and ποιμήν:

| | STEM αἰων- | STEM ἡγεμον- | STEM ποιμεν- |
|---|---|---|---|
| | | *Singular* | |
| Nom | αἰών | ἡγεμών | ποιμήν |
| Gen. | αἰῶνος | ἡγεμόνος | ποιμένος |
| Abl. | αἰῶνος | ἡγεμόνος | ποιμένος |
| Loc. | αἰῶνι | ἡγεμόνι | ποιμένι |
| Ins. | αἰῶνι | ἡγεμόνι | ποιμένι |
| Dat. | αἰῶνι | ἡγεμόνι | ποιμένι |
| Acc. | αἰῶνα | ἡγεμόνα | ποιμένα |
| | | *Plural* | |
| Nom. | αἰῶνες | ἡγεμόνες | ποιμένες |
| Gen. | αἰώνων | ἡγεμόνων | ποιμένων |
| Abl. | αἰώνων | ἡγεμόνων | ποιμένων |
| Loc. | αἰῶσι | ἡγεμόσι | ποιμέσι |
| Ins. | αἰῶσι | ἡγεμόσι | ποιμέσι |
| Dat. | αἰῶσι | ἡγεμόσι | ποιμέσι |
| Acc. | αἰῶνας | ἡγεμόνας | ποιμένας |

*a.* Stems in -ν are sometimes called nasal stems.

**263.** Observe: 1. The nominative is formed from the mere stem. In the case of αἰών the stem vowel is unchanged; in the case of ἡγεμών and ποιμήν the short stem vowel is lengthened (formative lengthening), ο to ω, and ε to η. 2. In the loc., ins., and dat. plural the -ν- of the stem drops out, without any change in the stem vowel.

**264.** The declension of σωτήρ:

STEM σωτηρ-

| Singular | | Plural |
|---|---|---|
| Nom. | σωτήρ | σωτῆρες |
| Gen. | σωτῆρος | σωτήρων |
| Abl. | σωτῆρος | σωτήρων |
| Loc. | σωτῆρι | σωτῆρσι |
| Ins. | σωτῆρι | σωτῆρσι |
| Dat. | σωτῆρι | σωτῆρσι |
| Acc. | σωτῆρα | σωτῆρας |

Observe: 1. The nominative is made from the stem without any change. 2. In the loc., ins., and dat. plural the ending -σι is added to the stem without any change of the stem vowel or consonant.

*a.* χείρ, gen. χειρός, is declined regularly except in the loc. inst., and dat. plur., which have χερσί.

The real stem of χείρ is χερσ-.

**265.** A circumstantial participle (generally present or aorist) may be used in the genitive[1] case to agree with a substantive or pronoun in a construction grammatically independent of the rest of the sen-

---

[1] In fact the case may be either genitive or ablative.

tence. This construction is called the genitive absolute. Thus:

ταῦτα εἰπόντων τῶν μαθητῶν οἱ δοῦλοι ἦλθον εἰς τὸν οἶκον, *the disciples having said this* } *the servants went* *after (or when) the disciples said this* } *into the house*

γενομένης ἡμέρας οἱ ποιμένες ἀπῆλθον,
*day having come* } *the shepherds went away*
*when day came* }

αὐτοῦ λέγοντος ταῦτα οἱ δοῦλοι ἀπῆλθον, *while he was saying this the servants departed*

*a.* The genitive absolute is found also when the participle could have agreed with some substantive or pronoun in the sentence. *b.* Sometimes the genitive absolute is used without a substantive or pronoun—the participle alone.

**266.** EXERCISES

I. 1. ὁ λόγος σὰρξ ἐγένετο. 2. ἴδετε (behold) τὰς χεῖράς μου καὶ πόδας μου ὅτι ἐγώ εἰμι αὐτός. 3. ὁ ἐσθίων ἐκ τούτου τοῦ ἄρτου ζήσει εἰς τὸν αἰῶνα.[1] 4. τοῦ ὄχλου ἀπελθόντος ὁ δοῦλος ἔρχεται εἰς τὸν οἶκον τοῦ ποιμένος. 5. οἱ ποιμένες εἶδον τοὺς ἀποστόλους κηρύσσοντας τὸν σωτῆρα.

II. 1. Truth abides forever. 2. Behold his hands and feet. 3. I write these (things) with my hand. 4. The Saviour having departed, the crowd said this. 5. While he was going away he saw an angel.

[1] εἰς τὸν αἰῶνα, (*into the age*), *forever.*

110    BEGINNER'S GREEK GRAMMAR

LESSON XXXIII

Third Declension (Continued): Liquid Stems in -ερ
(Syncopated).   The Relative Pronoun

**267.**              VOCABULARY

ἀνήρ, ἀνδρός, ὁ,  *man*        μήτηρ, -τρός, ἡ,  *mother*
θυγάτηρ, -τρός, ἡ, *daughter*   πατήρ, -τρός, ὁ,  *father*
ὅς, ἥ, ὅ, relative pronoun, *who, which, that, what*

**268.** The declension of πατήρ and ἀνήρ:

STEM πατερ-              STEM ἀνερ-

*Singular*

| Nom. | πατήρ | Ncm. | ἀνήρ |
|------|-------|------|------|
| Gen. | πατρός | Gen. | ἀνδρός |
| Abl. | πατρός | Abl. | ἀνδρός |
| Loc. | πατρί | Loc. | ἀνδρί |
| Ins. | πατρί | Ins. | ἀνδρί |
| Dat. | πατρί | Dat. | ἀνδρί |
| Acc. | πατέρα | Acc. | ἄνδρα |
| Voc. | πάτερ | Voc. | ἄνερ |

*Plural*

| N. V. | πατέρες | N. V | ἄνδρες |
|-------|---------|------|--------|
| Gen. | πατέρων | Gen. | ἀνδρῶν |
| Abl. | πατέρων | Abl. | ἀνδρῶν |
| Loc. | πατράσι | Loc. | ἀνδράσι |
| Ins. | πατράσι | Ins. | ἀνδράσι |
| Dat. | πατράσι | Dat. | ἀνδράσι |
| Acc. | πατέρας | Acc. | ἄνδρας |

**269.** Observe:  1. The nom. is formed from the
simple stem;  and the short vowel ε is lengthened
(formative lengthening) to η.

2. Owing to the effect of the accent in the loc., ins., and dat. sing. of πατήρ the vowel ε of the stem is suppressed; and at the same time in the loc., ins., and dat. plural α is developed after ρ to facilitate pronunciation (also in ἀνδράσι[1]).

3. In ἀνήρ, when ε is suppressed, there is inserted sympathetically the consonant δ for the sake of euphony.

4. The voc. sing. is the simple stem, and has recessive accent.

**270.** μήτηρ, *mother*, and θυγάτηρ, *daughter*, are declined like πατήρ. The vocative of θυγάτηρ is θύγατερ. No voc. of μήτηρ occurs in the New Testament.

**271.** The declension of the relative pronoun ὅς, ἥ, ὅ is:

|  | *Singular* | | | *Plural* | | |
|---|---|---|---|---|---|---|
|  | *Masc.* | *Fem.* | *Neut.* | *Masc.* | *Fem.* | *Neut.* |
| Nom. | ὅς | ἥ | ὅ | οἵ | αἵ | ἅ |
| Gen. | οὗ | ἧς | οὗ | ὧν | ὧν | ὧν |
| Abl. | οὗ | ἧς | οὗ | ὧν | ὧν | ὧν |
| Loc. | ᾧ | ᾗ | ᾧ | οἷς | αἷς | οἷς |
| Ins. | ᾧ | ᾗ | ᾧ | οἷς | αἷς | οἷς |
| Dat. | ᾧ | ᾗ | ᾧ | οἷς | αἷς | οἷς |
| Acc. | ὅν | ἥν | ὅ | οὕς | ἅς | ἅ |

It will be noticed that this pronoun is declined in the first and second declensions. Observe that every form has the rough breathing (ʼ) and an accent.

**272.** The relative pronoun generally agrees with its antecedent in gender and number; but it may have

---

[1] -ρα- actually represent the vocalic sound of ρ.

112 BEGINNER'S GREEK GRAMMAR

its own case in its clause, or it may be attracted to
the case of its antecedent.

EXAMPLES: ἐπίστευεν ὁ ἄνθρωπος τῷ λόγῳ ὃν εἶπεν αὐτῷ
ὁ Ἰησοῦς, *the man was believing the word that
Jesus spoke to him.*

τὰ ῥήματα ἃ ἐγὼ εἶπον ὑμῖν πνεῦμά ἐστιν καὶ ζωή ἐστιν,
*the words which I spoke to you are spirit and are
life.*

μένετε ἐν αὐτῷ ὅς ἐστιν ὁ σωτὴρ τοῦ κόσμου, *you are abiding in him who is the Saviour of the world.*

**273.** Usually the attraction of the relative to the
case of the antecedent is from the accusative (in
which it naturally would be in its own clause) to
some other oblique case:

μνημονεύετε[1] τοῦ λόγου οὗ ἐγὼ εἶπον ὑμῖν, *remember the
word that I said to you.*

Here οὗ has been attracted to the case of λόγου.
In its own clause it naturally would be in the accusative.

**274.** Often the relative has no antecedent expressed:

μὴ γινώσκοντες ὃ λέγει ἀπέρχονται, *not knowing what
(that which) he says they go away.*

ὃς δέχεταί με δέχεται ὑμᾶς, *he who receives me receives
you.*

**275.**            EXERCISES

I.  1. ἡ ἐντολή ἐστιν ὁ λόγος ὃν ἀκούετε.  2. ἄνδρα οὐ
γινώσκω.  3. ἔλεγον οὖν αὐτῷ Ποῦ[2] ἐστιν ὁ πατήρ σου;  4. ἐν

---

[1] μνημονεύω, *to remember*, with genitive.   [2] ποῦ, *where.*

ἐκείνῃ τῇ ἡμέρᾳ ἐν τῷ ὀνόματί μου αἰτήσεσθε, καὶ οὐ λέγω ὑμῖν ὅτι ἐγὼ ἐρωτήσω τὸν πατέρα περὶ ὑμῶν. 5. ὃ ἀκούετε ἀπ' ἀρχῆς γινώσκετε. 6. χάριτι δὲ τοῦ θεοῦ εἰμι ὃ εἰμι. 7. οὗτός ἐστιν ὑπὲρ οὗ εἶπον.

II. 1. The hope which we have is eternal. 2. This is my father and my mother. 3. We believe in him who died for us. 4. He shall ask the father concerning us. 5. This is the daughter concerning whom I spoke.

# LESSON XXXIV

### Third Declension (Continued): Stems in ι
### The Interrogative and Indefinite Pronouns

276.                          VOCABULARY

ἀνάστασις, -εως, ἡ,   *resurrection*
ἄφεσις, -εως, ἡ,      *remission, forgiveness*
γνῶσις, -εως, ἡ,      *knowledge*
δύναμις, -εως, ἡ,     *power*
θλίψις, -εως, ἡ,      *tribulation, distress*
κρίσις, -εως, ἡ,      *judgment*
κτίσις, -εως, ἡ,      *creation*
παράκλησις, -εως, ἡ,  *exhortation*
πίστις, -εως, ἡ,      *faith*
πόλις, -εως, ἡ,       *city*
τίς, τί, interrogative pronoun, *who, which, what?*
τις, τι, indefinite pronoun, *one, a certain one. a certain thing; some one, something.*
ποῦ, interrogative adverb, *where?*

**277.** The declension of πόλις is:

STEM πολι- (πολει-)

| *Singular* | | *Plural* | |
|---|---|---|---|
| Nom. | πόλις | πόλεις | |
| Gen. | πόλεως | πόλεων | |
| Abl. | πόλεως | πόλεων | |
| Loc. | πόλει | πόλεσι | |
| Ins. | πόλει | πόλεσι | |
| Dat. | πόλει | πόλεσι | |
| Acc. | πόλιν | πόλεις | |

The voc. sing. πόλι does not occur in the New Testament.

**278.** Observe: 1. In the nom. and acc. sing. the stem is πολι-. 2. In the other cases the stem is πολει (ι is here a semi-vowel). 3. πόλεως and πόλεων of the gen. and abl. are for πολε(ι)ως and πολε(ι)ων. ε here preserves the semivowel sound of ι which is dropped. Note the apparent exception to rule of accent, that the accent cannot stand on antepenult when the ultima is long. -ως is lengthened from -ος. 4. In the loc., ins., and dat. sing. πόλει is for πόλε(ι)ι; ι of the case ending and ε contract, ε + ι = ει (diphthong). 5. In acc. sing. -ν is the case ending, not -α. 6. The nom. plural πόλεις is for πολε(ι)ες; ε + ε contract to ει (diphthong). 7. The acc. plural (old form πόλεας) is assimilated to the nominative.

**279.** Like πόλις are declined all substantives (not having accent on ultima) in -σις, -ξις, -ψις. They are mainly abstract substantives of the feminine gender.

**280.** The declension of the interrogative pronoun τίς, τί is:

| | Singular | | Plural | |
|---|---|---|---|---|
| | Masc.and Fem. | Neut. | Masc. and Fem. | Neut. |
| Nom. | τίς | τί | τίνες | τίνα |
| Gen. | τίνος | τίνος | τίνων | τίνων |
| Abl. | τίνος | τίνος | τίνων | τίνων |
| Loc. | τίνι | τίνι | τίσι | τίσι |
| Ins. | τίνι | τίνι | τίσι | τίσι |
| Dat. | τίνι | τίνι | τίσι | τίσι |
| Acc. | τίνα | τί | τίνας | τίνα |

*a.* Note that this pronoun is declined in the third declension; the masculine and feminine genders are alike; the neuter differs from the masculine and feminine only in the nom. and acc. *b.* The interrogative pronoun has the acute accent on the first syllable; it is never changed to the grave.

**281.** The declension of the indefinite pronoun τὶς, τὶ is:

| | Singular | | Plural | |
|---|---|---|---|---|
| | Masc. and Fem. | Neut. | Masc. and Fem. | Neut. |
| Nom. | τὶς | τὶ | τινές | τινά |
| Gen. | τινός | τινός | τινῶν | τινῶν |
| Abl. | τινός | τινός | τινῶν | τινῶν |
| Loc. | τινί | τινί | τισί | τισί |
| Ins. | τινί | τινί | τισί | τισί |
| Dat. | τινί | τινί | τισί | τισί |
| Acc. | τινά | τὶ | τινάς | τινά |

Note that the indefinite pronoun is declined like the interrogative, except that the accent is placed on the ultima because it is an enclitic and loses or retains its accent according to the principles given in 138.

**282.** Examine carefully the following examples of the use of the interrogative pronoun:

1. σὺ τίς εἶ; *who art thou?*
2. τίνα μισθὸν ἔχετε; *what pay* (reward) *have you?*
3. τίς ἐστιν ὁ ἄνθρωπος οὗτος; *who is this man?*
4. τίνα ζητεῖτε; *whom are you seeking?*
5. τί ποιήσω; *what shall I do?*
6. γινώσκετε τίς ἐστιν ὁ ἀνήρ, *you know who the man is.*

Note: 1. The interrogative τίς is used as a substantive (1, 3 and 4) or as an adjective (2). 2. It is used in both direct (1–5) and indirect (6) questions.

**283.** The neuter accusative τί is frequently used adverbially in the sense of "why."

τί με λέγεις ἀγαθόν; *why do you call me good?*

**284.** In indirect questions the same mode and tense is generally found as in the direct; and the same interrogative words:

εἶδε ποῦ μένετε, *he saw where you are staying.*

ἐγίνωσκε τί ἐστιν ἐν ἀνθρώπῳ, *he knew what is in man.*

**285.** Study carefully the following examples of the use of the indefinite pronoun:

| | |
|---|---|
| 1. εἶπέν τις αὐτῷ, | *one* (a certain man) *said to him.* |
| 2 τινὲς δὲ ἐξ αὐτῶν εἶπον, | *some* (certain ones) *of them said.* |
| 3. εἰσῆλθεν εἰς κώμην τινά, | *he went into a certain village.* |

4. ἄνθρωπός τις εἶχεν δύο υἱούς, *a certain man had two sons.*

Note that the indefinite τὶς is used as a substantive (1 and 2), or as an adjective (3 and 4).

**286.** EXERCISES

I. 1. τί θέλετε ποιήσω ὑμῖν; 2. ἡ πίστις σου σώζει σε. 3. ἀλλὰ εἰσὶν ἐξ ὑμῶν τινὲς οἳ οὐ πιστεύουσιν. 4. ἐν τῇ δυνάμει τοῦ πνεύματος εἰς Γαλιλαίαν εἰσέρχεται. 5. εἴδομέν τινα ἐν τῷ ὀνόματί σου ἐκβάλλοντα δαιμόνια. 6. γράψω ἐπ᾽ αὐτὸν τὸ ὄνομα τοῦ θεοῦ μου καὶ τὸ ὄνομα τῆς πόλεως τοῦ θεοῦ μου.

II. 1. What shall we say? 2. Ye have power to become the children of God. 3. In a certain city he was preaching the word. 4. A certain man said, "Lord, I will follow thee." 5. Why are you going away? 6. The faith which we have saves men.

## LESSON XXXV

**Third Declension (Continued): Stems in -ευ (εϝ) and -εσ.**

**287.** VOCABULARY

| | | | |
|---|---|---|---|
| ἀρχιερεύς, -έως, ὁ, | chief priest | ἔλεος, -ους, τό, | pity, mercy |
| βασιλεύς, -έως, ὁ, | king | ἔτος, -ους, τό, | year |
| γραμματεύς, -έως, ὁ, | scribe | μέλος, -ους, τό, | member |
| ἱερεύς, -έως, ὁ, | priest | μέρος, -ους, τό, | part |
| γένος, -ους, τό, | race | πλῆθος, -ους, τό, | crowd, multitude |
| ἔθνος, -ους, τό, | nation | σκότος, -ους, τό, | darkness |
| ἔθος, -ους, τό, | custom | τέλος, -ους, τό, | end |

**288.** The declension of βασιλεύς is:

STEM βασιλευ(ϝ)- [1]

| Singular | | Plural | |
|---|---|---|---|
| Nom. | βασιλεύς | N. V. βασιλεῖς | |
| Gen. | βασιλέως | | βασιλέων |
| Abl. | βασιλέως | | βασιλέων |
| Loc. | βασιλεῖ | | βασιλεῦσι |
| Ins. | βασιλεῖ | | βασιλεῦσι |
| Dat. | βασιλεῖ | | βασιλεῦσι |
| Acc. | βασιλέα | | βασιλεῖς |
| Voc. | βασιλεῦ | | |

Observe: 1. The final υ (ϝ) of the stem is dropped when it would come between two vowels; it is retained when final (vocative) or followed by a consonant (nom. sing.; loc., ins., and dat. plur.). 2. In the loc., ins., and dat. sing., and in the nom. and acc. plural contraction takes place. 3. In the acc. sing. -α is the case ending and not -ν. The acc. plural has been assimilated to the nominative. Compare βασιλεύς with πόλις.

**289.** All substantives with nom. sing. in -εύς are masculine, and are declined like βασιλεύς.

**290.** The declension of γένος is:

STEM γενεσ-

| Singular | | Plural |
|---|---|---|
| Nom. | γένος | γένη |
| Gen. | γένους | γενῶν (γενέων) |
| Abl. | γένους | γενῶν (γενέων) |

---

[1] ϝ, vau, called also *digamma*, an old letter standing in the alphabet after ε, and pronounced like *w*. Its presence as a semi-vowel is often shown by υ.

| Loc. | γένει | γένεσι |
|------|-------|--------|
| Ins. | γένει | γένεσι |
| Dat. | γένει | γένεσι |
| Acc. | γένος | γένη |

Observe: 1. The nom. (and acc.) is the stem with vowel ε strengthened to ο. 2. In all other cases the σ of the stem is dropped, and contraction of the concurrent vowels takes place.

*a.* In the gen. and abl. sing. γένους came from γένεσος; σ dropped out, ε + ο contracted to ου. *b.* In the loc., ins., and dat. sing. γένει came from γένεσι; σ dropped out, ε + ι contracted to -ει. *c.* The nom. and acc. plural γένη came from γένεσα; σ dropped out, ε + α contracted to η. *d.* In the gen. and abl. plural γενῶν (γενέων) came from γενέσων; σ dropped out, ε + ω contracted to ω, or remained uncontracted as γενέων. 3. The accent of the contracted gen. and abl. plural is a circumflex over the ultima.

**291.** Like γένος are declined all neuters with nom. sing. in -ος (stem -εσ).

**292.**                     EXERCISES

I.  1. σὺ εἶ ὁ βασιλεὺς τῶν 'Ιουδαίων.  2. οἱ βασιλεῖς τῶν ἐθνῶν κυριεύουσιν¹ αὐτῶν.  3. ἀλλ' οὔπω²τὸ τέλος ἐστίν.  4. ἔμελλεν 'Ιησοῦς ἀποθνήσκειν ὑπὲρ τοῦ ἔθνους, καὶ οὐχ ὑπὲρ τοῦ ἔθνους μόνον.⁸  5. οὐκ ἔχεις μέρος μετ' ἐμοῦ.  6. οἱ ἀρχιερεῖς εἶπον Οὐκ ἔχομεν βασιλέα.

II.  1. The multitude will follow him.  2. That one is not king of this world.  3. This is the gospel

---
¹ κυριεύω, *to be lord of*, or *to rule* (*over*), with the genitive.
² οὔπω, *not yet.*
⁸ μόνον. adv.. *only.*

which I proclaim among (ἐν) the nations.    4. You
have a part in the kingdom of heaven.    5. The
scribes and priests have not mercy.


## LESSON XXXVI

### First Aorist Indicative Active and Middle

**293.**                          VOCABULARY

ἁγιάζω,   *I sanctify*        καθαρίζω, *I purify*
βασιλεύω, *I reign, I am king*  καταλύω, *I destroy*
θεάομαι,   *I behold*         τυφλόω, *I make blind, blind*

**294.** The second aorist tense (178) is older than
the first aorist.  As tense the first aorist is not a different tense from the second aorist.  The second and
first aorists are just two different forms of the same
tense.

**295.** The first aorist indicative active of λύω is:

STEM  λυσ(α)-

| *Singular* | *Plural* |
|---|---|
| 1. ἔλυσα,  *I loosed,* | 1. ἐλύσαμεν |
| 2. ἔλυσας   etc. | 2. ἐλύσατε |
| 3. ἔλυσε | 3. ἔλυσαν |

First aorist active infinitive,   λῦσαι

For translation of the aorist, see 187.

**296.** On the formation of the first aorist it is to be
observed:

  1. The first aorist stem is formed by adding -σα to
the verb stem.

  2. The secondary active personal endings (see 66)

are used. But -ν is not used in the first singular; and -ε of the third sing. seemingly takes the place of α.

3. In the indicative there is an augment as in the second aorist (182. 3, and 70).

4. The infinitive ending is -αι; the accent is on the penult.

**297.** The first aorist indicative middle of λύω is:

| *Singular* | | *Plural* |
|---|---|---|
| 1. ἐλυσάμην | *I loosed* | 1. ἐλυσάμεθα |
| 2. ἐλύσω | *(for) myself,* | 2. ἐλύσασθε |
| 3. ἐλύσατο | etc. | 3. ἐλύσαντο |

First aorist middle infinitive, λύσασθαι

*a.* The second pers. sing. ἐλύσω came from ἐλύσασο; σ dropped out, and the concurrent vowels α and ο contracted to ω.

**298.** Observe: 1. That the secondary middle endings (see 80) are added directly to the theme λυσα-.

2. The middle infinitive ending -σθαι is added to the theme λυσα-.

**299.** The same principles of augment are found in the first aorist indicative as in the second aorist (182. 3) and imperfect (70).

**300.** The form ἐλύσατο may be analyzed thus: ἐ-λύ-σα-το; ἐ is the augment; λυ- is the verb-stem, σα is the tense suffix; λυσ(α) is the tense stem, λυσα is the tense theme, and το is the secondary middle personal ending of the third person. Analyze the active ἐλύσατε.

For the meaning of the aorist middle see Lesson XXIV, and 52.

**301.** Verbs with stems ending in a vowel (except α, ε, o) regularly form the first aorist (if they have a first aorist) like λύω.

Thus: κωλύω, *I hinder*—first aorist ἐκώλυσα.

πιστεύω, *I believe*—first aorist ἐπίστευσα.

**302.** Generally, verbs that have a first aorist do not have a second aorist; and verbs that have a second aorist do not have a first aorist.

*a.* A few verbs have both aorists. When they occur, the first aorist is usually transitive and the second aorist intransitive.

In the New Testament it is common for a second aorist stem to have α of the first aorist: thus εἶδα, εἶδας, εἴδαμεν, etc.; εἶπα, etc.

**303.** 1. Verbs with stems ending in a short vowel α, ε, or o, form the first aorist by lengthening the vowel before the tense suffix σα (as in the future before σο/ε, 215):

α is lengthened to η (except after ε, ι, or ρ, when
ε is lengthened to η    it is lengthened to α.)
o is lengthened to ω.

Thus:

|  |  |
|---|---|
| ἀγαπάω, *I love,* | first aorist ἠγάπησα. |
| ποιέω, *I do, make,* | first aorist ἐποίησα. |
| πληρόω, *I fill,* | first aorist ἐπλήρωσα. |

Active infinitives, ἀγαπῆσαι, ποιῆσαι, πληρῶσαι.

2. But a few verbs like καλέω, *I call,* and τελέω, *I end, I complete,* do not lengthen ε before the aorist tense suffix. Thus:

|  |  |
|---|---|
| καλέω, *I call,* | first aorist ἐκάλεσα |
| τελέω, *I finish,* | first aorist ἐτέλεσα |

3. Verb stems with endings in mutes make the same changes with σ of -σα to form the aorist, as was made with σ of the future, 215–16–17.

Thus: Labial (πβφ): πέμπω,       aorist ἔπεμψα
                    γράφω,       aorist ἔγραψα
      Palatal (κγχ): διώκω,       aorist ἐδίωξα
                    διαλέγω,     aorist διέλεξα
      Lingual (τδθ): σώζω (σωδ-), aorist ἔσωσα
                    πείθω,       aorist ἔπεισα

**304.** There is no difference in meaning between a first aorist and a second aorist. Both express *punctiliar* action—point action. See 178–179.

**305.** There were originally two verb-types, the one denoting durative or linear action, the other momentary, or punctiliar action. Thus in ἐσθίω the verb-stem is durative or linear, and in ἔφαγον the verb-stem is punctiliar. So in English "blink the eye" is a different kind of action from "live a life." In Greek this matter of the "kind of action" in the verb-stem (or root), called *Aktionsart*, applies to all verbs. This "kind of action" of the verb-stem itself was before there was any idea of the later tense development.

The aorist tense at first was used with verb-stems of punctiliar sense. The verb-stem itself may accent the beginning of the action, the end of the action, or the action as a whole. *The aorist tense itself always means point-action* (punctiliar action). But the individual verb-stem meaning may deflect the punctiliar action to the beginning or to the end. Consequently, in the aorist the tense idea is to be combined with the verb-stem meaning. Thus in punctiliar action three distinctions arise: (1) the unmodified point-action, called *constative;* (2) the point action with the stress on the beginning of the action, called *ingressive;* (3) the point-action with the stress on the conclusion or end of the action, called *effective.* Thus:

ἐκ τοῦ πληρώματος αὐτοῦ ἡμεῖς ἐλάβομεν, *of his fulness we received.* (Effective.)

ὁ λόγος σὰρξ ἐγένετο, *the word became flesh.* (Ingressive.)

ἐσκήνωσεν ἐν ἡμῖν, *he dwelt among us.* (Constative.)

Sometimes the same word can be used for each of these ideas; as βαλεῖν may mean "*throw*" (constative), or "*let fly*" (ingressive), or "*hit*" (effective).

**306.** The aorist tense, although at first it was confined to verbs of punctiliar action, came gradually to be made on verbs of durative action. (So also verbs of durative action came to have the tenses of punctiliar action.) Thus the tenses came to be used for the expression of the idea that once belonged only to the verb-stem (or root). That is, the aorist tense imposed a punctiliar idea on a durative verb-stem. (So also the present tense imposed a durative idea on a punctiliar verb-stem.) Thus the aorist just treats as punctiliar an act which is not in itself point-action. This is the advance that the tense makes on the verb-stem (or root). So all aorists are punctiliar, in fact or statement.

**307.** Of course the "kind of action" of the tense (punctiliar) and the "kind of action" of the verb-stem (Aktionsart) run through the whole tense (modes, infinitive, and participle).

**308.** What was said in Lessons XXIV and XXV about the meaning of the second aorist applies also to the first aorist; and what is said in this lesson applies to the second aorist. Review the meaning of the modes.

**309.** Exercises

I. 1. εἰς τοῦτο γὰρ Χριστὸς ἀπέθανεν καὶ ἔζησεν. 2. οὐκ ἦλθον καταλῦσαι τὸν νόμον ἀλλὰ πληρῶσαι. 3. ἔγραψα ὑμῖν, παιδία, ὅτι γινώσκετε τὸν πατέρα. 4. καὶ ἔζησαν καὶ ἐβασίλευσαν μετὰ τοῦ χριστοῦ χίλια (thousand) ἔτη. 5. αὐτὸς ἠγάπησεν ἡμᾶς. 6. ἐθεάσαντο ἃ ἐποίησεν καὶ ἐπίστευσαν εἰς αὐτόν.

II. 1. Darkness blinded his eyes. 2. We did not receive the gospel because we did not hear the word. 3. They made him king. 4. He came to destroy the works of the devil. 5. He sanctified them in truth.

## LESSON XXXVII

### First Aorist Subjunctive Active and Middle

**310.** Vocabulary

| | |
|---|---|
| ἄνεμος, ὁ, *wind* | νομίζω, *I think, suppose* |
| θαυμάζω, *I wonder, marvel* | πρεσβύτερος, ὁ, *elder* |
| ἰσχυρός, -ά, -όν, *strong* | σκανδαλίζω, *I cause to stumble, offend* |
| κρίμα, τό, *judgment* | |
| μισέω, *I hate* | φόβος, ὁ, *fear* |
| νικάω, *I conquer* | χρεία, ἡ, *need* |

**311.** The first aorist subjunctive active and middle of λύω:

ACTIVE

| Singular | Plural |
|---|---|
| 1. λύσω | 1. λύσωμεν |
| 2. λύσῃς | 2. λύσητε |
| 3. λύσῃ | 3. λύσωσι |

MIDDLE

| | |
|---|---|
| 1. λύσωμαι | 1. λυσώμεθα |
| 2. λύσῃ | 2. λύσησθε |
| 3. λύσηται | 3. λύσωνται |

*a.* λύσῃ, the second pers. sing. middle, came from λυσησαι; σ dropped out, and η and αι contracted to η.

**312.** Observe: 1. There is no augment. Augment belongs to the secondary tenses of the indicative only. 2. The stem λυσ(α) (σ(α) is the tense suffix) is the same stem as in the aorist indicative. 3. The long thematic vowel ω/η is added to the stem. Compare the present subjunctive 165 and 172. 4. The personal endings are the primary active and middle endings, the same as in the present subjunctive (165 and 172).

**313.** In the formation of the first aorist subjunctive of verbs with stems ending in a short vowel or a mute, the same changes are made at the end of the stem as in the first aorist indicative (see 303. 1, 3). Thus the first aorist subjunctive of

| | | |
|---|---|---|
| ἀγαπάω | is ἀγαπήσω, ἀγαπήσῃς, | etc. |
| ποιέω | is ποιήσω, ποιήσῃς, | etc. |
| πληρόω | is πληρώσω, πληρώσῃς, | etc. |

πέμπω        is πέμψω, πέμψης,        etc.
ἄρχομαι      is ἄρξωμαι, ἄρξῃ,        etc.
πείθω        is πείσω, πείσῃς,        etc.
σώζω (σωδ-) is σώσω, σώσῃς,          etc.

**314.** Write the first aorist subjunctive of

αἰτέω, *I ask;* ἐρωτάω, *I ask* (question); φανερόω, *I make manifest;* δέχομαι, *I receive;* γράφω, *I write;* βλέπω, *I see;* σώζω, *I save.*

**315.** Of course the "kind of action" of the aorist subjunctive is punctiliar; and Aktionsart is present as in the indicative. What was said in 304–306 about punctiliar action and Aktionsart applies to the aorist subjunctive.

**316.** It needs to be repeated that the difference in the meaning between the present subjunctive and the aorist subjunctive is in the "kind of action" expressed by the two tenses: durative action in the present, and punctiliar action in the aorist.

**317.** The aorist subjunctive (in the second and third persons) with μή is used to express a prohibition.

1. Generally in the second person:

   μὴ ἄρξησθε λέγειν, *do not begin to say.*

2. Less often in the third person:

   μή τις ὑμᾶς πλανήσῃ, *let no one cause you to err.*

**318.**              EXERCISES

I.  1. τινὲς δὲ ἐξ αὐτῶν ἀπῆλθον πρὸς τοὺς Φαρισαίους καὶ εἶπαν αὐτοῖς ἃ ἐποίησεν Ἰησοῦς. 2. ἐτύφλωσεν αὐτῶν

128 BEGINNER'S GREEK GRAMMAR

τοὺς ὀφθαλμοὺς ἵνα μὴ ἴδωσι τοῖς ὀφθαλμοῖς. 3. μὴ νομίσητε ὅτι ἦλθον καταλῦσαι τὸν νόμον ἢ τοὺς προφήτας. 4. οὗτος ἦλθε εἰς μαρτυρίαν ἵνα μαρτυρήσῃ περὶ τοῦ φωτὸς ἵνα πάντες (all) πιστεύσωσιν δι' αὐτοῦ. 5. ζητήσωμεν αὐτόν. 6. μὴ περὶ τούτων γράψῃς.

II. 1. What shall we do? 2. Let us receive the Gospel. 3. Do not love the world. 4. They asked him concerning the parable. 5. If we do his will, he will love us.

## LESSON XXXVIII

**First Aorist Active and Middle Participle.  Adjectives of the Third Declension.  Declension of πᾶς**

**319.**  VOCABULARY

ἄδικος, -η, -ον, *unrighteous*
ἀδύνατος, -ον, *unable, impossible*
ἀκάθαρτος, -ον, *unclean*
ἀμήν, adv., *truly, verily*
ἅπας, ἅπασα, ἅπαν, *all, altogether*
ἀπολύω, *I release*
βιβλίον, τό, *book, a written document*
θεραπεύω, *I heal*
ὅτε, relative temporal adv. with the indicative, *when*
ὅταν, relative temporal adv. with the subj. and indicative, *whenever, when*
πᾶς, πᾶσα, πᾶν, *all, every*

**320.**  The first aorist active participle of λύω is λύσας (masc.), λύσασα (fem.), λῦσαν (neut.).

STEM λυσαντ-

*Singular*

| | Masc. | Fem. | Neut. |
|------|-------|------|-------|
| Nom. | λύσας | λύσασα | λῦσαν |
| Gen. | λύσαντος | λυσάσης | λύσαντος |
| Abl. | λύσαντος | λυσάσης | λύσαντος |
| Loc. | λύσαντι | λυσάσῃ | λύσαντι |
| Ins. | λύσαντι | λυσάσῃ | λύσαντι |
| Dat. | λύσαντι | λυσάσῃ | λύσαντι |
| Acc. | λύσαντα | λύσασαν | λῦσαν |

*Plural*

| | | | |
|------|-------|------|-------|
| Nom. | λύσαντες | λύσασαι | λύσαντα |
| Gen. | λυσάντων | λυσασῶν | λυσάντων |
| Abl. | λυσάντων | λυσασῶν | λυσάντων |
| Loc. | λύσασι | λυσάσαις | λύσασι |
| Ins. | λύσασι | λυσάσαις | λύσασι |
| Dat. | λύσασι | λυσάσαις | λύσασι |
| Acc. | λύσαντας | λυσάσας | λύσαντα |

*a.* All participles with masc. nom. in -ας are declined like λύσας, λύσασα, λῦσαν.

**321.** Observe: 1. The aorist tense suffix σα appears throughout. 2. To the aorist theme is added the participial ending -ντ. 3. The stem is λυσαντ-; and (1) to this is added ς to form the nominative masc. sing.; ντ cannot stand before ς and drops out, and α is lengthened; (2) the neuter nom. sing. is the mere stem, τ being dropped (234, 4); (3) the fem. nom. sing. λύσασα is from λυσανσα from λυσαντια (see 234, 3 footnote). 4. The masc. and neuter are declined according to the third declension, and the fem. is declined according to the first declension.

**322.** The first aorist middle participle of λύω is λυσάμενος, λυσαμένη, λυσάμενον.   Note the middle participle ending -μενος, -μενη, -μενον is added to the aorist theme λυσα-.   The first aorist middle participle, like the present and second aorist middle participles, is declined like an adjective of the first and second declensions.

**323.** Of course the kind of action (punctiliar) and the Aktionsart of the verb-stem apply to the participle.

**324.** The declension of πᾶς, πᾶσα, πᾶν is:

STEM παντ-

*Singular*

| | Masc. | Fem. | Neut. |
|---|---|---|---|
| Nom. | πᾶς | πᾶσα | πᾶν |
| Gen. | παντός | πάσης | παντός |
| Abl. | παντός | πάσης | παντός |
| Loc. | παντί | πάση | παντί |
| Ins. | παντί | πάση | παντί |
| Dat. | παντί | πάση | παντί |
| Acc. | πάντα | πᾶσαν | πᾶν |

*Plural*

| | | | |
|---|---|---|---|
| Nom. | πάντες | πᾶσαι | πάντα |
| Gen. | πάντων | πασῶν | πάντων |
| Abl. | πάντων | πασῶν | πάντων |
| Loc. | πᾶσι | πάσαις | πᾶσι |
| Ins. | πᾶσι | πάσαις | πᾶσι |
| Dat. | πᾶσι | πάσαις | πᾶσι |
| Acc. | πάντας | πάσας | πάντα |

*a.* ἅπας is a strengthened form of πᾶς and except for the accent is declined like πᾶς.

**325.** 1. Note that except for the accent πᾶς is declined like the first aorist participle λύσας; and the formation of genders and cases is like λύσας.

2. Observe that the accent in the masculine and neuter singular is that of monosyllables of the third declension (226), while in the plural the accent is on the penult.

**326.** Examine carefully the following examples of the use of πᾶς:

  1. In the predicate position:

      *a.* πᾶσα ἡ πόλις,   *all the city*
      *b.* πᾶσαι αἱ πόλεις, *all cities*

  2. In the attributive position:

      *a.* ἡ πᾶσα πόλις,   *the city as a whole*
      *b.* ὁ πᾶς νόμος,    *the entire law, the whole law*
      *c.* οἱ πάντες ἄνδρες, *the total number of the men*

  3. With a singular substantive, without the article; πᾶσα πόλις or πόλις πᾶσα, *every city*

  4. πᾶς ὁ and the participle is a common construction in the New Testament.

| | |
|---|---|
| πᾶς ὁ ἀκούων, | *every one hearing, every one who hears* |
| πάντες οἱ ἀκούοντες, | *all those hearing, all those who hear* |
| παντὶ τῷ ἀκούοντι, | *to every one hearing, to every one who hears* |
| πάντες οἱ ἀκούσαντες, | *all those having heard, all those who heard* |

**327.** ὥστε, *so that* (to be distinguished from ὥστε used as an inferential conjunction, *and so, therefore*) is used with the infinitive (twice with the indicative) to express result:

καὶ ἐθεράπευσεν αὐτὸν ὥστε τὸν τυφλὸν βλέπειν, *and he healed him so that the blind man was seeing.*

*a.* The accusative τὸν τυφλόν is not the subject of the infinitive βλέπειν. The infinitive does not have a subject; it has no personal endings, and is not a finite verb. The acc. limits an idea in content, scope, and direction. The action in βλέπειν is limited by the acc. to τὸν τυφλόν. This use of the acc. is generally called the acc. of *general reference.*

**328.**    Exercises

I.  1. ὁ πέμψας με δίκαιός ἐστιν. 2. ταῦτα πάντα ἐλάλησεν ὁ Ἰησοῦς ἐν παραβολαῖς τοῖς ὄχλοις. 3. πᾶς ὁ ἐν αὐτῷ μένων οὐχ ἁμαρτάνει. 4. ἀκούσας ταῦτα εἶπεν αὐτῷ Τί τοῦτο ἀκούω περὶ σοῦ; 5. ἦλθον ποιῆσαι τὸ θέλημα τοῦ πέμψαντός με. 6. ὅταν ἀκούσωσιν τὸν λόγον, μετὰ χαρᾶς λαμβάνουσιν αὐτόν. 7. ἀμὴν ἀμὴν λέγω ὑμῖν ὅτι ἔρχεται ὥρα καὶ νῦν ἐστιν ὅτε οἱ νεκροὶ ἀκούσουσιν τῆς φωνῆς τοῦ υἱοῦ τοῦ θεοῦ καὶ οἱ ἀκούσαντες ζήσουσιν.

II.  1. Having heard this he went away. 2. He healed all the blind so that they marvelled. 3. Every one believing on him comes not into judgment. 4. When you hear his voice, you will believe. 5. Let us hear him who sent him.

## LESSON XXXIX

**Adjectives of the Third Declension: Stems in -ες. Irregular Adjectives, πολύς and μέγας**

**329.**  VOCABULARY

| | |
|---|---|
| ἀληθής, -ές, *true* | πολύς, πολλή, πολύ, *much,* |
| ἀσθενής, -ές, *weak, sick* | *many* |
| γάμος, ὁ, *marriage* | προσευχή, ἡ, *prayer* |
| μέγας, μεγάλη, μέγα, *great* | ὑπάγω, *I go away, depart* |
| μονογενής, -ές, *only begotten* | ὑγιής, -ές, *whole, healthy* |

**330.**  The declension of ἀληθής is:

STEM ἀληθεσ-

*Singular*

| | Masc. and Fem. | Neut. |
|---|---|---|
| Nom. | ἀληθής | ἀληθές |
| Gen. | ἀληθοῦς | ἀληθοῦς |
| Abl. | ἀληθοῦς | ἀληθοῦς |
| Loc. | ἀληθεῖ | ἀληθεῖ |
| Ins. | ἀληθεῖ | ἀληθεῖ |
| Dat. | ἀληθεῖ | ἀληθεῖ |
| Acc. | ἀληθῆ | ἀληθές |

*Plural*

| | Masc. and Fem. | Neut. |
|---|---|---|
| Nom. | ἀληθεῖς | ἀληθῆ |
| Gen. | ἀληθῶν | ἀληθῶν |
| Abl. | ἀληθῶν | ἀληθῶν |
| Loc. | ἀληθέσι | ἀληθέσι |
| Ins. | ἀληθέσι | ἀληθέσι |
| Dat. | ἀληθέσι | ἀληθέσι |
| Acc. | ἀληθεῖς | ἀληθῆ |

There are about sixty adjectives in the New
Testament declined like ἀληθής.
Compare the declension of ἀληθής with γένος (290).

**331.** In the declension of ἀληθής observe: 1. The
neuter nom. and acc. sing. is the mere stem. 2. The
masc. nom. sing. is the stem with the stem vowel
lengthened.    3. In the other cases σ of the stem
drops out and the concurrent vowels contract. The
gen. and abl. sing. ἀληθοῦς is from ἀληθέσος (ε + ο = ου);
the loc., ins., and dat. sing. ἀληθεῖ is from ἀληθέσι
(ε + ι = ει); the masc. acc. sing. ἀληθῆ is from ἀληθέσα
(ε + α = η); the masc. nom. plur. ἀληθεῖς is from
ἀληθέσες (ε + ε = ει); the neut. nom. and acc. plur.
ἀληθῆ is from ἀληθέσα (ε + α = η); the gen. plural ἀληθῶν
is from ἀληθέσων (ε + ω = ω); the masc. and fem. acc.
plur. ἀληθεῖς is like the nom. (probably borrowed
from the nom.).    4. The masc. and fem. forms are
alike.    (This is the first adjective given thus far, the
feminine of which is declined in the third declension.)    5. The gen., abl., loc., ins. and dat. in all
three genders are alike.

**332.** The declension of πολύς is:

STEMS πολυ- and πολλο-, -α-

*Singular*

|      | *Masc.* | *Fem.* | *Neut.* |
|------|---------|--------|---------|
| Nom. | πολύς   | πολλή  | πολύ    |
| Gen. | πολλοῦ  | πολλῆς | πολλοῦ  |
| Abl. | πολλοῦ  | πολλῆς | πολλοῦ  |
| Loc. | πολλῷ   | πολλῇ  | πολλῷ   |

|      | *Masc.* | *Fem.* | *Neut.* |
|------|---------|--------|---------|
| Ins. | πολλῷ | πολλῇ | πολλῷ |
| Dat. | πολλῷ | πολλῇ | πολλῷ |
| Acc. | πολύν | πολλήν | πολύ |

*Plural*

|      | | | |
|------|---------|--------|---------|
| Nom. | πολλοί | πολλαί | πολλά |
| Gen. | πολλῶν | πολλῶν | πολλῶν |
| Abl. | πολλῶν | πολλῶν | πολλῶν |
| Loc. | πολλοῖς | πολλαῖς | πολλοῖς |
| Ins. | πολλοῖς | πολλαῖς | πολλοῖς |
| Dat. | πολλοῖς | πολλαῖς | πολλοῖς |
| Acc. | πολλούς | πολλάς | πολλά |

Observe: 1. The masc. and neut. nom. and acc.
sing. are made on the stem πολυ-. 2. All the other
cases (masc. fem. and neut.) are made on the stem
πολλο- (fem. end. -η) and declined according to the
first and second declensions.

**333.** The declension of μέγας is:

STEMS μεγα- and μεγαλο-, -α-.

*Singular*

|      | *Masc.* | *Fem.* | *Neut.* |
|------|---------|--------|---------|
| Nom. | μέγας | μεγάλη | μέγα |
| Gen. | μεγάλου | μεγάλης | μεγάλου |
| Abl. | μεγάλου | μεγάλης | μεγάλου |
| Loc. | μεγάλῳ | μεγάλη | μεγάλῳ |
| Ins. | μεγάλῳ | μεγάλη | μεγάλῳ |
| Dat. | μεγάλῳ | μεγάλη | μεγάλῳ |
| Acc. | μέγαν | μεγάλην | μέγα |

*Plural*

| | Masc. | Fem. | Neut. |
|------|-------|------|-------|
| Nom. | μεγάλοι | μεγάλαι | μεγάλα |
| Gen. | μεγάλων | μεγάλων | μεγάλων |
| Abl. | μεγάλων | μεγάλων | μεγάλων |
| Loc. | μεγάλοις | μεγάλαις | μεγάλοις |
| Ins. | μεγάλοις | μεγάλαις | μεγάλοις |
| Dat. | μεγάλοις | μεγάλαις | μεγάλοις |
| Acc. | μεγάλους | μεγάλας | μεγάλα |

Observe: 1. The masc. and neut. nom. and acc. sing. are made on the short stem μεγα-.

2. All the other cases (masc., fem., and neut.) are made on the long stem μεγαλο- (fem. end. -η) and are declined like adjectives of the first and second declensions.

**334.** Study carefully the following examples of indirect discourse:

I. Indirect assertions. 1. After ὅτι (*that*):

σὺ λέγεις ὅτι βασιλεύς εἰμι, *thou sayest that I am a King.*
εἶδον ὅτι ἐσθίει, *they saw that he was eating.*

2. With the infinitive:

λέγουσιν αὐτὸν μένειν, *they say that he remains.*

3. With the participle:

εἴδαμέν τινα ἐκβάλλοντα δαιμόνια, *we saw one casting out demons.*

II. Indirect questions:

αὐτὸς γὰρ ἐγίνωσκεν τί ἦν ἐν τῷ ἀνθρώπῳ, *for he himself knew what was in man.*
εἶδαν ποῦ μένει, *they saw where he was abiding.*
ἠρώτησαν τί φάγωσι, *they asked what they were to eat.*

III. Indirect commands.

τῷ Παύλῳ ἔλεγον διὰ τοῦ πνεύματος μὴ ἐπιβαίνειν εἰς
    Ἱεροσόλυμα, *they said to Paul through the spirit
    that he should not go up to Jerusalem* (literally,
    *not to go up to Jerusalem*).

**335.** Observe:

1. Indirect assertions are expressed (1) by ὅτι
and the indicative; (2) by the infinitive; (3) by the
participle.

2. The same introductory words are generally
used in indirect questions as those which are found
in direct questions.

3. The infinitive is frequently used in indirect
commands.

*a.* Sometimes ἵνα and a finite mode is used.[1]

4. The tense generally remains unchanged in the
Greek indirect discourse.

*a.* Sometimes there is a change, as in the first
example under II; the imperfect ἦν seems to represent
a present in the direct.

5. The mode generally remains unchanged in the
Greek indirect discourse. The subjunctive mode
(φάγωσι) in the third example under II was in the
direct.

6. The person of the verb is or is not changed
according to the circumstances.

In the third example under II the third person was
first or second in the direct.

[1] Also used as object-clause after verbs of striving, beseeching, etc.

**336.**    Exercises

I. 1. καὶ ἐγένετο φόβος μέγας ἐπὶ πάντας. 2. τίς γάρ
ἐστιν ἀνθρώπων ὃς οὐ γινώσκει τὴν Ἐφεσίων ¹ πόλιν
νεωκόρον ² οὖσαν τῆς μεγάλης Ἀρτέμιδος; 3. λέγουσιν
ἀνάστασιν μὴ εἶναι. 4. καὶ πολὺ πλῆθος ἀπὸ τῆς Γαλιλαίας
ἠκολούθησεν αὐτῷ. 5. εἶπεν ὅτι μεγάλη ἐστὶν ἡ πίστις
αὐτοῦ. 6. ἔτι πολλὰ ἔχω ὑμῖν λέγειν. 7. μετὰ ταῦτα
ἤκουσα ὡς φωνὴν μεγάλην ὄχλου πολλοῦ. 8. γινώσκομεν
ὅτι ἀληθὴς εἶ.

II. 1. They did not know what they would see.
2. They know that there shall be great tribulation.
3. Many saw the Lord coming and said that he was
the Saviour of the world. 4. This one is the only
begotten son.

## LESSON XL

### First Aorist Passive Indicative and Subjunctive.
### Future Passive Indicative

**337.**    Vocabulary

ἀναγινώσκω, *I read*

ἄνωθεν, adv., *from above, again*

αὔριον, adv., *tomorrow*

ἐγγύς, adv., *near*

ἐπαύριον, adv., *on the morrow*

λυπέω, *I grieve*

ὅπου, rel. adv., *where*

πόθεν, interrogative adv., *whence*

σαλεύω, *I shake*

σταυρόω, *I crucify*

**338.** The stem of first aorist passive is formed by
adding θε directly to the verb-stem. Thus λυθε- is
the first aorist stem of λύω.

---

¹ Ἐφέσιος, -η, -ον, *Ephesian.*
² νεωκόρος, ὁ or ἡ, *temple-keeper*

**339.** The first aorist passive indicative of λύω is:

| *Singular* | *Plural* |
|---|---|
| 1. ἐλύθην, *I was loosed* | 1. ἐλύθημεν, *we were loosed* |
| 2. ἐλύθης, *you were loosed* | 2. ἐλύθητε, *you were loosed* |
| 3. ἐλύθη, *he was loosed* | 3. ἐλύθησαν, *they were loosed* |

First aorist passive infinitive—λυθῆναι, *to be loosed*

Observe: 1. The vowel ε of the aorist passive tense suffix θε is lengthened to η (θη) throughout the indicative, and in the infinitive. 2. The personal endings of the aorist passive indicative are the secondary active personal endings (**66**). 3. The endings are added directly to the aorist passive stem. 4. In the indicative there is an augment as in the aorist active ind. (182, 3 and 296, 3), and is formed on the same principles as in the imperfect (70). 5. The aorist passive infinitive ending is -ναι; the accent of the aorist passive infinitive is always on the penult.

**340.** The aorist passive subjunctive of λύω is:

| *Singular* | *Plural* |
|---|---|
| 1. λυθῶ | 1. λυθῶμεν |
| 2. λυθῇς | 2. λυθῆτε |
| 3. λυθῇ | 3. λυθῶσι |

Observe: 1. The subjunctive has the primary personal endings. 2. The subjunctive mode sign ω/η contracts with ε of the passive suffix. 3. The circumflex accent is written over the contracted syllable. 4. The subjunctive does not have an augment.

**341.** Review the "kind of action" (punctiliar) of the aorist tense and Aktionsart of the verb-stem,

178–180, 305–307. These of course apply to the aorist passive as well as to active and middle.

**342.** For the meaning of the passive voice see 51. Some defective (152) verbs have no aorist middle, but passive form; but not the passive meaning: the meaning is either middle or active (or intransitive):

$$\pi \text{ορεύομαι, } I \text{ go; } \text{ἐπορεύθην, } I \text{ went.}$$

Some verbs have both aorist middle and passive forms, as ἀπεκρινάμην, ἀπεκρίθην.

**343.** Verbs with stems ending in a short vowel (α, ε, ο) generally lengthen (ᾰ to ᾱ after ε, ι, or ρ) the vowel of the stem before the tense suffix θε in formation of the aorist passive. Thus:

>ποιέω;    aorist passive, ἐποιήθην.
>γεννάω;   aorist passive, ἐγεννήθην.
>φανερόω;  aorist passive, ἐφανερώθην.

*a.* A few verbs like τελέω do not lengthen ε; but have σ before θε, as ἐτελέσθην.

**344.** The future passive is made upon the aorist passive stem. Thus λυθήσομαι, *I shall be loosed*, is the aorist passive stem λυθη + σο (the future tense suffix and thematic vowel) + μαι (the primary middle ending). The future passive of λύω is:

*Singular*

1. λυθήσομαι, *I shall be loosed*
2. λυθήσῃ,    *you   shall   be loosed*
3. λυθήσεται *he, she or it shall be loosed*

*Plural*

1. λυθησόμεθα, *we shall be*
2. λυθήσεσθε   *loosed*, etc.
3. λυθήσονται

Observe that the future passive is conjugated like the future middle except that the stem of the passive is λυθησ-, whereas the stem of the middle is λυσ-.

**345.** In some verbs (having no first aorist passive) there is found a second aorist passive with suffix -ε (-η) added directly to the verb-stem. The conjugation is like that of the first aorist passive, except there is no θ.

Thus: the second aorist passive of γράφω is ἐγράφην,[1] ἐγράφης, etc.: στρέφω, ἐστράφην, etc. Second aorist passive infinitive γραφῆναι.

The second future passive is built on the second aorist stem. The second future passive of φαίνω (second aor. pass., ἐφάνην) is φανήσομαι.

**346.** EXERCISES

I. 1. καὶ ἐξελθὼν ἐπορεύθη εἰς ἕτερον τόπον. 2. ἀμὴν ἀμὴν λέγω σοι, ἐὰν μή τις γεννηθῇ ἄνωθεν, οὐ δύναται ἰδεῖν τὴν βασιλείαν τοῦ θεοῦ. 3. εἰς τοῦτο ἐφανερώθη ὁ υἱὸς τοῦ θεοῦ ἵνα λύσῃ τὰ ἔργα διαβόλου. 4. λέγει αὐτῷ Σίμων Πέτρος, Κύριε, ποῦ ὑπάγεις; ἀπεκρίθη Ἰησοῦς Ὅπου ὑπάγω οὐ δύνασαί μοι νῦν ἀκολουθῆσαι. 5. ἐγγὺς ἦν ὁ τόπος τῆς πόλεως ὅπου ἐσταυρώθη ὁ Ἰησοῦς.

II. 1. If he be made manifest, we shall be like (ὅμοιοι) him (associative-instrumental case). 2. Those who believed were begotten of (ἐκ) God. 3. It was written in order that the Scripture might be fulfilled. 4. The powers of the heavens shall be shaken.

---

[1] The second aorist passive is really an active form that came to have a passive meaning.

## LESSON XLI

### Aorist Passive (Continued)

**347.**    VOCABULARY

ἀληθῶς, adv., *truly, surely*    καλῶς, adv., *finely, well*
ἀνοίγω, *I open*    πειράζω, *I test, tempt*
διάνοια, ἡ, *mind, under-*    πρό, prep. with abl., *before*
   *standing*    τελειόω, *I end, complete,*
ἐπιθυμία, ἡ, *desire*    *fulfill*

**348.** The formation of the first aorist and future passive given in Lesson XL is typical of all verbs with stems ending in a vowel.

**349.** Verbs with stems ending in a mute (217–218) suffer euphonic changes in the mute before the passive suffix θε.

1. A labial mute, πβφ, before θ (of the suffix) becomes φ. πέμπω, stem πεμπ-, aorist passive ἐπέμφθην.

2. A palatal mute, κγχ, before θ, becomes χ. ἄγω, stem ἀγ-, aorist passive -ἤχθην.

3. A lingual mute, τδθ, before θ becomes σ. πείθω, stem πειθ-, aorist passive ἐπείσθην.

These changes may be represented to the eye in tabular form, thus:

$$\pi, \; \beta, \; \varphi \; \text{before} \; \theta = \varphi\theta.$$
$$\varkappa, \; \gamma, \; \chi \; \text{before} \; \theta = \chi\theta.$$
$$\tau, \; \delta, \; \theta, \; \text{before} \; \theta = \sigma\theta.$$

After these changes are made the conjugation follows the form of ἐλύθην. Thus λείπω:

Aorist passive indicative    ἐλείφθην, etc.
Aorist passive subjunctive    λειφθῶ, etc.
Aorist passive infinitive    λειφθῆναι
Future passive indicative    λειφθήσομαι, etc.

**350.** The stem of the aorist passive participle is made on the aorist passive stem with the participial ending -ντ. The stem of the aorist passive participle of λύω is λυθεντ-.

The declension of the aorist passive participle of λύω is:

### Singular

|       | *Masc.* | *Fem.* | *Neut.* |
|-------|---------|--------|---------|
| Nom.  | λυθείς    | λυθεῖσα   | λυθέν     |
| Gen.  | λυθέντος  | λυθείσης  | λυθέντος  |
| Abl.  | λυθέντος  | λυθείσης  | λυθέντος  |
| Loc.  | λυθέντι   | λυθείσῃ   | λυθέντι   |
| Ins.  | λυθέντι   | λυθείσῃ   | λυθέντι   |
| Dat.  | λυθέντι   | λυθείσῃ   | λυθέντι   |
| Acc.  | λυθέντα   | λυθεῖσαν  | λυθέν     |

### Plural

|       | *Masc.* | *Fem.* | *Neut.* |
|-------|---------|--------|---------|
| Nom.  | λυθέντες  | λυθεῖσαι  | λυθέντα   |
| Gen.  | λυθέντων  | λυθεισῶν  | λυθέντων  |
| Abl.  | λυθέντων  | λυθεισῶν  | λυθέντων  |
| Loc.  | λυθεῖσι   | λυθείσαις | λυθεῖσι   |
| Ins.  | λυθεῖσι   | λυθείσαις | λυθεῖσι   |
| Dat.  | λυθεῖσι   | λυθείσαις | λυθεῖσι   |
| Acc.  | λυθέντας  | λυθείσας  | λυθέντα   |

Observe: 1. The masc. nom. sing. is formed by adding -ς to the stem λυθεντ = λυθεντς; ντ cannot stand before ς and drops out; the ε is lengthened (compensatory) to ει. 2. The fem. nom. sing. is formed from λυθεντια = λυθενσα = λυθεισα; ε is lengthened (compensatory) to ει; see 321, 3 (3); 234, 3 footnote. 3. The neut. nom. (and acc.) sing. is the

mere stem, without τ (see 234, 3).   4. For the forms
of the masc. and neut. loc., ins., and dat. plural see
229, 2, and lengthening of ε to ει see above.   5. Note
the position of the accent on the aorist passive participle in comparison with the other participles.

**351.** The aorist passive participle of

πέμπω is πεμφθείς, -θεῖσα, -θέν.
ἄγω is ἀχθείς, -θεῖσα, -θέν.
πείθω is πεισθείς, -θεῖσα, -θέν.
γεννάω is γεννηθείς, -θεῖσα, -θέν.
φανερόω is φανερωθείς, -θεῖσα, -θέν.

The second aorist passive participle of

γράφω is γραφείς, -εῖσα, -έν.
φαίνω is φανείς, -εῖσα, -έν.
στρέφω is στραφείς, -εῖσα, -έν.

**352.** The aorist passive participle is used in all the
participial constructions that have been studied.

**353.** It cannot certainly be told beforehand what
form of the aorist passive a verb will have.   The
aorist passive stem must be known.

  1. Some of the second aorist passives found in
the New Testament (besides those already given)
are:

-ἐκόπην (fut. pass. κοπήσομαι),  pres. κόπτω, I *beat, strike*
ἐκρύβην,                          pres. κρύπτω, I *hide*
ἐσπάρην,                          pres. σπείρω, I *sow*
(ἀπ)εστάλην,                      pres. (ἀπο)στέλλω, I *send*
ἠνοίγην (fut. pass. ἀνοιχθήσομαι, ἀνοιγήσομαι),  pres. ἀνοίγω,
     I *open*

2. Some verbs have apparently irregular forms in the first aorist and future passive:

| Present | First aorist passive | Future passive |
|---|---|---|
| ἀκούω | ἠκούσθην | ἀκουσθήσομαι |
| βάλλω | ἐβλήθην | βληθήσομαι |
| γινώσκω | ἐγνώσθην | γνωσθήσομαι |
| ἐγείρω | ἠγέρθην | ἐγερθήσομαι |
| καλέω | ἐκλήθην | κληθήσομαι |
| λαμβάνω | ἐλήμφθην | -λημφθήσομαι |
| Stem ὀπ- | ὤφθην | ὀφθήσομαι. |

(Presents used, βλέπω, ὁράω, and ὀπτάνομαι).

**354.** EXERCISES

I. 1. ἐκλήθη δὲ ὁ Ἰησοῦς εἰς τὸν γάμον. 2. καὶ τῇ τρίτῃ ἡμέρᾳ ἐγερθήσεται. 3. ὁ δὲ διεκώλυεν[1] αὐτὸν λέγων Ἐγὼ χρείαν ἔχω ὑπὸ σοῦ βαπτισθῆναι. 4. οὗτος μέγας κληθήσεται ἐν τῇ βασιλείᾳ τῶν οὐρανῶν. 5. ὑμεῖς δὲ τίνα με λέγετε εἶναι; ἀποκριθεὶς ὁ Πέτρος λέγει αὐτῷ Σὺ εἶ ὁ Χριστός. 6. πίστει Μωυσῆς γεννηθεὶς ἐκρύβη τρίμηνον (three months) ὑπὸ τῶν πατέρων αὐτοῦ. 7. ἤχθη ὁ Ἰησοῦς ὑπὸ τοῦ πνεύματος εἰς τὴν ἔρημον πειρασθῆναι ὑπὸ τοῦ διαβόλου. 8. μετὰ ταῦτα ὤφθη πᾶσι τοῖς ἀποστόλοις.

II. 1. The prince of this world will be cast out. 2. Let us be led by the spirit. 3. If I touch him, I shall be saved. 4. He who was begotten of God will keep you. 5. If we be raised from the dead, they shall be raised.

[1] διακωλύω, I hinder.

## LESSON XLII

**Some Irregular Substantives of the Third Declension.
Some Uses of the Infinitive**

**355.**              VOCABULARY

ἀντί, prep. (original meaning "at ends" [face to face])
    with the gen., *opposite, against; instead of, in
    place of, for*

ἄξιος, -α, -ον, *fitting, worthy*

ἐπιθυμέω, *I desire*

νεφέλη, ἡ, *cloud*

πάσχα, τό (indeclinable), *the Passover*

πάσχω, *I suffer;* second aorist ἔπαθον

σιγάω, *I am silent, keep silent*

συνεσθίω, *I eat with* (someone)

φοβέομαι, *I am afraid, I fear*

φωνέω, *I call, speak aloud*

χρονίζω, *I spend time, tarry*

**356.** Learn the forms of the following irregular
substantives of the third declension given in § 12:
γόνυ, τό, *knee;* γυνή, ἡ, *woman;* θρίξ, ἡ, *hair;* κύων, ὁ,
*dog;* οὖς, τό, *ear;* ὕδωρ, τό, *water.*

Note especially the forms not in parentheses—
the forms in parentheses do not occur in the New
Testament.

**357.** The infinitive, as we have learned, has tense
and voice; but it has no manner of affirmation and
is not a mode.

There are a great many uses of the infinitive.
Note carefully some of the uses of the infinitive in
the following:

1. As an indeclinable verbal substantive (of

neuter gender) the infinitive may be used in any case (not vocative) with or without the article. With the article it is indeclinable; but the neuter article with the infinitive is declined and shows the case of the infinitive.

(1) καλόν σοί ἐστιν εἰσελθεῖν εἰς ζωήν, *it is good for thee to enter into life.* εἰσελθεῖν is in the nominative case.

(2) ἤλθομεν προσκυνῆσαι, *we came to worship.* προσκυνῆσαι is in the dative case. In this construction the infinitive is common for the expression of purpose.

(3) ἐζήτησαν τοῦ καταλῦσαι τὰ ἔργα αὐτοῦ, *they sought to destroy his work.* τοῦ καταλῦσαι is in the genitive case. τοῦ and the infinitive is common in the New Testament to express purpose.

2. The infinitive with the article is used in most of the constructions in which any other substantive is used.

(1) The infinitive is used with such verbs as: δύναμαι, θέλω, ζητέω, ἄρχομαι, etc. In fact, the infinitive can be used with almost any verb that can be used with a substantive.

θέλει ἀκούειν τὸ εὐαγγέλιον, *he wishes to hear the gospel.*
οὐ δύναται αὐτῷ δουλεύειν, *he is not able to serve him.*

(2) The infinitive is used with substantives, most frequently with those expressing time, fitness, ability, need, etc.

ἔχομεν ἐξουσίαν γενέσθαι τὰ τέκνα τοῦ θεοῦ, *we have power to become the children of God.*
ἔχει πίστιν τοῦ σωθῆναι, *he has faith to be healed (saved).*

(3) The infinitive is used with adjectives, commonly with

ἄξιος, δυνατός, ἱκανός.

οὐκέτι εἰμὶ ἄξιος κληθῆναι υἱός σου, *I am no longer worthy to be called a son of thine.*

δυνατός ἐστιν αὐτὸ φυλάξαι, *he is able to guard (keep) it.*

(4) The infinitive with the article is used with many prepositions.

πρὸ τοῦ σε Φίλιππον φωνῆσαι εἶδόν σε, *before Philip called thee, I saw thee.*

εἶπεν παραβολὴν διὰ τὸ ἐγγὺς εἶναι Ἰερουσαλὴμ αὐτόν, *he spoke a parable because he was near Jerusalem.*

μετὰ τὸ ἀποθανεῖν αὐτὸν ἀπῆλθον, *after he died, they went away.*

ταῦτα εἶπον ὑμῖν εἰς τὸ μὴ μένειν ὑμᾶς ἐν τῇ ἁμαρτίᾳ, *I said this to you in order that you might not remain in sin.*

Note: εἰς τὸ and an infinitive is a common construction to express purpose.

καὶ ἐθαύμαζον ἐν τῷ χρονίζειν ἐν τῷ ναῷ αὐτόν, *and they marvelled while he was tarrying in the temple.*

*a.* Observe that the case of the infinitive has its proper meaning. The prepositions, as with cases of other substantives, help out the meaning of the cases. What the resultant meaning is depends on the meaning of the word, the case with the preposition, and the context. In the first example the resultant meaning of πρὸ τοῦ φωνῆσαι (abl. case) is temporal; of the second example, διὰ τὸ εἶναι, causal; of the third, μετὰ τὸ ἀποθανεῖν, temporal; of the fourth, εἰς τὸ μὴ μένειν, purpose; of the fifth, ἐν τῷ χρονίζειν (loc. case), temporal. *b.* The voices of the infinitive have the usual significance. *c.* The tenses have their force in the infinitive, as in the modes and participle. Tense in the infinitive has no time except in indirect discourse. *d.* It is not necessary for the article to come next to the infinitive. Several words may intervene (see first example under (4)) and the clause may be one of considerable extent. *e.* The infinitive is not a mode and is not limited by personal endings; and, therefore, does not have a subject. See 327, *a.*

**358.** EXERCISES

I. 1. πρὸ γὰρ τοῦ ἐλθεῖν τινὰς ἀπὸ 'Ιακώβου μετὰ τῶν ἐθνῶν συνήσθιεν ὁ Πέτρος. 2. οὐκ ἔστιν καλὸν λαβεῖν τὸν ἄρτον τῶν τέκνων καὶ βαλεῖν τοῖς κυσίν. 3. μετὰ δὲ τὸ σιγῆσαι αὐτοὺς ἀπεκρίθη 'Ιάκωβος. 4. ἐπεθύμησα τοῦτο τὸ πάσχα φαγεῖν μεθ' ὑμῶν πρὸ τοῦ με παθεῖν. 5. ἐφοβήθησαν δὲ ἐν τῷ εἰσελθεῖν αὐτοὺς εἰς τὴν νεφέλην.

II. 1. After he entered the house, the crowd went away. 2. While the woman was going away, he spoke to his disciples. 3. The son of man has power to save men. 4. He was worthy to receive the glory. 5. Before he saw you I called you.

## LESSON XLIII

### The Perfect and Pluperfect Indicative Active

**359.** VOCABULARY

ἀπαγγέλλω, *I announce, declare*

σύρω, *I drag, draw*

ψεύστης, -ου, ὁ, *liar*

ἔξω, adv., *without;* used also
with abl.

μακάριος, -α,- ον, *blessed, happy*

ὁράω, *I see;* fut. ὄψομαι; second aor. εἶδον.

φεύγω, *I flee, take flight;*
second aorist,
ἔφυγον.

**360.** The perfect indicative active of λύω is:

| *Singular* | *Plural* |
|---|---|
| 1. λέλυκα, *I have loosed,* | 1. λελύκαμεν |
| 2. λέλυκας    etc. | 2. λελύκατε |
| 3. λέλυκε | 3. λελύκασι or λέλυκαν |

Perfect active infinitive, λελυκέναι

*a.* In the second pers. sing. a form like λέλυκες occurs a few times. *b.* In the third pers. plur. a form like λέλυκαν occurs ten times in the New Testament.

**361.** Observe: 1. To the verb-stem (λυ-) is prefixed its initial consonant (λ) with ε.   This is called *reduplication.*   2. The suffix -κα is added to the reduplicated verb-stem: thus is formed, in the indicative, the first (or κ) perfect stem (active). 3. The personal endings seem to be the secondary personal endings, except -ασι in the third plur.

**362.** The first (or κ) perfect (active) is generally formed from verb-stems ending in a vowel, a liquid (λ, ρ), or a lingual (dental) mute (τ, δ, θ).

1. Vowel stems.   If the final vowel of the stem is long (or a diphthong) -κα is added to the reduplicated verb-stem without change, as πεπίστευκα.

If the final vowel of the stem is short, it is lengthened before -κα as νικάω, *I conquer,* νενίκηκα; ποιέω, *I do,* πεποίηκα; πληρόω, πεπλήρωκα.

Here α, ε, and ο follow the same principle of lengthening as in the future and first aorist active and passive.

2. **Liquid stems.** -κα is added to the reduplicated verb-stem, as στέλλω (σταλ-), ἔσταλκα (for reduplication see below).

3. **Lingual mute stems.** τ, δ, or θ is dropped before -κα, as σώζω (σωδ), σέσωκα.

**363.** Verbs beginning with a vowel, two consonants (except a mute and liquid), a double consonant (ζ, ξ, ψ), or ῥ, form the reduplication like the augment. ρ is generally doubled. Thus: ἀγαπάω, ἠγάπηκα; στέλλω, ἔσταλκα; ξηραίνω, ἐξήραμμαι.

**364.** Verbs beginning with a rough mute (φ, χ, θ) have the corresponding smooth mute (π, κ, τ), in reduplication. Thus: φιλέω, πεφίληκα; -θνήσκω, τέθνηκα.

**365.** A few verbs have a seemingly irregular perfect, as

γινώσκω, perf. act. ἔγνωκα.

ὁράω, perf. act. ἑώρακα.

**366.** In formation of the perfect active a few verbs add -α and not -κα to the reduplicated verb-stem. These are called *second* or *strong* perfects, and are older than the κ- perfects. Conj. like κ- perf.

| *Present* | *Second perfect* |
|---|---|
| ἀκούω | ἀκήκοα |
| γίνομαι | γέγονα |
| γράφω | γέγραφα |
| ἔρχομαι | ἐλήλυθα |
| πάσχω | πέπονθα |
| πείθω | πέποιθα |
| φεύγω | πέφευγα. |

**367.** The tense in Greek called perfect is really a present perfect. The perfect presents the action of the verb in a completed state or condition. When the action was completed the perfect tense does not tell. It is still complete at the time of the use of the tense by the speaker or writer. The perfect expresses the continuance of completed action. It is then a combination of punctiliar action and durative action. This kind of action expressed by the perfect tense is sometimes called *perfective* action.

**368.** The perfect tense as tense is timeless. But in the indicative the time element is present. The perfect indicative generally expresses the present result of a past action. It then has to do with the past and the present. The English perfect is not an equivalent to the Greek perfect. The translations given in the paradigms are not at all to be taken as equivalent to the Greek perfect, but as a means of associating the verb meaning with the verb. Aktionsart of the verb applies to the perfect. E.g.,

γέγραφα, *I wrote and the statement is still on record.*

ἐλήλυθα, *I came* (punctiliar) *and am still here* (durative).

**369.** The pluperfect (past perfect) indicative active of λύω is

| Singular | | Plural | |
|---|---|---|---|
| 1. [(ἐ)λελύκειν], | *I had loosed,* | 1. [(ἐ)λελύκειμεν] | |
| 2. [(ἐ)λελύκεις] | etc. | 2. (ἐ)λελύκειτε | |
| 3. (ἐ)λελύκει, | | 3. (ἐ)λελύκεισαν | |

*a.* The forms in brackets do not occur in the New Testament.

Observe: 1. The pluperf. is made upon the perfect stem. 2. The thematic vowel is ει. 3. The personal endings are the secondary personal endings. 4. There is an augment before the reduplication. The augment is usually dropped in the pluperf. in the New Testament.

**370.** If a second perfect has a pluperfect, the pluperf. is made on the second perfect stem and is called the second pluperfect. Thus:

| Present | Second perf. | Second pluperf. (third pers. sing.) |
|---------|-------------|------------------------------------|
| γίνομαι | γέγονα | (ἐ)γεγόνει |
| ἔρχομαι | ἐλήλυθα | ἐληλύθει |

The pluperfect expresses continuance of the completed state in past time up to a prescribed limit in the past.

**371.**       EXERCISES

I. 1. ὃ ἑωράκαμεν καὶ ἀκηκόαμεν ἀπαγγέλλομεν καὶ ὑμῖν. 2. ἐν τούτῳ ἐστὶν ἡ ἀγάπη, οὐχ ὅτι ἡμεῖς ἠγαπήκαμεν τὸν θεόν, ἀλλ' ὅτι αὐτὸς ἠγάπησεν ἡμᾶς. 3. λέγει αὐτῷ Ἰησοῦς Ὅτι ἑώρακάς με πεπίστευκας, μακάριοι οἱ μὴ ἰδόντες καὶ πιστεύσαντες. 4. ψεύστην πεποίηκε αὐτὸν ὅτι οὐ πεπίστευκεν εἰς τὴν μαρτυρίαν ἣν μεμαρτύρηκεν ὁ θεὸς περὶ τοῦ υἱοῦ αὐτοῦ. 5. αὕτη δέ ἐστιν ἡ κρίσις ὅτι τὸ φῶς ἐλήλυθεν εἰς τὸν κόσμον. 6. τὸν Παῦλον ἔσυρον ἔξω τῆς πόλεως, νομίζοντες αὐτὸν τεθνηκέναι.

II. 1. We have made him King. 2. He said "What I have written, I have written." 3. We have kept the faith. 4. I have come to do the will of him who sent me.

## LESSON XLIV

### The Perfect Tense (Continued)

**372.**                    VOCABULARY

ἑορτή, ἡ, *feast*

ἥλιος, ὁ, *sun*

θεραπεύω, *I heal*

ἐμός, -ή, -όν, poss. pron. of first pers. *my, mine*

σός,- ή,- όν, poss. pron. of the second pers., *thy, thine*

ἡμέτερος, -α, -ον, poss. pron. of the first pers., *our*

ὑμέτερος, -α, -ον, poss. pron. of the second pers., *your*

**373.** The declension of the perfect active participle of λύω is

*Singular*

|      | *Masc.* | *Fem.* | *Neut.* |
|------|---------|--------|---------|
| Nom. | λελυκώς | λελυκυῖα | λελυκός |
| Gen.<br>Abl. | λελυκότος | λελυκυίας | λελυκότος |
| Loc.<br>Ins.<br>Dat. | λελυκότι | λελυκυίᾳ | λελυκότι |
| Acc. | λελυκότα | λελυκυῖαν | λελυκός |

*Plural*

|      | *Masc.* | *Fem.* | *Neut.* |
|------|---------|--------|---------|
| Nom. | λελυκότες | λελυκυῖαι | λελυκότα |
| Gen.<br>Abl. | λελυκότων | λελυκυιῶν | λελυκότων |
| Loc.<br>Ins.<br>Dat. | λελυκόσι | λελυκυίαις | λελυκόσι |
| Acc. | λελυκότας | λελυκυίας | λελυκότα |

Observe: 1. The perfect act. part. is made on the perfect act. stem. 2. In the masc. and neut. it is declined according to the third declension, and in the fem. according to the first declension. 3. The accent seemingly is irregular.

**374.** The second perfect act. part. is made on the second perfect act. stem, and is commonly declined like λελυκώς, -κυῖα, -κός. Thus,

| Present | Second perf. | Second perf. part. |
|---------|--------------|--------------------|
| λαμβάνω | εἴληφα | εἰληφώς, -φυῖα,-φός |

**375.** The perfect indicative middle and passive of λύω is:

|  | Singular |  | Plural |
|--|----------|--|--------|
| 1. | λέλυμαι | 1. | λελύμεθα |
| 2. | λέλυσαι | 2. | λέλυσθε |
| 3. | λέλυται | 3. | λέλυνται |

Perf. midd. and pass. infinitive, λελύσθαι

Observe: 1. The stem of the perf. middle and pass. is the reduplicated verb-stem. 2. The primary middle personal endings are attached directly to the reduplicated verb-stem. 3. There is no thematic vowel.

*a.* The translations *I have loosed (for) myself* (midd.) and *I have been loosed* (pass.) do not give accurately the meaning of the perfect tense in Greek.

**376.** Verbs with stems in a short vowel (α, ε, ο) lengthen the vowel (as in the fut., aor., etc.) before the personal endings, as,

πληρόω, πεπλήρωμαι; θεάομαι, τεθέαμαι.

**377.** Of verbs with stems in a labial mute (π, β, φ), a palatal mute (κ, γ, χ), a liquid (λ, ρ), or a nasal (μ, ν), the third pers. sing. only of the perf. middle and passive occurs in the New Testament. Of verbs with stems in a lingual mute (τ, δ, θ) the first and third pers. sing. and the first pers. plur. occur in the New Testament. See p. 240, § 31.

**378.** The pluperfect indicative middle (and passive) is formed by adding the secondary middle endings to the perfect middle stem. Sometimes there is also an augment. The pluperf. indic. middle third pers. plur. of λύω is (ἐ)λέλυντο. The pluperfect indic. middle (and passive) of verbs with stems in a consonant is so rare that the forms are not given here.

**379.** The perfect middle (and passive) participle is formed by adding the middle participle endings, -μένος, -μένη, -μένον, to the perfect middle stem. Thus the perfect middle (and passive) participle of λύω is:

| Masc. | Fem. | Neut. |
|-------|------|-------|
| λελυμένος | λελυμένη | λελυμένον |

With the exception of the accent, it is declined like other participles in μενος, -η, -ον.

**380.** It needs to be remembered that *perfective* action runs through the whole perfect tense, and that *Aktionsart* of the verb-stem modifies the tense action.

The perf. participle, then, may represent a state or a completed action. The time of the perf. part. is relative to the time of the principal verb. The action of the participle may be:

1. Coincident with that of the principal verb; e.g.,

εἶδον ἤδη αὐτὸν τεθνηκότα, *they saw that he was already dead.*

2. Antecedent to that of the principal verb; e.g.,

πολλοὶ τῶν πεπιστευκότων ἤρχοντο, *many of those having believed were coming.*

The perf. part. may be used in any of the constructions in which other participles are used.

**381.** The second class conditional sentence. It is the *condition determined as unfulfilled.* The condition is assumed to be contrary to fact. The thing in itself may be true, but it is treated as untrue. The condition has only to do with the *statement*, not with the actual fact. The condition has εἰ + a past tense of the indicative; the conclusion has a past tense of the indicative usually with ἄν.

ἄν cannot be really translated into English. It seems to have a definite sense, *in that case*, and an indefinite sense. It is a particle used to give more color to the mode with which it occurs.

1. The imperf. ind. is used in unfulfilled conditions about *present time;* e.g.,

εἰ ἦν ὁ προφήτης, ἐγίνωσκεν ἄν, *if he were the prophet, he would know.*

2. The aorist ind. or pluperf. ind. is used in unfulfilled conditions about *past time;* e.g.,

εἰ γὰρ ἔγνωσαν, οὐκ ἂν τὸν κύριον τῆς δόξης ἐσταύρωσαν, *for if they had known, they would not have crucified the Lord of glory.*

*a.* Sometimes one tense occurs in one clause,

another tense in the other clause.  *b.* Each tense has
its proper *kind of action*.  *c.* The negative with the
protasis (if-clause) is μή, with the apodosis οὐ.

**382.**                    EXERCISES

I.  1. ἀπεκρίθη ὁ Ἰησοῦς Ἀμὴν ἀμὴν λέγω σοι, ἐὰν μή
τις γεννηθῇ ἐξ ὕδατος καὶ πνεύματος, οὐ δύναται εἰσελθεῖν
εἰς τὴν βασιλείαν τοῦ θεοῦ.  τὸ γεγεννημένον ἐκ τῆς σαρκὸς
σάρξ ἐστιν, καὶ τὸ γεγεννημένον ἐκ τοῦ πνεύματος πνεῦμά
ἐστιν.  2. ἐν τούτῳ ἡ ἀγάπη τοῦ θεοῦ τετελείωται.  3. ἐξ
ἡμῶν ἐξῆλθαν, ἀλλ' οὐκ ἦσαν ἐξ ἡμῶν. εἰ γὰρ ἐξ ἡμῶν ἦσαν,
μεμενήκεισαν ἂν μεθ' ἡμῶν.  4. γέγραπται ἐν τῷ νόμῳ καὶ τοῖς
προφήταις.  5. ἡμεῖς δὲ κηρύσσομεν Χριστὸν ἐσταυρωμένον.

II.  1. If we had seen him, we would have loved
him.  2. The days have been fulfilled.  3. We
receive those who have believed on the Lord.

### LESSON XLV

**Reflexive Pronoun.  Reciprocal Pronoun.
Indefinite Relative Pronoun**

**383.**                    VOCABULARY

ἐλπίζω, *I hope*                    ὁ πλησίον, *neighbor*
μυστήριον, τό, *mystery*            ταπεινόω, *I make low,*
πλησίον, adv., *near*                    *humble*

**384.** The reflexive pronouns are:

ἐμαυτοῦ, -ῆς, *myself*          σεαυτοῦ, -ῆς, *thyself*
ἑαυτοῦ, -ῆς, -οῦ (rarely αὐτοῦ, -ῆς, -οῦ), *himself, herself,*
        *itself*

They are declined as follows:

1. First person:

|  | Singular | | Plural | |
|---|---|---|---|---|
|  | *Masc.* | *Fem.* | *Masc.* | *Fem.* |
| Gen. Abl. | ἐμαυτοῦ | ἐμαυτῆς | ἑαυτῶν | ἑαυτῶν |
| Loc. Ins. Dat. | ἐμαυτῷ | ἐμαυτῇ | ἑαυτοῖς | ἑαυταῖς |
| Acc. | ἐμαυτόν | ἐμαυτήν | ἑαυτούς | ἑαυτάς |

2. Second person:

|  | Singular | | Plural | |
|---|---|---|---|---|
|  | *Masc.* | *Fem.* | *Masc.* | *Fem.* |
| Gen. Abl. | σεαυτοῦ | σεαυτῆς | ἑαυτῶν | ἑαυτῶν |
| Loc. Ins. Dat. | σεαυτῷ | σεαυτῇ | ἑαυτοῖς | ἑαυταῖς |
| Acc. | σεαυτόν | σεαυτήν | ἑαυτούς | ἑαυτάς |

3. Third person:

|  | Singular | | |
|---|---|---|---|
|  | *Masc.* | *Fem.* | *Neut.* |
| Gen. Abl. | ἑαυτοῦ | ἑαυτῆς | ἑαυτοῦ |
| Loc. Ins. Dat. | ἑαυτῷ | ἑαυτῇ | ἑαυτῷ |
| Acc. | ἑαυτόν | ἑαυτήν | ἑαυτό |

*Plural*

|  | *Masc.* | *Fem.* | *Neut.* |
|---|---|---|---|
| Gen.<br>Abl. | ἑαυτῶν | ἑαυτῶν | ἑαυτῶν |
| Loc.<br>Ins.<br>Dat. | ἑαυτοῖς | ἑαυταῖς | ἑαυτοῖς |
| Acc. | ἑαυτούς | ἑαυτάς | ἑαυτά |

Observe: 1. These pronouns occur in the oblique cases only. 2. They are formed from the personal pronouns plus αὐτός. 3. There is no neuter gender in the reflexive pronouns of the first and second persons. 4. The plural form is the same for all three persons.

**385.** Examine carefully the following examples of the use of the reflexive pronouns.

1. ἐγὼ δοξάζω ἐμαυτόν, *I glorify myself.*
2. ἔχει ζωὴν ἐν ἑαυτῷ, *he has life in himself.*
3. τί λέγεις περὶ σεαυτοῦ; *what dost thou say concerning thyself?*
4. αὐτοὶ ἐν ἑαυτοῖς στενάζομεν, *we ourselves groan within ourselves.*

In these examples it is seen that the pronoun refers back to the subject of the clause, hence the name reflexive.

**386.** The reciprocal pronoun is ἀλλήλων, *of one another.* It occurs in the New Testament only in the masculine forms ἀλλήλων, ἀλλήλοις, ἀλλήλους. No fem. and neut. forms occur.

ἔλεγον πρὸς ἀλλήλους, *they said to one another.*

**387.** οἶδα, *I know*, an old perfect with a present (durative) meaning is conjugated in the indicative active as follows:

| Singular | | Plural | |
|---|---|---|---|
| 1. οἶδα, | *I know*, | 1. οἴδαμεν | |
| 2. οἶδας | etc. | 2. οἴδατε | |
| 3. οἶδε | | 3. οἴδασι | |

Infinitive, εἰδέναι

**388.** The forms of the (indefinite) relative pronoun ὅστις, ἥτις, ὅτι, given below are the forms found in the New Testament.

*Singular*

| | Masc. | Fem. | Neut. |
|---|---|---|---|
| Nom. | ὅστις | ἥτις | ὅτι |
| Acc. | | | ὅτι |

*Plural*

| | | | |
|---|---|---|---|
| Nom. | οἵτινες | αἵτινες | ἅτινα |

*a.* An old form ὅτου (gen.) is found in certain set phrases.

This pronoun is made from the relative ὅς and the indefinite τις. It is used with the meanings "anyone" (indefinite) and "somebody" in particular (definite), i.e., "whoever" (indef.) and "who" (def.).

**389.** EXERCISES

I. 1. ἐμὲ οἴδατε καὶ οἴδατε πόθεν εἰμί. καὶ ἀπ' ἐμαυτοῦ οὐκ ἐλήλυθα, ἀλλ' ἔστιν ἀληθινὸς ὁ πέμψας με, ὃν ὑμεῖς οὐκ οἴδατε. 2. καὶ ὑπὲρ αὐτῶν ἐγὼ ἁγιάζω ἐμαυτόν. 3. ἀγαπήσεις τὸν πλησίον σου ὡς σεαυτόν. 4. ὅστις οὖν ταπεινώσει ἑαυτὸν ὡς τὸ παιδίον τοῦτο, οὗτός ἐστιν ὁ μείζων (greatest) ἐν τῇ βασιλείᾳ τῶν οὐρανῶν. 5. οὐ γὰρ ἑαυτοὺς

κηρύσσομεν ἀλλὰ Χριστὸν 'Ιησοῦν Κύριον, ἑαυτοὺς δὲ
δούλους ὑμῶν διὰ 'Ιησοῦν. 6. καὶ πολλοὶ μισήσουσιν
ἀλλήλους.

II. 1. You shall love one another. 2. I have not
spoken concerning myself. 3. We preached not ourselves, but Christ. 4. They said that he made himself the son of God.

## LESSON XLVI

### Future and Aorist Active and Middle of Liquid Verbs

**390.**    VOCABULARY

ἀποκτείνω, *I kill, slay*        πρόβατον, τό, *sheep*
ἐκτείνω, *I stretch out*        σωτηρία, ἡ, *salvation*
κράβαττος, ὁ, *pallet, bed*     ὀφείλω, *I owe, ought;* (sec.
                                aorist without augment,
                                ὄφελον)

**391.** Verbs with stems in a liquid (λ, ν, ρ) form the
futures by adding -ε ᵒ/ε¹ to the stem. The ε of the
suffix contracts with the thematic vowel ᵒ/ε. (Remember that the present stem is not always the
same as the verb-stem.)

**392.** The conjugation of κρίνω in the future indicative is:

ACTIVE

*Singular*                    *Plural*
1. κρινῶ (κρινέω)            1. κρινοῦμεν (κρινέομεν)
2. κρινεῖς (κρινέεις)        2. κρινεῖτε (κρινέετε)
3. κρινεῖ (κρινέει)          3. κρινοῦσι (κρινέουσι)

¹ Originally -εσᵒ/ε.    σ was expelled.

## MIDDLE

| *Singular* | *Plural* |
|---|---|
| 1. κρινοῦμαι (κρινέομαι) | 1. κρινούμεθα (κρινεόμεθα) |
| 2. κρινῇ (κρινέῃ) | 2. κρινεῖσθε (κρινέεσθε) |
| 3. κρινεῖται (κρινέεται) | 3. κρινοῦνται (κρινέονται) |

Observe that when one of the uncontracted syllables has an accent the contracted form has an accent (the circumflex, if possible).

*a.* The uncontracted forms do not occur. They are given to exhibit the vowels that are contracted.

*b.* Table of the vowel contractions.

$$\varepsilon + \omega = \omega \qquad\qquad \varepsilon + o = ou$$
$$\varepsilon + \varepsilon\iota = \varepsilon\iota \qquad\qquad \varepsilon + ou = ou$$
$$\varepsilon + \varepsilon + \varepsilon\iota$$

**393.** Verbs with stems in a liquid form the aorist active and middle by lengthening the stem vowel and adding -α.[1] α of the stem is lengthened to η (but ᾱ before ρ), ε to ει, ῐ to ι and ῠ to ῡ. The conjugation through all the modes, infinitives, and participles is like the regular first aorist; thus the aor. ind. act. of μένω is ἔμεινα, etc.; the subj., μείνω, etc.; infinitive, μεῖναι part., μείνας. The aor. ind. middle of κρίνω is ἐκρινάμην, etc. Notice that these verbs have no σ in the aorist.

**394.** Liquid verbs may have a second aorist, as βάλλω (βαλ-), ἔβαλον.

[1] Originally σ was expelled after a liquid.

**395.** Learn the stem, the future, and aorist of the following verbs:

| Present | Stem | Future | Aorist act. |
|---------|------|--------|-------------|
| ἀγγέλλω | ἀγγελ- | ἀγγελῶ | ἤγγειλα |
| αἴρω | ἀρ- | ἀρῶ | ἦρα |
| ἀποκτείνω | (ἀπο)κτεν- | ἀποκτενῶ | ἀπέκτεινα |
| ἀποστέλλω | (ἀπο)στελ- | ἀποστελῶ | ἀπέστειλα |
| βάλλω | βαλ- | βαλῶ | ἔβαλον |
| ἐγείρω | ἐγερ- | ἐγερῶ | ἤγειρα |

Of course the.compound forms of these verbs form their tenses in the same way as the uncompounded forms, as

ἐπαγγέλλω, ἐπαγγελῶ, ἐπήγγειλα
ἀποκτείνω and ἀποστέλλω are compound verbs.

**396.** The tenses of the verb in Greek are divided into nine tense-systems. As we have seen each tense-system has a distinct stem, called tense-stem.

| *Systems* | | *Tenses* |
|-----------|--|----------|
| 1. Present, | including | present and imperfect in all voices. |
| 2. Future, | " | future active and middle. |
| 3. First aorist, | " | first aorist act. and middle (and liquid aorists also). |
| 4. Second aorist, | " | second aorist act. and middle. |
| 5. First perfect, | " | first perfect and pluperf. active. |
| 6. Second perfect, | " | second perfect and pluperf. active. |

7. Perfect middle, including perfect and pluperf.
middle and passive
(and future perfect).

8. First passive, " first aorist and future
passive.

9. Second passive, " second aorist and future
passive.

*a.* Most verbs have only six of these nine systems, since very few verbs have both the first and second forms of the same tense; many verbs have less than six. No verb occurring in the New Testament is used in all nine systems.

**397.** The principal parts of a Greek verb are the first person singular indicative of every system used in it; e.g.,

λύω, λύσω, ἔλυσα, λέλυκα, λέλυμαι, ἐλύθην.

βάλλω, βαλῶ, ἔβαλον, βέβληκα, βέβλημαι, ἐβλήθην.

γίνομαι, γενήσομαι, ἐγενόμην, γέγονα, γεγένημαι, ἐγενήθην.

To know a verb one must know its principal parts.

**398.** Exercises

I. 1. καθὼς ἐμὲ ἀπέστειλας εἰς τὸν κόσμον, κἀγὼ[1] ἀπέστειλα αὐτοὺς εἰς τὸν κόσμον, καὶ ὑπὲρ αὐτῶν ἐγὼ ἁγιάζω ἐμαυτόν, ἵνα καὶ αὐτοὶ ὦσιν ἡγιασμένοι ἐν ἀληθείᾳ. 2. ὁ ἐγείρας τὸν Ἰησοῦν καὶ ἡμᾶς σὺν Ἰησοῦ[2] ἐγερεῖ. 3. καὶ ἀποκτενοῦσιν αὐτόν, καὶ τῇ τρίτῃ ἡμέρᾳ ἐγερθήσεται. 4. ἐὰν ἐν ὑμῖν μείνῃ ὃ ἀπ᾽ ἀρχῆς ἠκούσατε, καὶ[3] ὑμεῖς ἐν τῷ υἱῷ καὶ[3] ἐν τῷ πατρὶ μενεῖτε. 5. καὶ ἦρε τὸν κράβαττον αὐτοῦ. 6. ἐξῆλθεν ὁ σπείρων τοῦ σπεῖραι.

[1] κἀγὼ = καὶ ἐγώ, see § 4.
[2] Associative-ins. case. [3] See καὶ ... καὶ in 415

II. 1. They sought to kill him. 2. The disciples sowed the word. 3. I will send unto them prophets and apostles. 4. If we remain in the truth, the truth will remain in us.

## LESSON XLVII

### The Imperative Mode

**399.**                    VOCABULARY

ἄρχομαι, *I begin*          νηστεύω, *I fast*
ναός, ὁ, *temple*          ὑποκριτής-, -οῦ, ὁ, *pretender,*
                              *hypocrite*

**400.** The imperative is comparatively a late development in Greek. More of its forms came from an old injunctive mode than from any other source.

**401.** The personal endings of the imperative are:

ACTIVE

| *Singular* | *Plural* |
|---|---|
| 2. —, -θι, -ς | -τε |
| 3. -τω. | -τωσαν. |

MIDDLE (AND PASSIVE)

| | |
|---|---|
| 2. -σο | -σθε |
| 3. -σθω | -σθωσαν. |

*a.* -θι (probably an old adverb) is found in a few old verbs, and, except in the aor. pass., is not used in the active forms of the imperative of most verbs. The ending -ς is found only in a few old verbs.
*b.* -τω is probably an old ablative form of a demonstrative pronoun.

**402.** The present imperative active, middle, and passive is made on the present tense-stem. See 396.

**403.** The present active imperative of λύω is:

| Singular | Plural |
|---|---|
| 2. λῦε, *loose (thou)* | 2. λύετε, *loose (ye)* |
| 3. λυέτω, *let him loose* | 3. λυέτωσαν, *let them loose* |

*a.* λῦε is the verb-stem with the thematic vowel ε. Note the thematic vowel ε in all persons.

**404.** The present middle imperative of λύω is:

| Singular | Plural |
|---|---|
| 2. λύου, *loose (for) thyself* | 2. λύεσθε, *loose (for) yourself* |
| 3. λυέσθω, *let him loose (for) himself* | 3. λυέσθωσαν, *let them loose (for) themselves* |

*a.* λύου is for λύεσο, σ is expelled, and ε and ο contract to ου.

**405.** The present passive imperative of λύω is:

| Singular | Plural |
|---|---|
| 2. λύου, *be (thou) loosed* | 2. λύεσθε, *be (ye) loosed* |
| 3. λυέσθω, *let him be loosed* | 3. λυέσθωσαν, *let them be loosed* |

Observe that the pres. passive imperative is like the pres. middle in form.

**406.** The second aorist active imperative of βάλλω is:

| Singular | Plural |
|---|---|
| 2. βάλε | 2. βάλετε |
| 3. βαλέτω | 3. βαλέτωσαν |

*a.* The second pers. sing. of some second aorists is accented on the ultima, as εἰπέ, ἐλθέ, εὑρέ; accent of imps. recessive.   *b.* No augment.

**407.** The second aorist middle imperative of βάλλω is

<table>
<tr><td colspan="2" align="center">*Singular*</td><td colspan="2" align="center">*Plural*</td></tr>
<tr><td>2.</td><td>βαλοῦ</td><td>2.</td><td>βάλεσθε</td></tr>
<tr><td>3.</td><td>βαλέσθω</td><td>3.</td><td>βαλέσθωσαν</td></tr>
</table>

*a.* Note the accent of βαλοῦ.

Observe that in the endings the imperative of the second aor. act. and middle is like that of the present act. and middle.   The difference between them is the difference in tense-stem: the present tense-stem is βαλλ-, the second aorist tense-stem is βαλ-.

**408.** The imperative, like the subjunctive, is always future in time, though it may apply to the immediate future.

The difference in meaning between the present imperative and the aorist imperative is in the *kind of action,*—*durative* action in the present, and *punctiliar* action in the aorist.   The pres. imperative, then, has to do with action in progress.   The aorist imperative has to do with the simple act without regard to progress.   E.g.,

βάλλε λίθους, *keep on* (or *go on*) *throwing stones.*

μὴ βάλλε, *stop* (or *quit*) *throwing stones.*

εἴσελθε εἰς τὸν οἶκον, *enter the house.*

μὴ εἰσέλθῃς εἰς τὸν οἶκον, *do not* (*do not begin to*) *enter the house.*

It will be observed that the first and second examples (present) have reference to the continuance of the action, while the third and fourth examples (aorist) have reference to the simple act. In the second example μὴ with the pres. imperative forbids the *continuance* of the action; while in the fourth example μὴ with the aor. subjunctive forbids the beginning (ingressive) of the action. In the second example the action is *going on;* in the fourth example the action has not begun. Thus Aktionsart must be considered. In prohibitions to forbid a thing not yet done the aor. subj. (not the imperative) is used with μή (see fourth example above).

**409.** The first aorist act. imperative of λύω is:

| Singular | Plural |
|---|---|
| 2. λῦσον | 2. λύσατε |
| 3. λυσάτω | 3. λυσάτωσαν |

*a.* The origin of -ον of the second pers. sing. is obscure.

Observe that the stem is the aorist stem λυσα-.

**410.** The first aorist middle imperative of λύω is:

| Singular | Plural |
|---|---|
| 2. λῦσαι | 2. λύσασθε |
| 3. λυσάσθω | 3. λυσάσθωσαν |

*a.* The second pers. sing. ending -αι probably came from the aorist infinitive. Note accent, βάπτισαι.

**411.** The aorist passive imperative of λύω is:

| Singular | | Plural |
|---|---|---|
| 2. λύθητι, *be (thou) loosed,* | | 2. λύθητε |
| 3. λυθήτω | etc. | 3. λυθήτωσαν |

*a.* -τι of the second pers. sing. was -θι. θ **was** changed to τ to avoid the repetition of the rough **mute.**

Observe that the forms are made on the aor. pass. stem λυθε(η).

**412.** In the imperative in Greek there is no first person form. In the first person the subjunctive is used instead of the imperative.

**413.** The original significance of the imperative was demand or exhortation; but it was not confined to this idea.

The imperative is used in:

1. Commands or exhortations—

   ἀκουέτω, *let him hear.*

   εἴσελθε εἰς τὸν οἶκον, *enter the house.*

2. Prohibitions—

   μὴ κρίνετε *quit (don't go on) judging*

3. Entreaties—

πάτερ ἅγιε, τήρησον αὐτοὺς ἐν τῷ ὀνόματί σου, *Holy Father, keep them in thy name.*

Note.—The negative of the imperative is μή.

**414.**               EXERCISES

I.   1. μὴ κρίνετε ἵνα μὴ κριθῆτε.   2. ἁγιασθήτω τὸ ὄνομά σου, ἐλθάτω ἡ βασιλεία σου, γενηθήτω τὸ θέλημά σου, ὡς ἐν οὐρανῷ καὶ ἐπὶ γῆς.   3. ὅταν δὲ νηστεύητε, μὴ γίνεσθε ὡς οἱ ὑποκριταὶ σκυθρωποί.[1]   4. ὁ ἔχων ὦτα ἀκούειν ἀκουέτω. 5. πορεύθητι πρὸς τὸν λαὸν τοῦτον.   6. ἄρθητι καὶ βλήθητι εἰς τὴν θάλασσαν.   7. λέγει αὐτῷ Ἔρχου καὶ ἴδε.

II.  1. Let him depart.   2. Guard thyself from the evil one.   3. Say to this people all the words of this life.   4. Quit saying evil things.

_____
[1] σκυθρωπός, adj., *of a gloomy countenance.*

## LESSON XLVIII

### Numerals.  οὐδείς

**415.**                    VOCABULARY

διψάω, *I thirst*                    πάλιν, adv., *again*
καί...καί, *both—and*         πεινάω, *I hunger, am hun-*
μήτε...μήτε, *neither—nor*        *gry*
οὐκέτι, *no longer, no more*   πώποτε, *ever yet*
οὔτε...οὔτε, *neither—nor*    τὲ...καί, *both—and*

**416.** Learn the numerals (cardinal and ordinal) from one (first) to twelve (twelfth).

| *Cardinals* | *Ordinals* |
|---|---|
| *1.* εἷς, *one*, etc. | πρῶτος, *first*, etc. |
| 2. δύο | δεύτερος |
| 3. τρεῖς | τρίτος |
| 4. τέσσαρες | τέταρτος |
| 5. πέντε | πέμπτος |
| 6. ἕξ | ἕκτος |
| 7. ἑπτά | ἕβδομος |
| 8. ὀκτώ | ὄγδοος |
| 9. ἐννέα | ἔνατος |
| 10. δέκα | δέκατος |
| 11. ἕνδεκα | ἐνδέκατος |
| 12. δώδεκα | δωδέκατος |
| δεκαδύο | |

Other numerals may be learned from a lexicon as they are needed.

**417.** The ordinals have the regular terminations of adjectives of the first and second declensions, as τρίτος (masc.), τρίτη (fem.), τρίτον (neut.), and are so declined.

**418.** The cardinals are indeclinable, except the first four and from 200 onward.

The first four are declined as follows:

I. εἷς, μία, ἕν, *one*                    2. δύο, *two*

| | Masc., | Fem. | Neut. | | Masc., Fem., and Neut. |
|---|---|---|---|---|---|
| Nom. | εἷς | μία | ἕν | Nom. | δύο |
| Gen. | ⎫ | | | Gen. | ⎫ |
| | ⎬ ἑνός | μιᾶς | ἑνός | | ⎬ δύο |
| Abl. | ⎭ | | | Abl. | ⎭ |
| Loc. | ⎫ | | | Loc. | ⎫ |
| Ins. | ⎬ ἑνί | μιᾷ | ἑνί | Ins. | ⎬ δυσί |
| Dat. | ⎭ | | | Dat. | ⎭ |
| Acc. | ἕνα | μίαν | ἕν | Acc. | δύο. |

3. τρεῖς, τρία, *three*              4. τέσσαρες, τέσσαρα, *four*

| | Masc. and Fem. | Neut. | | Masc. and Fem. | Neut. |
|---|---|---|---|---|---|
| Nom. | τρεῖς | τρία | Nom. | τέσσαρες | τέσσαρα |
| Gen. | ⎫ | | Gen. | ⎫ | |
| | ⎬ τριῶν | τριῶν | | ⎬ τεσσάρων | τεσσάρων |
| Abl. | ⎭ | | Abl. | ⎭ | |
| Loc. | ⎫ | | Loc. | ⎫ | |
| Ins. | ⎬ τρισί | τρισί | Ins. | ⎬ τέσσαρσι | τέσσαρσι |
| Dat. | ⎭ | | Dat. | ⎭ | |
| Acc. | τρεῖς | τρία | Acc. | τέσσαρας | τέσσαρα. |

These cardinals agree with the substantives with which they are used.

**419.** The declension of οὐδείς, οὐδεμία, οὐδέν, *no one* (*nobody*), *nothing*, is:

|  | *Masc.* | *Fem.* | *Neut.* |
|---|---|---|---|
| Nom. | οὐδείς | οὐδεμία | οὐδέν |
| Gen. }<br>Abl. } | οὐδενός | οὐδεμιᾶς | οὐδενός |
| Loc. }<br>Ins. }<br>Dat. } | οὐδενί | οὐδεμιᾷ | οὐδενί |
| Acc. | οὐδένα | οὐδεμίαν | οὐδέν |

Like οὐδείς is declined μηδείς, μηδεμία, μηδέν, *no one, nothing.* μηδείς is generally used wherever μή would be the appropriate negative.

**420.** A negative sentence in Greek may have more than one negative particle. In Greek the succession of negatives merely strengthens the first negative if the second (and third) is a compound form like οὐδέ, οὐδείς, οὔπω, μηδείς, etc., e.g.,

μηδενὶ μηδὲν ὀφείλετε, *owe no one anything.*

**421.** οὐ and μή are used in direct questions to indicate the kind of answer expected.

1. οὐ expects the answer *yes.*

οὐ τῷ ὀνόματι ἐπροφητεύσαμεν; *Did we not prophesy by thy name?*

2. μή expects the answer *no.*

παιδία, μή τι προσφάγιον ἔχετε; *Little children, have you anything to eat?* (*You haven't anything to eat, have you?*)

**422.** οὐ μή is used with the aorist subjunctive (rarely present) or occasionally the future ind. in the sense of an emphatic negative future indicative.

καὶ τὸν ἐρχόμενον πρός με οὐ μὴ ἐκβάλω ἔξω, *and him who comes to me I will* NOT *cast out.*

**423.**            EXERCISES

I.   1. καὶ οὐκ ἔφαγεν οὐδὲν ἐν ταῖς ἡμέραις ἐκείναις, καὶ συντελεσθεισῶν αὐτῶν ἐπείνασεν.   2. οὐδεὶς δύναται δυσὶ κυρίοις δουλεύειν, τὸν γὰρ ἕνα μισήσει καὶ τὸν ἕτερον ἀγαπήσει.   3. ὁ ἐρχόμενος πρὸς ἐμὲ οὐ μὴ πεινάσῃ, καὶ ὁ πιστεύων εἰς ἐμὲ οὐ μὴ διψήσει πώποτε.   4. εἶπεν οὖν ὁ Ἰησοῦς τοῖς δώδεκα Μὴ καὶ ὑμεῖς θέλετε ὑπάγειν;   5. οὐκ εἰμὶ ἐλεύθερος; οὐκ εἰμὶ ἀπόστολος;   6. ὁ θεὸς φῶς ἐστιν καὶ σκοτία οὐκ ἔστιν ἐν αὐτῷ οὐδεμία.   7. οὐδεὶς ἀγαθὸς εἰ μὴ[1] εἷς ὁ θεός.   8. οὔτε ἐμὲ οἴδατε οὔτε τὸν πατέρα μου.

II.   1. Let no one enter the house.   2. Did he not see me?   3. I will not serve him.   4. Is he able to serve two masters?

## LESSON XLIX

### Present System of Contract Verbs in -έω.

**424.**            VOCABULARY

| | | | |
|---|---|---|---|
| ἀρνέομαι, | *I deny* | οἰκοδομέω, | *I build* |
| δοκέω, | *I think, suppose;* impers. *it seems* | ὁμολογέω, | *I agree with, confess* |
| θεωρέω, | *I look at, gaze, see* | περιπατέω, | *I walk* (*live*) |
| μετανοέω, | *I repent* | φιλέω, | *I love* |

**425.** The conjugation of verbs with stems in α, ε, or o, has been given in all tenses except the present and imperfect. The conjugation of these verbs (stems in α, ε, or o) differs from that of regular ω- verbs in the present and imperfect tenses only.

---

[1] εἰ μή (or ἐὰν μή) with a substantive means *except*.

**426.** In the present and imperfect tenses the vowel (α, ε, or o) of the stem unites with the thematic vowel (and in some forms the personal ending also) and forms a diphthong or a single long vowel. This is called *contraction*.

**427.** The conjugation of φιλέω in the present system is as follows:

1. The present indicative:

ACTIVE

| *Singular* | *Plural* |
|---|---|
| 1. φιλῶ (φιλέω) | 1. φιλοῦμεν (φιλέομεν) |
| 2. φιλεῖς (φιλέεις) | 2. φιλεῖτε (φιλέετε) |
| 3. φιλεῖ (φιλέει) | 3. φιλοῦσι (φιλέουσι) |

MIDDLE AND PASSIVE

| *Singular* | *Plural* |
|---|---|
| 1. φιλοῦμαι (φιλέομαι) | 1. φιλούμεθα (φιλεόμεθα) |
| 2. φιλῇ (φιλέη) | 2. φιλεῖσθε (φιλέεσθε) |
| 3. φιλεῖται (φιλέεται) | 3. φιλοῦνται (φιλέονται) |

2. The present subjunctive:

ACTIVE

| *Singular* | *Plural* |
|---|---|
| 1. φιλῶ (φιλέω) | 1. φιλῶμεν (φιλέωμεν) |
| 2. φιλῇς (φιλέης) | 2. φιλῆτε (φιλέητε) |
| 3. φιλῇ (φιλέη) | 3. φιλῶσι (φιλέωσι) |

MIDDLE AND PASSIVE

| *Singular* | *Plural* |
|---|---|
| 1. φιλῶμαι (φιλέωμαι) | 1. φιλώμεθα (φιλεώμεθα) |
| 2. [φιλῇ (φιλέη)] | 2. φιλῆσθε (φιλέησθε) |
| 3. φιλῆται (φιλέηται) | 3. φιλῶνται (φιλέωνται) |

3. The present imperative:

### ACTIVE

| *Singular* | *Plural* |
|---|---|
| 2. φίλει (φίλεε) | 2. φιλεῖτε (φιλέετε) |
| 3. φιλείτω (φιλεέτω) | 3. φιλείτωσαν (φιλεέτωσαν) |

### MIDDLE AND PASSIVE

| *Singular* | *Plural* |
|---|---|
| 2. φιλοῦ (φιλέου) | 2. φιλεῖσθε (φιλέεσθε) |
| 3. φιλείσθω (φιλεέσθω) | 3. φιλείσθωσαν (φιλεέσθωσαν) |

4. The present infinitive:

ACTIVE φιλεῖν (φιλέειν)

MIDDLE AND PASSIVE φιλεῖσθαι (φιλέεσθαι)

5. The present participle:

### ACTIVE

φιλῶν (φιλέων), φιλοῦσα (φιλέουσα), φιλοῦν (φιλέον)

### MIDDLE AND PASSIVE

φιλούμενος, -η, -ον (φιλεόμενος, -η, -ον)

6. The imperfect indicative:

### ACTIVE

| *Singular* | *Plural* |
|---|---|
| 1. ἐφίλουν (ἐφίλεον) | 1. ἐφιλοῦμεν (ἐφιλέομεν) |
| 2. ἐφίλεις (ἐφίλεες) | 2. ἐφιλεῖτε (ἐφιλέετε) |
| 3. ἐφίλει (ἐφίλεε) | 3. ἐφίλουν (ἐφίλεον) |

### MIDDLE AND PASSIVE

| *Singular* | *Plural* |
|---|---|
| 1. ἐφιλούμην (ἐφιλεόμην) | 1. ἐφιλούμεθα (ἐφιλεόμεθα) |
| 2. ἐφιλοῦ (ἐφιλέου) | 2. ἐφιλεῖσθε (ἐφιλέεσθε) |
| 3. ἐφιλεῖτο (ἐφιλέετο) | 3. ἐφιλοῦντο (ἐφιλέοντο) |

**428.** The declension of the present active participle
φιλῶν, -οῦσα, -οῦν is:

*Singular*

|  | *Masc.* | *Fem.* | *Neut.* |
|---|---|---|---|
| Nom. | φιλῶν (φιλέων) | φιλοῦσα (φιλέουσα) | φιλοῦν (φιλέον) |
| Gen. Abl. | φιλοῦντος (φιλέοντος) | φιλούσης | like masc. |
| Loc. Ins. Dat. | φιλοῦντι (φιλέοντι) | φιλούσῃ | like masc. |
| Acc. | φιλοῦντα (φιλέοντα) | φιλοῦσαν | φιλοῦν (φιλέον) |

*Plural*

|  | *Masc.* | *Fem.* |
|---|---|---|
| Nom. | φιλοῦντες (φιλέοντες) | φιλοῦσαι (φιλέουσαι) |
| Gen. Abl. | φιλούντων (φιλεόντων) | φιλουσῶν |
| Loc. Ins. Dat. | φιλοῦσι (φιλέουσι) | φιλούσαις |
| Acc. | φιλοῦντας (φιλέοντας) | φιλούσας |

*Neut.*

| Nom. | φιλοῦντα (φιλέοντα) |
|---|---|
| Gen. Abl. | like masc. |
| Loc. Ins. Dat. | like masc. |
| Acc. | φιλοῦντα (φιλέοντα). |

**429.** The scheme of contraction for regular -εω verbs is as follows:

ε + ε = ει          ε + ει = ει
ε + ο = ου          ε + η = η
ε + ω = ω          ε + ου = ου

**430.** Observe that: 1. The syllable resulting from contraction has an accent if either one of the component syllables had an accent in the uncontracted form. 2. The accent is circumflex, if the first vowel (of the contracting vowels) had the acute; but it is an acute, if the second vowel had the acute.

**431.**            EXERCISES

I. 1. καλῶς ποιεῖτε τοῖς μισοῦσιν ὑμᾶς. 2. μὴ θαυμάζετε, ἀδελφοί, εἰ μισεῖ ὑμᾶς ὁ κόσμος. 3. ταῦτα αὐτοῦ λαλοῦντος πολλοὶ ἐπίστευσαν. 4. τί δὲ ὑμῖν δοκεῖ; 5. ἐάν τι αἰτώμεθα κατὰ τὸ θέλημα αὐτοῦ ἀκούει ἡμῶν. 6. καὶ μετὰ ταῦτα περιεπάτει Ἰησοῦς ἐν τῇ Γαλιλαίᾳ, οὐ γὰρ ἤθελεν ἐν τῇ Ἰουδαίᾳ περιπατεῖν, ὅτι ἐζήτουν αὐτὸν οἱ Ἰουδαῖοι ἀποκτεῖναι. 7. ἐφοβοῦντο τὸν λαόν.

II. 1. Who is seeking to kill you? 2. He who hates his brother walks in darkness. 3. Follow me. 4. Quit doing these things. 5. They feared the crowd.

## LESSON L

### Comparison of Adjectives and Adverbs

**432.**            VOCABULARY

ἔξεστιν,    *it is lawful, is possible*    παλαιός, -ά, -όν, *old, ancient*
                                                    περισσός, -ή, -όν, *abundant*
νέος, -α, -ον, *young, new*    πλούσιος, -α, -ον, *rich*

**433.** The comparative degree of an adjective in -ος is generally formed by adding -τερος, -α, -ον to the masc. stem of adj. as found in the positive degree. To form the superlative[1] degree, -τατος, -η, -ον is added to the masc. stem of adj. as found in the positive degree.

**434.** Examine carefully the following examples:

Positive          Comparative          Superlative

1. ἰσχῡρός, -ά, -όν, ἰσχυρότερος, -α, -ον, [ἰσχυρότατος,-η,-ον]
   *strong*          *stronger*          *strongest*
2. νέος, -α, -ον    νεώτερος, -α, -ον    [νεώτατος, -η, -ον]
3. σοφός, -ή, -όν   σοφώτερος, -α, -ον   [σοφώτατος, -η, -ον]

*a.* The forms enclosed in brackets are not found in the New Testament.

Similarly adjectives in -ες make the comparison.

4. ἀσθενής, -ές ἀσθενέστερος, -α, -ον [ἀσθενέστατος, -η, -ον]

**435.** Observe: 1. If the penult of the adjective (with nom. sing. masc. in -ος) is short[2] in the positive, the ο of the stem is lengthened to ω[3] in the comparative and superlative. 2. All comparatives and superlatives have recessive accent.

**436.** The stem from which the comparative is formed may be an adverb, e.g.,

ἔξω, *out*          ἐξώτερος, *outer*
ἄνω, *up, above*    ἀνώτερος, *higher*

[1] There are only three superlative forms in -τατος in the New Testament.
[2] A penult, although its vowel is short, is considered long if its vowel is followed by two consonants or a double consonant.
[3] Sometimes -ώτερος occurs instead of -ότερος, and *vice versa*.

**437.** With the comparative degree (of adverbs also) the *ablative* is commonly used to express the standard of comparison, e.g.,

τὸ μωρὸν τοῦ θεοῦ σοφώτερον τῶν ἀνθρώπων, *the foolishness of God* (is) *wiser than men.*

ἔρχεται δὲ ὁ ἰσχυρότερός μου, *but there comes one stronger* (*mightier*) *than I.*

**438.** The comparative may be followed by ἤ (*than*), then the standard of comparison is in the same case as the object compared, e.g.,

Σοδόμοις ἐν τῇ ἡμέρᾳ ἐκείνῃ ἀνεκτότερον ἔσται ἢ τῇ πόλει ἐκείνῃ, *it will be more tolerable in that day for Sodom than for that city.*

*a.* ἤ is used also in the comparison of clauses.

**439.** The superlative form is rare in the New Testament. When it occurs, it generally has, not the true superlative sense, but the *elative* sense of *very* or *exceedingly.*

In the New Testament the comparative with the article generally performs the peculiar functions of the superlative, e.g.,

ὁ δὲ μικρότερος ἐν τῇ βασιλείᾳ τῶν οὐρανῶν, *the least in the kingdom of heaven.*

**440.** Adverbs are made from adjectives also. Note carefully the following example.

| Positive | Comparative | Superlative |
|---|---|---|
| ἀκριβῶς, | ἀκριβέστερον, | [ἀκριβέστατα] |
| *accurately* | *more accurately* | *most accurately* |
| adj. ἀκριβό- | | |

Observe: 1. The positive degree of the adverb is made by adding the ablative ending -ως to the adjective stem. (In a mechanical way the positive degree of the adverb is formed from the positive degree of the adjective by changing final ν of the ablative plural neuter to ς and retaining the accent of the adjective.) 2. The comparative of the adverb is the neut. sing. acc. of the adjective. 3. The superlative of the adverb is the neut. plur. acc. of the superlative of the adjective.

**441.** ὁ δέ, ἡ δέ, οἱ δέ are used demonstratively to refer to persons already mentioned in an oblique case, e.g., πάλιν δὲ ὁ Πειλᾶτος προσεφώνησεν αὐτοῖς, θέλων ἀπολῦσαι τὸν Ἰησοῦν. οἱ δὲ ἐπεφώνουν λέγοντες Σταύρου σταύρου αὐτόν, *And again Pilate spoke to them, wishing to release Jesus. But they shouted, saying, "Crucify, crucify him."*
οἱ δέ refers to αὐτοῖς.

**442.** In comparisons μᾶλλον (*more, rather*) and ἤ are used with the positive degree.

**443.** EXERCISES

I. 1. καὶ τὸ ἀσθενὲς (weakness) τοῦ θεοῦ ἰσχυρότερον τῶν ἀνθρώπων. 2. μακάριόν ἐστιν μᾶλλον διδόναι (to give) ἢ λαμβάνειν. 3. ὁ δὲ ὀπίσω μου ἐρχόμενος ἰσχυρότερός μου ἐστίν. 4. Σάββατόν ἐστιν, καὶ οὐκ ἔξεστίν σοι ἆραι τὸν κράβαττον. ὃς δὲ ἀπεκρίθη αὐτοῖς Ὁ ποιήσας με ὑγιῆ ἐκεῖνός μοι εἶπεν Ἆρον τὸν κράβαττόν σου καὶ περιπάτει. 5. αὕτη δέ ἐστιν ἡ κρίσις ὅτι τὸ φῶς ἐλήλυθεν εἰς τὸν κόσμον καὶ ἠγάπησαν οἱ ἄνθρωποι μᾶλλον τὸ σκότος ἢ τὸ φῶς, ἦν γὰρ αὐτῶν πονηρὰ τὰ ἔργα. 6. ἀποκριθεὶς δὲ ὁ ἡγεμὼν εἶπεν αὐτοῖς Τίνα θέλετε ἀπὸ τῶν δύο ἀπολύσω ὑμῖν; οἱ δὲ εἶπαν Τὸν Βαραββᾶν.

II. 1. That man is stronger than I. 2. He said to them, "Come unto me." They said to him, "We are not able to go." 3. The children of God loved light rather (μᾶλλον) than darkness. 4. Seek ye rather to enter the kingdom than to die in sin.

## LESSON LI

**Comparison of Adjectives and Adverbs (Continued).**
**Declension of Adjectives with Stems in -ον-**

**444.**                     VOCABULARY

ἄφρων,-ον, *foolish*                 πολύ, adv., *much*
εὖ, *well*                                     ταχέως, ταχύ, adv., *quickly*
εὐθέως, adv., *straightway,*   σώφρων, -ον, *of sound mind,*
   *at once*                                *sober-minded*
τέλειος, -α, -ον, *finished,*    ὧδε, adv., *here, hither*
   *complete*

**445.** The following adjectives show irregularities of comparison.

Comparative suffix -ιων (masc.)
Superlative suffix -ιστος (masc.)

| Positive | Comparative | Superlative |
|---|---|---|
| ἀγαθός | κρείσσων | κράτιστος |
|  | κρείττων | (only as title) |
| κακός | χείρων |  |
|  | ἥσσων |  |
| μέγας | μείζων | μέγιστος |
| μικρός | μικρότερος |  |
|  | ἐλάσσων | ἐλάχιστος |
| πολύς | πλείων | πλεῖστος |
|  | πλέων |  |

**446.** The declension of μείζων, -ον, the comparative of μέγας, is:

STEM μειζον- (μειζοσ-)

*Singular*

|  | *Masc. and Fem.* | *Neut.* |
|---|---|---|
| Nom. | μείζων | μεῖζον |
| Gen. Abl. | μείζονος | μείζονος |
| Loc. Ins. Dat. | μείζονι | μείζονι |
| Acc. | μείζονα, μείζω | μεῖζον. |

*Plural*

|  | *Masc. and Fem.* | *Neut.* |
|---|---|---|
| Nom. | μείζονες, μείζους | μείζονα, μείζω |
| Gen. Abl. | μειζόνων | μειζόνων |
| Loc. Ins. Dat. | μείζοσι | μείζοσι |
| Acc. | μείζονας, μείζους | μείζονα, μείζω. |

**447.** Comparatives in -(ι)ων are declined like μείζων; so κρείσσων, πλείων, etc. The superlatives in -ιστος, -η, -ον are declined like adjectives of the first and second declensions.

**448.** Adjectives with stems in -ον- are declined like μείζων, except that they do not have the second forms like μείζω and μείζους: as ἄφρων, -ον, σώφρων, -ον, etc.

The voc. sing. of ἄφρων is ἄφρων (like nom.).

**449.** Observe carefully the following examples of the comparison of irregular adverbs. (See 438, 1-3):

| Positive | Comparative | Superlative |
|---|---|---|
| εὖ | βέλτιον | ———— |
| καλῶς | κάλλιον | ———— |
| κακῶς | ἧσσον | ———— |
| (μάλα) | μᾶλλον | μάλιστα |
| πολύ | πλεῖον | ———— |
|  | πλέον |  |
| ἐγγύς | ἐγγύτερον | ἔγγιστα |
| τάχα or | τάχιον | τάχιστα |
| ταχέως | τάχειον |  |

*a.* The positive of the adverb is sometimes made from the neut. acc. sing. of the adjective.

**450.**  EXERCISES

I.  1. ἤκουσαν οἱ Φαρισαῖοι ὅτι 'Ιησοῦς πλείονας μαθητὰς ποιεῖ καὶ βαπτίζει ἢ 'Ιωάνης.  2. ὁ πιστεύων εἰς ἐμὲ τὰ ἔργα ἃ ἐγὼ ποιῶ κἀκεῖνος¹ ποιήσει καὶ μείζονα τούτων ποιήσει, ὅτι ἐγὼ πρὸς τὸν πατέρα πορεύομαι.  3. ἄφρων, ταύτῃ τῇ νυκτὶ τὴν ψυχήν σου αἰτοῦσι ἀπὸ σοῦ.  4. λέγει οὖν αὐτῷ 'Ιησοῦς, "Ὃ ποιεῖς ποίησον τάχειον.  5. οὐκ ἔστιν δοῦλος μείζων τοῦ κυρίου αὐτοῦ οὐδὲ ἀπόστολος μείζων τοῦ πέμψαντος αὐτόν.  6. ἐγὼ γάρ εἰμι ὁ ἐλάχιστος τῶν ἀποστόλων.  7. τίς ἄρα² μείζων ἐστὶν ἐν τῇ βασιλείᾳ τῶν οὐρανῶν; ὅστις οὖν ταπεινώσει ἑαυτὸν ὡς τὸ παιδίον τοῦτο, οὗτός ἐστιν ὁ μείζων ἐν τῇ βασιλείᾳ τῶν οὐρανῶν.

II.  1. My brother is greater than I.  2. I hope to come unto you quickly.  3. I am able to do more work than this.  4. Is it lawful to do well on the sabbath?

¹ See § 4, p. 217.    ² ἄρα. an inferential particle, *then, therefore.*

## LESSON LII

### Present System of Contract Verbs in -άω

**451.** Vocabulary

| | | | |
|---|---|---|---|
| διαλογίζομαι, | *I consider, reason, discuss* | τελευτάω, | *(I finish) I die* |
| ἐπερωτάω, | *I question, ask (a question)* | τιμάω, | *I honor* |
| | | τολμάω, | *I dare* |
| ἰάομαι, | *I heal* | σιωπάω, | *I am silent, keep silence* |
| πλανάω, | *I cause to wander, lead astray* | | |

**452.** The conjugation of γεννάω, as an example of the -άω verbs, in the present system, is:

1. The present indicative:

Active

| Singular | Plural |
|---|---|
| 1. γεννῶ (γεννάω) | 1. γεννῶμεν (γεννάομεν) |
| 2. γεννᾷς (γεννάεις) | 2. γεννᾶτε (γεννάετε) |
| 3. γεννᾷ (γεννάει) | 3. γεννῶσι (γεννάουσι) |

Middle and Passive

| Singular | Plural |
|---|---|
| 1. γεννῶμαι (γεννάομαι) | 1. γεννώμεθα (γενναόμεθα) |
| 2. γεννᾶσαι (γεννάεσαι) | 2. γεννᾶσθε (γεννάεσθε) |
| 3. γεννᾶται (γεννάεται) | 3. γεννῶνται (γεννάονται) |

2. The present subjunctive:

Active

| Singular | Plural |
|---|---|
| 1. γεννῶ (γεννάω) | 1. γεννῶμεν (γεννάωμεν) |
| 2. γεννᾷς (γεννάῃς) | 2. γεννᾶτε (γεννάητε) |
| 3. γεννᾷ (γεννάῃ) | 3. γεννῶσι (γεννάωσι) |

Note that the contract forms of the indicative and subjunctive active are alike.

### MIDDLE AND PASSIVE

| Singular | Plural |
|---|---|
| 1. γεννῶμαι (γεννάωμαι) | 1. γεννώμεθα (γενναώμεθα) |
| 2. [γεννᾷ (γεννάῃ)] | 2. γεννᾶσθε (γεννάησθε) |
| 3. γεννᾶται (γεννάηται) | 3. γεννῶνται (γεννάωνται) |

3. The present imperative:

### ACTIVE

| Singular | Plural |
|---|---|
| 2. γέννα (γένναε) | 2. γεννᾶτε (γεννάετε) |
| 3. γεννάτω (γενναέτω) | 3. γεννάτωσαν (γενναέτωσαν) |

### MIDDLE AND PASSIVE

| Singular | Plural |
|---|---|
| 2. γεννῶ (γεννάου) | 2. γεννᾶσθε (γεννάεσθε) |
| 3. γεννάσθω (γενναέσθω) | 3. γεννάσθωσαν (γενναέσθωσαν) |

4. The present infinitive:

### ACTIVE

γεννᾶν (γεννάειν); some editors write γεννᾷν

Note. γεννᾶν really represents γενναεεν, for the inf. ending -ειν is a contraction of the thematic vowel ε and εν.

### MIDDLE AND PASSIVE

γεννᾶσθαι (γεννάεσθαι)

5. The present participle:

### ACTIVE

γεννῶν (γεννάων), γεννῶσα (γεννάουσα), γεννῶν (γεννάον)

### MIDDLE AND PASSIVE

γεννώμενος, -η, -ον (γενναόμενος)

6. The imperfect indicative:

ACTIVE

<table>
<tr><td colspan="2" align="center">*Singular*</td><td colspan="2" align="center">*Plural*</td></tr>
<tr><td>1.</td><td>ἐγέννων (ἐγένναον)</td><td>1.</td><td>ἐγεννῶμεν (ἐγεννάομεν)</td></tr>
<tr><td>2.</td><td>ἐγέννας (ἐγένναες)</td><td>2.</td><td>ἐγεννᾶτε (ἐγεννάετε)</td></tr>
<tr><td>3.</td><td>ἐγέννα (ἐγένναε)</td><td>3.</td><td>ἐγέννων (ἐγένναον)</td></tr>
</table>

Note. In the third plur. a form like ἐγέννουν is sometimes found. Thus from ἐρωτάω, imperfect ἠρώτουν. This confusion between -άω and -έω verbs began early in the Ionic.

MIDDLE AND PASSIVE

<table>
<tr><td>1.</td><td>ἐγεννώμην (ἐγενναόμην)</td><td>1.</td><td>ἐγεννώμεθα (ἐγενναόμεθα)</td></tr>
<tr><td>2.</td><td>ἐγεννῶ (ἐγεννάου)</td><td>2.</td><td>ἐγεννᾶσθε (ἐγεννάεσθε)</td></tr>
<tr><td>3.</td><td>ἐγεννᾶτο (ἐγεννάετο)</td><td>3.</td><td>ἐγεννῶντο (ἐγεννάοντο)</td></tr>
</table>

**453.** The declension of the present active participle γεννῶν, -ῶσα, ῶν is:

*Singular*

|  | *Masc.* | *Fem.* |
|---|---|---|
| Nom. | γεννῶν (γεννάων) | γεννῶσα (γεννάουσα) |
| Gen. Abl. | γεννῶντος (γεννάοντος) | γεννώσης (γενναούσης) |
| Loc. Ins. Dat. | γεννῶντι (γεννάοντι) | γεννώση (γενναούση) |
| Acc. | γεννῶντα (γεννάοντα) | γεννῶσαν (γενναούσαν) |

*Neut.*

| Nom. | γεννῶν (γεννάον) |
|---|---|
| Gen. Abl. | like masc. |

Loc. ⎫
Ins. ⎬ like masc.
Dat. ⎭

Acc.    γεννῶν  (γεννάον)

### Plural

|  | Masc. | Fem. |
|---|---|---|
| Nom. | γεννῶντες (γεννάοντες) | γεννῶσαι (γεννάουσαι) |

Gen. ⎫
Abl. ⎬  γεννώντων (γενναόντων)    γεννωσῶν (γενναουσῶν)

Loc. ⎫
Ins. ⎬  γεννῶσι (γεννάουσι)    γεννώσαις (γενναούσαις)
Dat. ⎭

Acc.    γεννῶντας (γεννάοντας)    γεννώσας (γενναούσας)

### Neut.

Nom.    γεννῶντα (γεννάοντα)

Gen. ⎫
Abl. ⎬ like masc.

Loc. ⎫
Ins. ⎬ like masc.
Dat. ⎭

Acc.    γεννῶντα (γεννάοντα)

**454.** The scheme of contraction for regular -άω verbs is as follows:

$$\alpha + \varepsilon = \alpha \qquad \alpha + o = \omega$$
$$\alpha + \eta = \alpha \qquad \alpha + \omega = \omega$$
$$\alpha + \varepsilon\iota = ᾳ$$

$\alpha + \varepsilon\iota (= \varepsilon + \varepsilon) = \alpha$    $\alpha + o\upsilon = \omega$ (since ου in these

$\alpha + \eta = ᾳ$    uncontracted forms is a spurious diphthong, i.e., υ is not present in the uncontracted form of ου).

For the accent see 430.

**455.** EXERCISES

I. 1. ἐὰν εἴπωμεν ὅτι ἁμαρτίαν οὐκ ἔχομεν, ἑαυτοὺς πλανῶμεν καὶ ἡ ἀλήθεια οὐκ ἔστιν ἐν ἡμῖν. 2. οἱ ἁμαρτωλοὶ τοὺς ἀγαπῶντας αὐτοὺς ἀγαπῶσιν. 3. καὶ ἐν τῇ οἰκίᾳ γενόμενος ἐπηρώτα αὐτοὺς Τί ἐν τῇ ὁδῷ διελογίζεσθε; οἱ δὲ ἐσιώπων. 4. Τίμα τὸν πατέρα σου καὶ τὴν μητέρα. 5. τεκνία, μηδεὶς πλανάτω ὑμᾶς. 6. καὶ πᾶς ὁ ὄχλος ἐζήτουν ἅπτεσθαι αὐτοῦ, ὅτι δύναμις παρ' αὐτοῦ ἐξήρχετο καὶ ἰᾶτο πάντας. 7. Τί ἐξήλθατε εἰς τὴν ἔρημον θεάσασθαι; 8. ὁ μὴ ἀγαπῶν τὸν ἀδελφὸν αὐτοῦ ὃν ἑώρακεν, τὸν θεὸν ὃν οὐχ ἑώρακεν οὐ δύναται ἀγαπᾶν.

II. 1. Let us love one another. 2. He who loves his brother keeps the commandment of God. 3. The disciples were not able to heal him. 4. They were asking him concerning the kingdom.

## LESSON LIII

**Impersonal Verbs.** πρίν (ἤ) **and the Infinitive.**
**Constructions with** καὶ ἐγένετο

**456.** VOCABULARY

ἀλέκτωρ, -ορος, ὁ, *cock*
ἀπαρνέομαι, *I deny*
διακονέω, *I serve, minister*
διάκονος, ὁ, *servant, minister, deacon*
κοινός, -ή, -όν, *common, unclean*
κοινόω, *I make common, unclean*
μανθάνω, *I learn;* second aor. ἔμαθον
σταυρός, ὁ, *cross*
θανατόω, *I put to death*

**457.** There are some verbs used in the third person singular with an impersonal subject, called impersonal verbs. Examine the following examples:

1. δεῖ, *it is necessary.*   δεῖ με καὶ 'Ρώμην ἰδεῖν, *I must see Rome also* (it is necessary for me to see Rome also).  με is the acc. of general reference with ἰδεῖν; 'Ρώμην is the object of ἰδεῖν.  Observe that the subject of δεῖ is ἰδεῖν.

2. δοκεῖ, *it seems (good).*  τί ὑμῖν δοκεῖ; *what think you?* (What seems (good) to you?)  Observe the case of ὑμῖν.  δοκέω is used in the personal construction also.

3. ἔξεστι, *it is possible, it is lawful.*  οὐκ ἔξεστίν σοι ἔχειν αὐτήν, *it is not lawful for thee to have her.*  Observe that ἔχειν is the subject of ἔξεστιν, and that σοι is in the dative case.

4. μέλει, *it concerns, it is a care.*  καὶ οὐ μέλει αὐτῷ περὶ τῶν προβάτων, *he cares not for the sheep* (it is not a care to him concerning the sheep).

**458.** πρίν (or πρὶν ἤ), *before,* is frequently used with the infinitive (in the ablative case).  E.g.,

πρὶν 'Αβραὰμ γενέσθαι ἐγὼ εἰμί, *before Abraham came into being, I am.*

**459.** The idioms containing καὶ ἐγένετο (or ἐγένετο δέ), *and it came to pass (and it happened),* are so common in the New Testament that they call for a special note.  The New Testament has four constructions with καὶ ἐγένετο.

1. καὶ ἐγένετο καὶ + the verb.

καὶ ἐγένετο ἐν μιᾷ τῶν ἡμερῶν καὶ αὐτὸς ἦν διδάσκων, *and it came to pass, on one of the days, that he was teaching.*

2. καὶ ἐγένετο + the verb.

καὶ ἐγένετο ἀπῆλθεν εἰς τὸν οἶκον αὐτοῦ, *and it came to pass that he departed to his home.*

3. καὶ ἐγένετο καὶ ἰδού + the verb.

καὶ ἐγένετο καὶ ἰδοὺ ἄνδρες δύο ἐπέστησαν αὐταῖς, *and it came to pass that, behold, two men stood by them.*

4. καὶ ἐγένετο + an infinitive.

καὶ ἐγένετο αὐτὸν ἐν τοῖς σάββασιν διαπορεύεσθαι διὰ τῶν σπορίμων, *and it came to pass that he was going through the grain-fields on the Sabbath.*

**460.** EXERCISES

I. 1. δεῖ ὑμᾶς γεννηθῆναι ἄνωθεν. 2. πρὶν ἀλέκτορα φωνῆσαι τρὶς ἀπαρνήσῃ με. 3. τί με δεῖ ποιεῖν ἵνα σωθῶ; 4. ἐγένετο δὲ ἐν ἑτέρῳ σαββάτῳ εἰσελθεῖν αὐτὸν εἰς τὴν συναγωγὴν καὶ διδάσκειν. 5. τί δοκεῖ σοί; 6. ἡμῖν οὐκ ἔξεστιν ἀποκτεῖναι οὐδένα. 7. δοκῶ γὰρ κἀγὼ πνεῦμα θεοῦ ἔχειν. 8. διδάσκαλε, οἴδαμεν ὅτι ἀληθὴς εἶ καὶ οὐ μέλει σοι περὶ οὐδενός.

II. 1. It is necessary to go into the house. 2. He does not care for any one. 3. It came to pass before he went into the house that his brothers came to him. 4. It is not lawful for a man to kill any one.

## LESSON LIV

### Present System of Contract Verbs in -όω

**461.** VOCABULARY

διακονία, ἡ, *service, ministry*
δικαιόω, *I declare righteous, justify*
ἐκπορεύομαι, *I go out*
ἐνώπιον, prep. with gen., *before, in presence of*

ζηλόω, *I am jealous, desire eagerly*
λῃστής, οῦ, ὁ, *robber*
ὁμοιόω, *I make like*
προφητεύω, *I prophesy*

**462.** The conjugation of πληρόω, as an example of the -όω verbs, in the present system, is:

1. The present indicative:

ACTIVE

| Singular | Plural |
|---|---|
| 1. πληρῶ (πληρόω) | 1. πληροῦμεν (πληρόομεν) |
| 2. πληροῖς (πληρόεις) | 2. πληροῦτε (πληρόετε) |
| 3. πληροῖ (πληρόει) | 3. πληροῦσι (πληρόουσι) |

MIDDLE AND PASSIVE

| Singular | Plural |
|---|---|
| 1. πληροῦμαι (πληρόομαι) | 1. πληρούμεθα (πληροόμεθα) |
| 2. πληροῖ (πληρόῃ) | 2. πληροῦσθε (πληρόεσθε) |
| 3. πληροῦται (πληρόεται) | 3. πληροῦνται (πληρόονται) |

2. The present subjunctive:

ACTIVE

| Singular | Plural |
|---|---|
| 1. πληρῶ (πληρόω) | 1. ⎫ |
| 2. πληροῖς (πληρόῃς) | 2. ⎬ Like the present indicative (probably) |
| 3. πληροῖ (πληρόῃ) | 3. ⎭ |

The plural of the present subjunctive active of -οω verbs in New Testament seems to be like the pres. indic. Note that the pres. indic. and subj. active are alike. The pres. subj. act. was probably assimilated to the pres. ind. act. There is doubt concerning the plur. forms that occur in the New Testament.

MIDDLE AND PASSIVE

| Singular | Plural |
|---|---|
| 1. πληρῶμαι (πληρόωμαι) | The plural does not occur in the New Testament |
| 2. [πληροῖ (πληρόῃ)] | |
| 3. πληρῶται (πληρόηται) | |

If the plural had been used in the New Testament it would have probably been like the pres. ind.

Forms in brackets [] are not found in the New Testament.

3. The present imperative:

ACTIVE

| *Singular* | *Plural* |
|---|---|
| 2. πλήρου (πλήροε) | 2. πληροῦτε (πληρόετε) |
| 3. πληρούτω (πληροέτω) | 3. πληρούτωσαν (πληροέτωσαν) |

MIDDLE AND PASSIVE

| *Singular* | *Plural* |
|---|---|
| 2. πληροῦ (πληρόου) | 2. πληροῦσθε (πληρόεσθε) |
| 3. πληρούσθω (πληροέσθω) | 3. πληρούσθωσαν (πληροέσθωσαν) |

4. The present infinitive:

ACTIVE

πληροῦν (πληρόειν); some editors write πληροῖν. πληροῦν is for πληροεεν. See note to 452, 4.

MIDDLE AND PASSIVE

πληροῦσθαι (πληρόεσθαι).

5. The present participle:

ACTIVE

πληρῶν (πληρόων), πληροῦσα (πληρόουσα), πληροῦν (πληρόον)

MIDDLE AND PASSIVE

πληρούμενος, -η, -ον (πληροόμενος).

6. The imperfect indicative:

ACTIVE

| Singular | Plural |
|---|---|
| I. ἐπλήρουν (ἐπλήροον) | I. ἐπληροῦμεν (ἐπληρόομεν) |
| 2. ἐπλήρους (ἐπλήροες) | 2. ἐπληροῦτε (ἐπληρόετε) |
| 3. ἐπλήρου (ἐπλήροε) | 3. ἐπλήρουν (ἐπλήροον) |

In the third plur. a form like ἐπληροῦσαν (ἐπληρόοσαν) is found.

MIDDLE AND PASSIVE

| Singular | Plural |
|---|---|
| I. ἐπληρούμην (ἐπληροόμην) | I. ἐπληρούμεθα (ἐπληροόμεθα) |
| 2. ἐπληροῦ (ἐπληρόου) | 2. ἐπληροῦσθε (ἐπληρόεσθε) |
| 3. ἐπληροῦτο (ἐπληρόετο) | 3. ἐπληροῦντο (ἐπληρόοντο) |

**463.** The present active participle πληρῶν, πληροῦσα, πληροῦν is declined like φιλῶν, φιλοῦσα, φιλοῦν (427). The result of contraction is the same in both cases: ε + ο = ου; and ο + ο = ου.

**464.** The scheme of contraction for regular -όω verbs is as follows:

| | | |
|---|---|---|
| ο + ε = ου | ο + ω = ω | ο + ου = ου |
| ο + ο = ου | ο + ει = οι | |
| ο + η = ω | ο + ῃ = οι | |

**465.**          EXERCISES

I. 1. ὥστε, ἀδελφοί μου, ζηλοῦτε τὸ προφητεύειν. 2. τὰ δὲ ἐκπορευόμενα ἐκ τοῦ στόματος ἐκ τῆς καρδίας ἐξέρχεται, κἀκεῖνα κοινοῖ τὸν ἄνθρωπον. 3. καὶ σὺν αὐτῷ σταυροῦσιν δύο λῃστάς. 4. καὶ εἶπεν αὐτοῖς Ὑμεῖς ἐστὲ οἱ δικαιοῦντες ἑαυτοὺς ἐνώπιον τῶν ἀνθρώπων. 5. καὶ εἴπατε Ἀρχίππῳ Βλέπε τὴν διακονίαν ἣν παρέλαβες ἐν κυρίῳ, ἵνα αὐτὴν πληροῖς. 6. ἔλεγον τὴν ἔξοδον (departure) αὐτοῦ ἣν ἤμελλεν πληροῦν ἐν Ἰερουσαλήμ.

II. 1. They were crucifying him with two robbers. 2. Let us love him who justifies us. 3. The works of the righteous are being made manifest. 4. That which goes into the mouth does not defile man.

## LESSON LV

Conjugation of μι-verbs: δίδωμι. Second Aorist of γινώσκω

**466.** VOCABULARY

δίδωμι, *I give, deliver*

ἀποδίδωμι, *I give up* or *back; restore; pay;* midd., *sell*

ἐπιγινώσκω, *I recognize, discover*

ἐπιδίδωμι, *I give over*

παραδίδωμι, *I give over* (to another), *deliver up, betray*

**467.** Greek verbs are of two main conjugations, the ω-conjugation and the μι-conjugation. The conjugation which has been studied thus far, except εἰμί, is the ω-conjugation (ω-verbs). The verbs in -ω are by far more common than the verbs in -μι. The verbs (or conjugations) are so named because the ending of the first person singular present indicative active of one is -ω and of the other is -μι.

**468.** μι-verbs differ from ω-verbs only in the present and second aorist (called μι-aorist) systems. The essential difference between the μι-verbs and ω-verbs in these systems is that the μι-verbs do not have the thematic vowel °/ε which the ω-verbs have, before the personal endings. The subjunctive of the μι-verbs, however, has the thematic vowel ω/η (mode-sign). In the other tense systems the μι-verbs and the ω-verbs are conjugated alike.

**469.** The principal parts of δίδωμι[1] are:

δίδωμι, δώσω, ἔδωκα, δέδωκα, δέδομαι, ἐδόθην

Observe that: 1. The verb stem is δο-. 2. The present stem is the reduplicated verb-stem, with the vowel ι in the reduplication.

**470.** The present active of δίδωμι is:

**1.** Indicative:

| Singular | Plural |
|---|---|
| 1. δίδωμι | 1. [δίδομεν] |
| 2. δίδως | 2. [δίδοτε] |
| 3. δίδωσι | 3. διδόασι |

In the first sing. a form διδῶ (from διδόω) occurs.

**2.** Subjunctive:

| Singular | Plural |
|---|---|
| 1. [διδῶ] | 1. [διδῶμεν] |
| 2. [διδῷς or διδοῖς] | 2. [διδῶτε] |
| 3. διδῷ or διδοῖ | 3. [διδῶσι] |

**3.** Imperative:

| Singular | Plural |
|---|---|
| 2. δίδου | 2. δίδοτε |
| 3. διδότω | 3. [διδότωσαν] |

**4.** Infinitive:

διδόναι

---

[1] μι-verbs compounded with prepositions are numerous. The uncompounded forms of all μι-verbs are given as quotable in the New Testament, although the form may be found only in compounds.

5. Participle:

διδούς, διδοῦσα, διδόν

The participle is declined like λύων except for the nom. sing. masc., and the accent.

**471.** The imperfect indicative active of δίδωμι is:

| Singular | Plural |
|---|---|
| 1. [ἐδίδουν] | 1. [ἐδίδομεν] |
| 2. [ἐδίδους] | 2. [ἐδίδοτε] |
| 3. ἐδίδου | 3. ἐδίδοσαν, ἐδίδουν |

**472.** The present middle and passive of δίδωμι is:

1. Indicative:

| Singular | Plural |
|---|---|
| 1. [δίδομαι] | 1. διδόμεθα |
| 2. [δίδοσαι] | 2. [δίδοσθε] |
| 3. δίδοται | 3. [δίδονται] |

2. Subjunctive:

Does not occur in the New Testament.

3. Imperative:

Does not occur in the New Testament.

4. Infinitive:

δίδοσθαι

5. Participle:

διδόμενος, -η, -ον

**473.** The imperfect indicative middle and passive of δίδωμι is:

| Singular | Plural |
|---|---|
| 1. [ἐδιδόμην] | 1. [ἐδιδόμεθα] |
| 2. [ἐδίδοσο] | 2. [ἐδίδοσθε] |
| 3. ἐδίδοτο, ἐδίδετο | 3. [ἐδίδοντο] |

**474.** The aorist (μι-aorist) active of δίδωμι is:

1. Indicative:

| Singular | Plural |
|---|---|
| 1. ἔδωκα | 1. ἐδώκαμεν |
| 2. ἔδωκας | 2. ἐδώκατε |
| 3. ἔδωκε | 3. ἔδωκαν, ἔδοσαν |

Aorists made with the suffix -κα are called κ-aorists.  Actually they are not μι- aorists.

2. Subjunctive:

| Singular | Plural |
|---|---|
| 1. δῶ | 1. δῶμεν |
| 2. δῷς, δοῖς | 2. δῶτε |
| 3. δῷ, δοῖ, δώη | 3. δῶσι |

Some forms like δώσῃ, δώσωμεν are probably aorist subjunctives from a first aorist ἔδωσα (found in the papyri).

3. Imperative:

| Singular | Plural |
|---|---|
| 2. δός | 2. δότε |
| 3. δότω | 3. [δότωσαν] |

4. Infinitive:

δοῦναι

5. Participle:

δούς, [δοῦσα], [δόν]

Declined like the present act. participle.

**475.** The aorist middle of δίδωμι is:

1. Indicative:

| Singular | Plural |
|---|---|
| 1. [ἐδόμην] | 1. [ἐδόμεθα] |
| 2. [ἔδου] | 2. ἔδοσθε |
| 3. ἔδοτο, ἔδετο | 3. ἔδοντο |

2. Subjunctive:
Does not occur in the New Testament.

3. Imperative:
Does not occur in the New Testament.

4. Infinitive:
Does not occur in the New Testament.

5. Participle:
Does not occur in the New Testament.

**476.** Some ω-verbs have aorists conjugated like those of μι-verbs.

1. The aorist (μι-aorist) indicative active of γινώσκω is:

| Singular | Plural |
|---|---|
| 1. ἔγνων | 1. ἔγνωμεν |
| 2. ἔγνως | 2. ἔγνωτε |
| 3. ἔγνω | 3. ἔγνωσαν |

2. The subjunctive is γνῶ, γνῷς, etc., with ω throughout. But third sing. is γνοῖ.

3. The imperative is γνῶθι, γνώτω, γνῶτε, [γνώτωσαν]

4. The infinitive is γνῶναι

5. The participle γνούς, γνοῦσα, [γνόν].

**477.** EXERCISES

I. 1. ὑμῖν τὸ μυστήριον δέδοται τῆς βασιλείας τοῦ θεοῦ.
2. Κύριε, τίς ἐστιν ὁ παραδιδούς σε; 3. παντὶ αἰτοῦντί σε
δίδου. 4. εἰ δὲ οὐ ποιῶ τὰ ἔργα τοῦ πατρός μου, μὴ
πιστεύετε μοι. εἰ δὲ ποιῶ, κἂν¹ ἐμοὶ μὴ πιστεύητε, τοῖς
ἔργοις πιστεύετε, ἵνα γνῶτε καὶ γινώσκητε ὅτι ἐν ἐμοὶ ὁ
πατὴρ κἀγὼ ἐν τῷ πατρί. 5. δότε αὐτοῖς ὑμεῖς φαγεῖν.
6. λέγω δὲ ὑμῖν ὅτι Ἡλείας ἤδη ἦλθεν, καὶ οὐκ ἐπέγνωσαν
αὐτόν. 7. ἀπόδοτε πᾶσι τὰς ὀφειλάς (dues). 8. ἔξεστιν
δοῦναι κῆνσον (poll-tax, tribute) Καίσαρι ἢ οὔ; δῶμεν ἢ
μὴ δῶμεν;

II. 1. If I know all mysteries and have not love,
I am nothing. 2. I give you power to cast out demons. 3. Jesus was giving bread to the disciples
that they might give it to the multitude.

## LESSON LVI

**Conjugation of μι-Verbs (cont'd):** ἵστημι. **Present
Imperative of** εἰμί. **Second Aorist of** βαίνω φημί

**478.** VOCABULARY

| | | | |
|---|---|---|---|
| ἵστημι, | I make to stand, place, stand | ἐφίστημι, | I stand upon or by, come upon |
| ἀνθίστημι, | I set against, withstand | καθίστημι, | I set down, appoint |
| ἀνίστημι, | I raise up, rise, arise | μεταβαίνω, | I pass over, depart |
| ἀφίστημι, | I put away, depart from | παρίστημι, | I place beside, stand by |
| ἐμβαίνω, | I go into, embark | | |

¹ κἄν = καὶ ἐάν, "even if," "though."

ἐξίστημι, *I am amazed, am beside myself*    συνίστημι, *I commend, establish*

**479.** The principal parts of ἵστημι are:

ἵστημι, στήσω, ἔστησα, ἔστηκα, [ἔσταμαι], ἐστάθην, second aor. act. ἔστην.

Observe that: 1. The verb-stem is στα- 2. The present stem is the verb-stem reduplicated, with the vowel ι in the reduplication. ἱστα- is for σιστα- (initial σ is represented by the rough breathing).

**480.** The conjugation of ἵστημι in the present active is:

1. Indicative:

| *Singular* | *Plural* |
|---|---|
| 1. ἵστημι | 1. [ἵσταμεν] |
| 2. [ἵστης] | 2. [ἵστατε] |
| 3. ἵστησι | 3. [ἱστᾶσι] |

Many forms from ἱστάνω occur. They are regular in their conjugation.

2. Subjunctive:

Does not occur in the New Testament.

3. Imperative:

Does not occur in the New Testament.

4. Infinitive:

ἱστάναι

5. Participle:

ἱστάς, [ἱστᾶσα], [ἱστάν]. ἱστάς is declined like πᾶς.

**481.** Imperfect indicative active forms of ἵστημι do not occur in the New Testament.

**482.** The conjugation of the present middle and passive of ἵστημι is:

1. Indicative:

| Singular | Plural |
|---|---|
| 1. ἵσταμαι | 1. ἱστάμεθα |
| 2. ἵστασαι | 2. ἵστασθε |
| 3. ἵσταται | 3. ἵστανται |

2. Subjunctive:

Does not occur in the New Testament.

3. Imperative:

| Singular | Plural |
|---|---|
| 2. ἵστασο | 2. [ἵστασθε] |
| 3. [ἱστάσθω] | 3. [ἱστάσθωσαν] |

4. Infinitive:

ἵστασθαι

5. Participle:

ἱστάμενος, -η, -ον

**483.** The imperfect indicative middle and passive of ἵστημι is:

| Singular | Plural |
|---|---|
| 1. ἱστάμην[1] | 1. ἱστάμεθα |
| 2. [ἵστασο] | 2. ἵστασθε |
| 3. ἵστατο | 3. ἵσταντο |

**484.** φημί, *I say*, is found in the pres. ind. act. first pers. sing. φημί, third pers. sing. φησί, third pers. plur. φασί, and in the imperfect ind. act. third pers. sing. ἔφη. The present forms are enclitic.

**485.** The present imperative of εἰμί, *I am*, is:

| Singular | Plural |
|---|---|
| 2. ἴσθι | 2. [ἔστε] |
| 3. ἔστω, ἤτω | 3. ἔστωσαν |

[1] Long. See 70, 2.

**486.** The aorist (μι-aorist) active of ἵστημι is:

1. Indicative:

| Singular | Plural |
|---|---|
| 1. ἔστην | 1. ἔστημεν |
| 2. [ἔστης] | 2. ἔστητε |
| 3. ἔστη | 3. ἔστησαν |

The difference in meaning between ἔστην and ἔστησα (first aorist) is that ἔστην, *I stood*, is intransitive, and ἔστησα, *I set* or *placed*, is transitive.

2. Subjunctive:

| Singular | Plural |
|---|---|
| 1. [στῶ] | 1. [στῶμεν] |
| 2. [στῇς] | 2. στῆτε |
| 3. στῇ | 3. στῶσι |

3. Imperative:

| Singular | Plural |
|---|---|
| 2. στῆθι, | 2. στῆτε |
| -στα | |
| 3. στήτω | 3. [στήτωσαν] |

-στα occurs only in compounds.

4. Infinitive:

στῆναι

5. Participle:

στάς, [στᾶσα], [στάν]

στάς is declined like πᾶς.

**487.** Like ἔστην is conjugated ἔβην the second (or μι-) aorist of βαίνω. Thus:

Ind. act. ἔβην, ἔβης, etc.

Subj. act. third sing. βῇ.

Imperative act. βῆθι and -βα, βάτω, -βατε.

Infinitive act. βῆναι

Participle act. βάς, declined like πᾶς.

In the New Testament βαίνω occurs only in compounds (see vocabulary).

**488.** EXERCISES

I. 1. καὶ ἀναστὰς ἦλθεν πρὸς τὸν πατέρα ἑαυτοῦ 2. καὶ ἤκουσαν φωνῆς μεγάλης ἐκ τοῦ οὐρανοῦ λεγούσης αὐτοῖς Ἀνάβατε ὧδε,¹ καὶ ἀνέβησαν εἰς τὸν οὐρανόν ἐν τῇ νεφέλῃ. 3. εἶπεν δὲ τῷ ἀνδρί Ἔγειρε καὶ στῆθι εἰς τὸ μέσον (midst) καὶ ἀναστὰς ἔστη. 4. καταβὰς δὲ Πέτρος πρὸς τοὺς ἄνδρας εἶπεν Ἰδοὺ ἐγώ εἰμι ὃν ζητεῖτε. 5. παρέστη γάρ μοι ταύτῃ τῇ νυκτὶ τοῦ θεοῦ οὗ εἰμί, ᾧ καὶ λατρεύω (serve), ἄγγελος λέγων Μὴ φοβοῦ, Παῦλε. Καίσαρί σε δεῖ παραστῆναι. 6. ὁ νόμος γὰρ ἀνθρώπους καθίστησιν ἀρχιερεῖς ἔχοντας ἀσθένειαν.

II. 1. An angel stood by Paul in the night. 2. Two men went up into the temple. 3. Who appointed you a ruler of the people? 4. The disciples went into the boat.

## LESSON LVII

### Conjugation of μι-Verbs (Continued): τίθημι

**489.** VOCABULARY

| | |
|---|---|
| τίθημι, | *I place, lay, put (down)* |
| ἐπιτίθημι, | *I lay upon, place upon* |
| μνημεῖον, τό, | *sepulchre, tomb* |
| παρατίθημι, | *I set before, commit* |
| προστίθημι, | *I add, give in addition* |

¹ ὧδε, adv. *hither, here.*

**490.** The principal parts of τίθημι are:

τίθημι, θήσω, ἔθηκα, τέθεικα, τέθειμαι, ἐτέθην

Observe that: 1. The verb-stem is θε-. 2. The present stem is the reduplicated verb-stem, with the vowel ι in the reduplication. 3. The aorist indic. has -κα as suffix.

**491.** The present active of τίθημι is:

1. Indicative:

| Singular | Plural |
|---|---|
| 1. τίθημι | 1. τίθεμεν |
| 2. [τίθης] | 2. τίθετε |
| 3. τίθησι | 3. τιθέασι |

2. Subjunctive:

| Singular | Plural |
|---|---|
| 1. τιθῶ | 1. τιθῶμεν |
| 2. τιθῇς | 2. τιθῆτε |
| 3. τιθῇ | 3. τιθῶσι |

3. Imperative:

| Singular | Plural |
|---|---|
| 2. τίθει | 2. τίθετε |
| 3. τιθέτω | 3. [τιθέτωσαν] |

4. Infinitive:

τιθέναι

5. Participle:

τιθείς, τιθεῖσα, τιθέν

Declined like the aorist passive participle of λύω: λυθείς, -εῖσα, -έν, **(350).**

**492.** The imperfect indicative active of τίθημι is:

| Singular | Plural |
|----------|--------|
| 1. [ἐτίθην] | 1. [ἐτίθεμεν] |
| 2. [ἐτίθεις] | 2. [ἐτίθετε] |
| 3. ἐτίθει | 3. ἐτίθεσαν |

A third pers. plur. ἐτίθουν is from τιθέω.

**493.** The conjugation of the present middle and passive of τίθημι is:

1. Indicative:

| Singular | Plural |
|----------|--------|
| 1. τίθεμαι | 1. [τιθέμεθα] |
| 2. [τίθεσαι] | 2. τίθεσθε |
| 3. τίθεται | 3. τίθενται |

2. Subjunctive:
Does not occur in the New Testament.

3. Imperative:

| Singular | Plural |
|----------|--------|
| 2. [τίθεσο] | 2. [τίθεσθε] |
| 3. [τιθέσθω] | 3. τιθέσθωσαν |

4. Infinitive:

τίθεσθαι

5. Participle:

τιθέμενος, -η, -ον

**494.** The imperfect indicative middle and passive of τίθημι is:

| Singular | Plural |
|----------|--------|
| 1. [ἐτιθέμην] | 1. [ἐτιθέμεθα] |
| 2. [ἐτίθεσο] | 2. [ἐτίθεσθε] |
| 3. ἐτίθετο | 3. ἐτίθεντο |

**495.** The aorist active of τίθημι is:

1. Indicative:

| *Singular* | *Plural* |
|---|---|
| 1. ἔθηκα | 1. ἐθήκαμεν |
| 2. ἔθηκας | 2. ἐθήκατε |
| 3. ἔθηκε | 3. ἔθηκαν |

As is the case with δίδωμι, so τίθημι has the κ-aorist in the indicative active. Other modes are of the μι- aorist type.

2. Subjunctive:

| *Singular* | *Plural* |
|---|---|
| 1. θῶ | 1. θῶμεν |
| 2. θῇς | 2. [θῆτε] |
| 3. θῇ | 3. θῶσι |

3. Imperative:

| *Singular* | *Plural* |
|---|---|
| 2. θές | 2. θέτε |
| 3. [θέτω] | 3. [θέτωσαν] |

4. Infinitive:

θεῖναι

5. Participle:

θείς, [θεῖσα], [θέν]

Declined like τιθείς.

**496.** The aorist middle of τίθημι is:

1. Indicative:

| *Singular* | *Plural* |
|---|---|
| 1. ἐθέμην | 1. [ἐθέμεθα] |
| 2. ἔθου | 2. ἔθεσθε |
| 3. ἔθετο | 3. ἔθεντο |

2. Subjunctive:

Singular

1. [θῶμαι]
2. [θῇ]
3. [θῆται]

Plural

1. θώμεθα
2. [θῆσθε]
3. [θῶνται]

3. Imperative:

Singular

2. θοῦ
3. [θέσθω]

Plural

2. θέσθε
3. [θέσθωσαν]

4. Infinitive:

θέσθαι

5. Participle

θέμενος, -η, -ον

**497.**    EXERCISES

I. 1. πᾶς ἄνθρωπος πρῶτον τὸν καλὸν οἶνον τίθησιν. 2. καὶ φωνήσας φωνῇ μεγάλῃ ὁ Ἰησοῦς εἶπεν Πάτερ, εἰς χεῖράς σου παρατίθεμαι τὸ πνεῦμά μου. 3. ἦραν τὸν κύριον ἐκ τοῦ μνημείου, καὶ οὐκ οἴδαμεν ποῦ ἔθηκαν αὐτόν. 4. ὁ δὲ κύριος προσετίθει τοὺς σωζομένους καθ᾽ ἡμέραν[1] ἐπὶ τὸ αὐτό.[2] 5. διὰ τοῦτό με ὁ πατὴρ ἀγαπᾷ ὅτι ἐγὼ τίθημι τὴν ψυχήν μου, ἵνα πάλιν λάβω αὐτήν. οὐδεὶς ἦρεν αὐτὴν ἀπ᾽ ἐμοῦ, ἀλλ᾽ ἐγὼ τίθημι αὐτὴν ἀπ᾽ ἐμαυτοῦ.

II. 1. The good shepherd lays down his life for the sheep. 2. The apostle commends the disciple to the Lord. 3. I do not know where they laid him. 4. He was placing his hands upon the children.

NOTE: *The students may now begin to read I John and continue it as Lessons after Lesson LIX is finished.*

[1] καθ᾽ ἡμέραν, daily.    [2] ἐπὶ τὸ αὐτό, (to the same), together.

## LESSON LVIII

**Conjugation of μι-Verbs (Continued):** ἀφίημι, συνίημι
**Other Verbs: Old Forms**

**498.**                    VOCABULARY

ἀφίημι, *I send away, for-*      συνίημι, *I perceive, under-*
  *give, leave, let*        *stand*
εἰδώς, -υῖα, -ός, *knowing*      τότε, adv., *then*
ἑστώς, ῶσα, ός, *standing*      ἤγαγον, second aor. ind.
ᾔδειν, old pluperf. (with        act. of ἄγω
  imp. meaning) of οἶδα.      κλίνη, ἡ, *bed*

**499.** The verb ἵημι, *I send*, occurs in the New Testament only in compounds. Of this verb the most common compounds are ἀφίημι (ἀπό + ἵημι) and συνίημι.

The verb-stem of ἵημι is ἑ-. The present stem is the reduplicated verb-stem, with ι in the reduplication.

The principal parts of ἀφίημι are:

ἀφίημι, ἀφήσω, ἀφῆκα, ἀφέωνται (third plur.), ἀφέθην.

**500.** The following forms of ἀφίημι are those which occur most frequently in the New Testament.

Present indicative active:

   *Singular*         *Plural*

  1. [ἀφίημι]        1. ἀφίεμεν, ἀφίομεν
  2. ἀφεῖς (from ἀφίω)  2. ἀφίετε
  3. ἀφίησι        3. ἀφίουσι

Imperfect indicative active:

    Third sing. ἤφιεν (notice augment
      of the preposition)

Present active imperative:
Third sing. ἀφιέτω.

Present active infinitive:

ἀφιέναι

Present indicative middle and passive:

| Singular | Plural |
|---|---|
| 3. ἀφίεται | 3. ἀφίενται |
| | ἀφίονται |

The aorist (κ-aorist) indicative active ἀφῆκα is conjugated like ἔθηκα.

The second (μι-) aorist subjunctive active:

| Singular | Plural |
|---|---|
| 1. ἀφῶ | 1. ——— |
| 2. ——— | 2. ἀφῆτε |
| 3. ἀφῇ | 3. ἀφῶσι |

The second aor. imperative active:

| Singular | Plural |
|---|---|
| 2. ἄφες | 2. ἄφετε |

The second aor. infinitive active ἀφεῖναι
The second aor. participle active ἀφείς (masc.).

**501.** The following forms of συνίημι occur.
Present ind. act. third plur. συνιᾶσι and συνίουσι.
Present subj. act. third plur. συνιῶσι.
Present act. participle συνιείς and συνίων.
Second aor. subj. third plur. συνῶσι.

**502.** The verb ἄγω has a reduplicated second **aorist** ἤγαγον.

Ind.  ἤγαγον, ἤγαγες, etc.
Subj. ἀγάγω, ἀγάγῃς, etc.;

and the rest like ἔλιπον, except the reduplication throughout the aorist.

**503.** The old pluperfect of οἶδα with the meaning of the imperfect is

1. Indicative active:

| Singular | Plural |
|---|---|
| 1. ᾔδειν, *I knew* | 1. [ᾔδειμεν] |
| 2. ᾔδεις | 2. ᾔδειτε |
| 3. ᾔδει | 3. ᾔδεισαν |

2. The old perfect subjunctive (with meaning of the present) of this verb is

ACTIVE

| Singular | Plural |
|---|---|
| 1. εἰδῶ | 1. εἰδῶμεν |
| 2. εἰδῇς | 2. εἰδῆτε |
| 3. εἰδῇ | 3. [εἰδῶσι] |

3. The old perf. infinitive, εἰδέναι

4. The old perf. participle, εἰδώς, εἰδυῖα, εἰδός (with meaning of the present). Declined like λελυκώς, -υῖα, -ός.

**504.** An old perfect active participle from ἵστημι is found also in the New Testament.

Nom.    ἑστώς, ἑστῶσα, ἑστός
Gen.    ἑστῶτος, ἑστώσης, ἑστῶτος

The other cases can be easily formed from these. ἑστώς has the intensive meaning, *standing*.

**505.**            EXERCISES

I.  1. ὁ μισθωτὸς (hireling) καὶ οὐκ ὢν ποιμήν, οὗ οὐκ ἔστιν τὰ πρόβατα ἴδια, θεωρεῖ τὸν λύκον (wolf) ἐρχόμενον καὶ ἀφίησιν τὰ πρόβατα καὶ φεύγει.  2. διὰ τοῦτο ἐν παραβολαῖς αὐτοῖς λαλῶ, ὅτι βλέποντες οὐ βλέπουσιν καὶ ἀκούοντες οὐκ ἀκούουσιν οὐδὲ συνίουσιν. 3. ἄγωμεν καὶ ἡμεῖς ἵνα ἀποθάνωμεν μετ' αὐτοῦ. 4. τί γάρ ἐστιν εὐκοπώτερον (easier), εἰπεῖν ᾿Αφίενταί σου αἱ ἁμαρτίαι, ἢ εἰπεῖν ᾿Εγειρε καὶ περιπάτει; ἵνα δὲ εἰδῆτε ὅτι ἐξουσίαν ἔχει ὁ υἱὸς τοῦ ἀνθρώπου ἐπὶ τῆς γῆς ἀφιέναι ἁμαρτίας—τότε λέγει¹ τῷ παραλυτικῷ (paralytic) ᾿Εγειρε ἆρόν σου τὴν κλίνην καὶ ὕπαγε εἰς τὸν οἶκόν σου. 5. καὶ θεωρεῖ τὸν ᾿Ιησοῦν ἑστῶτα, καὶ οὐκ ᾔδει ὅτι ᾿Ιησοῦς ἐστίν. 6. ᾿Ιησοῦς οὖν εἰδὼς πάντα τὰ ἐρχόμενα ἐπ' αὐτὸν ἐξῆλθεν, καὶ λέγει αὐτοῖς Τίνα ζητεῖτε;

II. 1. We saw him standing in the boat.  2. He said to the man, "Thy sins are forgiven."  3. I knew not who it was.  4. They led the servants to the house.

## LESSON LIX
### The Optative Mode.  Wishes
**506.**

εὐαγγελίζομαι, *I proclaim glad tidings (preach the gospel)*

ὀλίγος, -η, -ον, *few, little, small*

παρουσία, ἡ,  *coming, presence*

σημεῖον, τό,  *sign*

σήμερον,  adv., *to-day, this day*

**507.** Besides the indicative, subjunctive, and imperative modes, there is another mode in Greek, called the *Optative*.

In meaning the optative is a sort of weaker subjunctive.  The subjunctive and optative are really different forms of the same mode, the mode of *hesitating affirmation*.

---

¹ κλίνη, ἡ, *a couch, a bed.*

**508.** In the New Testament the optative mode occurs only sixty-seven times, and in the present and aorist tenses only.

**509.** Of the forms of the optative mode found in the New Testament the following are representative:

1. Present tense (act. and middle):

<table>
<tr><td>*Singular*</td><td>*Plural*</td></tr>
<tr><td>1. δυναίμην</td><td></td></tr>
<tr><td>3. { εἴη (from εἰμί)<br>   ἔχοι<br>   θέλοι</td><td>2. πάσχοιτε<br>3. { ἔχοιεν<br>   δύναιντο</td></tr>
</table>

2. Second aorist (act. and middle):

<table>
<tr><td>*Singular*</td><td>*Plural*</td></tr>
<tr><td>1. ὀναίμην (fr. ὀνίνημι)</td><td></td></tr>
<tr><td>3. { δῴη (fr. δίδωμι)<br>   λάβοι<br>   τύχοι<br>   φάγοι<br>   γένοιτο</td><td>3. εὕροιεν</td></tr>
</table>

3. First aorist (act. and middle):

<table>
<tr><td>*Singular*</td><td>*Plural*</td></tr>
<tr><td>1. εὐξαίμην</td><td></td></tr>
<tr><td>3. { περισσεύσαι<br>   πλεονάσαι<br>   καταρτίσαι<br>   κατευθύναι</td><td>3. { ποιήσαιεν<br>   ψηλαφήσειαν</td></tr>
</table>

4. First aorist passive:
Third sing., λογισθείη, πληθυνθείη, τηρηθείη.

Observe that: 1. There are two mode signs for the optative, either ι or ιη. 2. ι is used with thematic tense stems, as ἔχοι, εὐξαίμην. 3. ιη is used with

the non-thematic tense stems, as εἴη, δῴη.    4. ιε and
ια in the third person plural of both stems.    5. The
mode sign (ι) contracts with the vowel of the stem.

**510.**  A wish about the future is usually expressed
in the New Testament by the optative (generally
the aorist), e.g.,

αὐτὸς δὲ ὁ θεὸς τῆς εἰρήνης ἁγιάσαι ὑμᾶς ὁλοτελεῖς, *May
the God of peace himself sanctify you wholly.*

The commonest wish of this kind is the phrase
μὴ γένοιτο, *may it not become.*

A wish about the future may be expressed by
ὄφελον [1] and the future indicative — once in N. T.

**511.**  A wish about the present is expressed by ὄφελον
and the imperfect indicative, e.g.,

ὄφελον ψυχρὸς ἦς ἢ ζεστός, *would that thou wert cold or
hot.*

**512.**  A wish about the past is expressed by ὄφελον
and the aorist indicative, e.g.,

ὄφελον ἐβασιλεύσατε, *would that you did reign*

**513.**  The fourth class condition is the condition
undetermined and with remote prospect of determination.    εἰ and the optative in the protasis, and
the optative with ἄν in the apodosis.    In the New
Testament no whole example of this class of conditions occurs.    There is found the condition (protasis) or the conclusion (apodosis), but not both at
the same time.

εἰ καὶ πάσχοιτε, *if you should even suffer* (protasis)
εὐξαίμην ἄν, *I could pray* (potential optative).

---

[1] ὄφελον is just the second aor. of ὀφείλω without augment.

# PART II:[1] SUPPLEMENT TO PART I

[1] *Part II is based on "A Grammar of the Greek New Testament in the Light of Historical Research," by A. T. Robertson.*

## A. Sounds and Writing

**§ 1.** Syncope is the suppression of a short vowel between consonants for the sake of facility in pronunciation. Thus πατρός for πατέρος.

**§ 2.** Diaeresis (*separation*) is indicated by a double dot (¨), written over ι or υ to show that ι or υ does not form a diphthong with the preceding vowel. Thus πρωΐ, early; ἰσχύϊ, *by strength;* Μωϋσῆς, Moses.

**§ 3.** Elision is the dropping of a short vowel at the end of a word before a word beginning with a vowel. E.g., ἀπ' ἀρχῆς for ἀπὸ ἀρχῆς, οὐδ' ἵνα for οὐδὲ ἵνα, ἀφ' ἑαυτοῦ for ἀπὸ ἑαυτοῦ.

Note that an apostrophe marks the omission of the vowel.

**§ 4.** Crasis is the contraction of a vowel or diphthong at the end of a word with one at the beginning of the next word. Thus κἀμοί for καὶ ἐμοί; κἀκεῖνος for καὶ ἐκεῖνος; τοὔνομα for τὸ ὄνομα.

Note that crasis is indicated by the *coronis* (') over the contracted form.

**§ 5.** When a smooth mute (π, κ, τ) is brought before the rough breathing by elision or in forming compounds, it is changed to the corresponding rough mute. This is called aspiration. Thus ἀνθ' ὧν for ἀντὶ ὧν; ἐφ' ᾧ for ἐπὶ ᾧ; ἀφίημι (ἀπὸ + ἵημι).

§ 6. The vowels α, ε, ο are often interchanged in words of the same root. Sometimes there is an interchange among different vowels. This is called *interchange* or *gradation of vowels*. Thus πείθω, second perf. πέποιθα; τρέφω, *I nourish*, τροφή, *nourishment*, ἐτράφην, *I was nourished*.

§ 7. Modern editors of Greek texts use four punctuation marks: the comma and period are used as in English; the interrogation mark (;) is in form like the English semicolon; the point above the line (˙) corresponds to the English semicolon or colon.

## B. Paradigms of Nouns

### (a) Substantives

**§ 8.** Some masculines in -ας of the first declension.

βορρᾶς, ὁ, *north (wind)*

*Singular*

| | | |
|---|---|---|
| Nom. | βορρᾶς | So declined are some proper names in -ας. |
| Gen. Abl. | βορρᾶ | |
| Loc. Ins. Dat. | βορρᾷ | |
| Acc. | βορρᾶν | |
| Voc. | βορρᾶ | |

**§ 9.** The normal form of contract substantives (those with stems in -ε- or -ο- of the second declension) may be seen in the masculine and neuter of the contract adjective διπλοῦς (§14).

Frequently these substantives are found in the uncontracted form. Thus ὀστέα, acc. plur. of ὀστοῦν (ὀστέον).

**§ 10.** Substantives of the third declension with stems in -υ-.

στάχυς, ὁ, *ear of corn*

|  | Singular | Plural |
|------|----------|--------|
| Nom. | στάχυς | στάχυες |
| Gen. } Abl. | στάχυος | σταχύων |
| Loc. } Ins. } Dat. | στάχυϊ | στάχυσι |
| Acc. | στάχυν | στάχυας |

So are declined ἰσχύς, ἡ, *strength;* ὀσφύς, ἡ, *loins,* ἰχθύς, ὁ, *fish;* etc.

## § 11. Substantives of the third declension with stems in -ου- (-οϝ-).

βοῦς, ὁ, *ox*

|  | Singular | Plural |
|------|----------|--------|
| Nom. | βοῦς | [βόες] |
| Gen. } Abl. | βοός | βοῶν |
| Loc. } Ins. } Dat. | βοΐ | [βουσί] |
| Acc. | βοῦν | βόας |

So are declined νοῦς, ὁ, *mind;* πλοῦς, ὁ, *voyage;* and χοῦς, ὁ, *dust.*

## § 12. The following substantives show some peculiarities, either of form or accent: τὸ γόνυ, *knee;* ἡ γυνή, *woman;* ἡ θρίξ, *hair;* τὸ οὖς, *ear;* τὸ ὕδωρ, *water,* and ὁ κύων, [κυνός], [κυνί], [κύνα]. Plu. κύνες. [κυνῶν], κυσί, κύνας.

## Singular

| Nom. | [γόνυ] | γυνή | θρίξ | οὖς | ὕδωρ |
|---|---|---|---|---|---|
| Gen. Abl. | [γόνατος] | γυναικός | [τριχός] | [ὠτός] | ὕδατος |
| Loc. Ins. Dat. | [γόνατι] | γυναικί | [τριχί] | [ὠτί] | ὕδατι |
| Acc. | [γόνυ] | γυναῖκα | τρίχα | οὖς | ὕδωρ |
| Voc. | | γύναι | | | |

## Plural

| Nom. | γόνατα | γυναῖκες | τρίχες | ὦτα | ὕδατα |
|---|---|---|---|---|---|
| Gen. Abl. | γονάτων | γυναικῶν | τριχῶν | [ὤτων] | ὑδάτων |
| Loc. Ins. Dat. | γόνασι | γυναιξί | θριξί | ὠσί | ὕδασι |
| Acc. | γόνατα | γυναῖκας | τρίχας | ὦτα | ὕδατα |

### (b) Adjectives

§ 13. ἴδιος, one's own, and μικρός, small, of the α- and o- declension.

## Singular

| | M. | F. | N. | M. | F. | N. |
|---|---|---|---|---|---|---|
| Nom. | ἴδιος | ἰδία | ἴδιον | μικρός | μικρά | μικρόν |
| Gen. Abl. | ἰδίου | ἰδίας | ἰδίου | μικροῦ | μικρᾶς | μικροῦ |
| Loc. Ins. Dat. | ἰδίῳ | ἰδίᾳ | ἰδίῳ | μικρῷ | μικρᾷ | μικρῷ |
| Acc. | ἴδιον | ἰδίαν | ἴδιον | μικρόν | μικράν | μικρόν |
| Voc. | ἴδιε | ἰδία | ἴδιον | μικρέ | μικρά | μικρόν |

*Plural*

| Nom. | ἴδιοι | ἴδιαι | ἴδια | μικροί | μικραί | μικρά |
|------|-------|-------|------|--------|--------|-------|
| Gen. Abl. | ἰδίων | ἰδίων | ἰδίων | μικρῶν | μικρῶν | μικρῶν |
| Loc. Ins. Dat. | ἰδίοις | ἰδίαις | ἰδίοις | μικροῖς | μικραῖς | μικροῖς |
| Acc. | ἰδίους | ἰδίας | ἴδια | μικρούς | μικράς | μικρά |
| Voc. | like nominative | | | | | |

**§ 14.** Contract adjectives of the α- and o- declension. διπλοῦς, *twofold, double.*

*Singular*

|  | *Masc.* | *Fem.* | *Neut.* |
|------|---------|--------|---------|
|  | διπλοο- | διπλοη- | διπλοο- |
| Nom. | διπλοῦς | διπλῆ | διπλοῦν |
| Gen. Abl. | διπλοῦ | διπλῆς | διπλοῦ |
| Loc. Ins. Dat. | διπλῷ | διπλῇ | διπλῷ |
| Acc. | διπλοῦν | διπλῆν | διπλοῦν |

*Plural*

| Nom. | διπλοῖ | διπλαῖ | διπλᾶ |
|------|--------|--------|-------|
| Gen. Abl. | διπλῶν | διπλῶν | διπλῶν |
| Loc. Ins. Dat. | διπλοῖς | διπλαῖς | διπλοῖς |
| Acc. | διπλοῦς | διπλᾶς | διπλᾶ |

Of like form are those whose stems end in ε.

*a.* If ε, ι, or ρ precedes the stem vowel, α is found in the fem. sing. instead of η (sometimes η occurs). So are declined—

χρυσοῦς (χρύσεος), -ῆ, -οῦν, *golden*
ἀργυροῦς (ἀργύρεος), -ᾶ, -οῦν, *of silver*

**§ 15.** Adjectives (of the third declension) with stem in -υ- are declined like ὀξύς, *sharp.*

|  | *Singular* | | | *Plural* | | |
|---|---|---|---|---|---|---|
|  | M. | F. | N. | M. | F. | N. |
| Nom. | ὀξύς | ὀξεῖα | ὀξύ | ὀξεῖς | [ὀξεῖαι] | ὀξέα |
| Gen. Abl. | ὀξέως | ὀξείας | ὀξέως | ὀξέων | ὀξειῶν | ὀξέων |
| Loc. Ins. Dat. | ὀξεῖ | [ὀξείᾳ] | ὀξεῖ | [ὀξέσι] | ὀξείαις | [ὀξέσι] |
| Acc. | [ὀξύν] | ὀξεῖαν | ὀξύ | ὀξεῖς | ὀξείας | ὀξέα |

So βαρύς, *heavy;* βραχύς, *short;* εὐθύς, *straight.*

**§ 16.** Most of the participles with stems in -οντ- are declined like the present participle of εἰμί. Thus:

|  | M. | F. | N. | M. | F. | N. |
|---|---|---|---|---|---|---|
| Nόm. | ὤν | οὖσα | ὄν | ὄντες | οὖσαι | ὄντα |
| Gen. Abl. | ὄντος | οὔσης | ὄντος | ὄντων | οὐσῶν | ὄντων |
| Loc. Ins. Dat. | ὄντι | οὔσῃ | ὄντι | οὖσι | οὔσαις | οὖσι |
| Acc. | ὄντα | οὖσαν | ὄν | ὄντας | οὔσας | ὄντα |

## C. Pronouns

**§ 17.** A few forms of the demonstrative pronoun
ὅδε, ἥδε, τόδε, *this*, occur in the New Testament. It
is declined like the article (ὁ) with the enclitic δε
added.

**§ 18.** Most other pronouns (not personal) are declined in the first and second declensions, and may
be easily learned, as they are needed, from a lexicon.

## D. Paradigms of the Verb

**§ 19.** Simple ω-verb. λύω.

### ACTIVE VOICE

|        |    | Present | Imperfect | Future |
|--------|----|---------|-----------|--------|
| INDIC. |    |         |           |        |
| S.     | 1. | λύω | ἔλυον | λύσω |
|        | 2. | λύεις | ἔλυες | λύσεις |
|        | 3. | λύει | ἔλυε | λύσει |
| P.     | 1. | λύομεν | ἐλύομεν | λύσομεν |
|        | 2. | λύετε | ἐλύετε | λύσετε |
|        | 3. | λύουσι | ἔλυον | λύσουσι |
| SUBJ.  |    |         |           |        |
| S.     | 1. | λύω |  |  |
|        | 2. | λύῃς |  |  |
|        | 3. | λύῃ |  |  |
| P.     | 1. | λύωμεν |  |  |
|        | 2. | λύητε |  |  |
|        | 3. | λύωσι |  |  |
| OPT.   |    |         |           |        |
| S.     | 1. | [λύοιμι] |  |  |
|        | 2. | [λύοις] |  |  |
|        | 3. | λύοι |  |  |
| P.     | 1. | [λύοιμεν] |  |  |
|        | 2. | λύοιτε |  |  |
|        | 3. | λύοιεν |  |  |
| IMP.   |    |         |           |        |
| S.     | 2. | λῦε |  |  |
|        | 3. | λυέτω |  |  |
| P.     | 2. | λύετε |  |  |
|        | 3. | λυέτωσαν |  |  |
| INF.   |    | λύειν |  | λύσειν |
| PART.  |    | λύων, λύουσα, λῦον |  | λύσων,-ουσα,-ον |

|         |      |    | 1 *Aorist*   | 1 *Perfect*    | 1 *Pluperf.*        |
|---------|------|----|--------------|----------------|---------------------|
| Indic.  | S.   | 1. | ἔλυσα        | λέλυκα         | [ἐλελύκειν]         |
|         |      | 2. | ἔλυσας       | λέλυκας        | [ἐλελύκεις]         |
|         |      | 3. | ἔλυσε        | λέλυκε         | (ἐ)λελύκει          |
|         | P.   | 1. | ἐλύσαμεν     | λελύκαμεν      | [ἐλελύκειμεν]       |
|         |      | 2. | ἐλύσατε      | λελύκατε       | (ἐ)λελύκειτε        |
|         |      | 3. | ἔλυσαν       | λελύκασι,      | (ἐ)λελύκεισαν       |
|         |      |    |              | or -αν         |                     |

|        |      |    |            |                      |
|--------|------|----|------------|----------------------|
| Subj.  | S.   | 1. | λύσω       |                      |
|        |      | 2. | λύσῃς      | Periphrastic:        |
|        |      | 3. | λύσῃ       | Perf. act. par-      |
|        | P.   | 1. | λύσωμεν    | ticiple and          |
|        |      | 2. | λύσητε     | pres. subj. of       |
|        |      | 3. | λύσωσι     | εἰμί.                |

|      |      |    |                  |
|------|------|----|------------------|
| Opt. | S.   | 1. | [λύσαιμι]        |
|      |      | 2. | [λύσαις]         |
|      |      | 3. | λύσαι            |
|      | P.   | 1. | [λύσαιμεν]       |
|      |      | 2. | [λύσαιτε]        |
|      |      | 3. | λύσειαν or -αιεν |

|      |      |    |            |
|------|------|----|------------|
| Imp. | S.   | 2. | λῦσον      |
|      |      | 3. | λυσάτω     |
|      | P.   | 2. | λύσατε     |
|      |      | 3. | λυσάτωσαν  |

| Inf. | λῦσαι | λελυκέναι |
|------|-------|-----------|

| Part. | λύσας λύσασα λῦσαν | λελυκώς, -υῖα, -ός |
|-------|--------------------|--------------------|

## MIDDLE VOICE

|  |  | *Present* | *Imperfect* | *Future* |
|---|---|---|---|---|
| INDIC. | S. 1. | λύομαι | ἐλυόμην | λύσομαι |
|  | 2. | λύῃ | ἐλύου | λύσῃ |
|  | 3. | λύεται | ἐλύετο | λύσεται |
|  | P. 1. | λυόμεθα | ἐλυόμεθα | λυσόμεθα |
|  | 2. | λύεσθε | ἐλύεσθε | λύσεσθε |
|  | 3. | λύονται | ἐλύοντο | λύσονται |
| SUBJ. | S. 1. | λύωμαι |  |  |
|  | 2. | λύῃ |  |  |
|  | 3. | λύηται |  |  |
|  | P. 1. | λυώμεθα |  |  |
|  | 2. | λύησθε |  |  |
|  | 3. | λύωνται |  |  |
| OPT. | S. 1. | [λυοίμην] |  |  |
|  | 2. | [λύοιο] |  |  |
|  | 3. | λύοιτο |  |  |
|  | P. 1. | [λυοίμεθα] |  |  |
|  | 2. | [λύοισθε] |  |  |
|  | 3. | [λύοιντο] |  |  |
| IMP. | S. 2. | λύου |  |  |
|  | 3. | λυέσθω |  |  |
|  | P. 2. | λύεσθε |  |  |
|  | 3. | λυέσθωσαν |  |  |
| INF. |  | λύεσθαι |  | λύσεσθαι |
| PART. |  | λυόμενος, -η, -ον |  | λυσόμενος, -η, -ον |

|          |    |    | 1 *Aorist* | 1 *Perfect* | 1 *Pluperf.* |
|----------|----|----|-----------|-------------|--------------|
| INDIC.   | S. | 1. | ἐλυσάμην | λέλυμαι | [ἐλελύμην] |
|          |    | 2. | ἐλύσω | λέλυσαι | [ἐλέλυσο] |
|          |    | 3. | ἐλύσατο | λέλυται | (ἐ)λέλυτο |
|          | P. | 1. | ἐλυσάμεθα | λελύμεθα | [ἐλελύμεθα] |
|          |    | 2. | ἐλύσασθε | λέλυσθε | (ἐ)λέλυσθε |
|          |    | 3. | ἐλύσαντο | λέλυνται | (ἐ)λέλυντο |
| SUBJ.    | S. | 1. | λύσωμαι | | |
|          |    | 2. | λύσῃ | Periphrastic: | |
|          |    | 3. | λύσηται | Perf. midd. | |
|          | P. | 1. | λυσώμεθα | part. and | |
|          |    | 2. | λύσησθε | subj. of εἰμί. | |
|          |    | 3. | λύσωνται | | |
| OPT.     | S. | 1. | λυσαίμην | | |
|          |    | 2. | [λύσαιο] | | |
|          |    | 3. | [λύσαιτο] | | |
|          | P. | 1. | [λυσαίμεθα] | | |
|          |    | 2. | [λύσαισθε] | | |
|          |    | 3. | [λύσαιντο] | | |
| IMP.     | S. | 2. | λῦσαι | λέλυσο | |
|          |    | 3. | λυσάσθω | [λελύσθω] | |
|          | P. | 2. | λύσασθε | λέλυσθε | |
|          |    | 3. | λυσάσθωσαν | [λελύσθωσαν] | |
| INF.     |    |    | λύσασθαι | λελύσθαι | |
| PART.    |    |    | λυσάμενος, -η, -ον | λελυμένος, -η, -ον | |

## PASSIVE VOICE

The passive voice of the present, imperfect, perfect and pluperfect tenses is the same in form as the middle.

|  | 1 *Aorist* | 1 *Future* | 1 *Future Perf.* |
|---|---|---|---|
| **INDIC.** S. | 1. ἐλύθην | λυθήσομαι | [λελύσομαι] |
|  | 2. ἐλύθης | λυθήσῃ | [λελύσῃ] |
|  | 3. ἐλύθη | λυθήσεται | [λελύσεται] |
| P. | 1. ἐλύθημεν | λυθησόμεθα | [λελυσόμεθα] |
|  | 2. ἐλύθητε | λυθήσεσθε | [λελύσεσθε] |
|  | 3. ἐλύθησαν | λυθήσονται | [λελύσονται] |

**SUBJ.** S.
1. λυθῶ
2. λυθῇς
3. λυθῇ

P.
1. λυθῶμεν
2. λυθῆτε
3. λυθῶσι

**OPT.** S.
1. [λυθείην]
2. [λυθείης]
3. λυθείη

P.
1. [λυθείημεν]
2. [λυθείητε]
3. [λυθείησαν]

**IMP.** S.
2. λύθητι
3. λυθήτω

P.
2. λύθητε
3. λυθήτωσαν.

**INF.** λυθῆναι [λυθήσεσθαι]

**PART.** λυθείς, -εῖσα, -έν λυθησόμενος

**§ 20.** κάθημαι (κατα + ἡμαι), *I sit, I am seated.*

STEM ἡσ-

|  |  | *Present* | *Imperfect* |
|---|---|---|---|
| INDIC. | S. | 1. κάθημαι | 1. [ἐκαθήμην] |
|  |  | 2. κάθη | 2. [ἐκάθησο] |
|  |  | 3. κάθηται | 3. ἐκάθητο |
|  | P. | 1. [καθήμεθα] | 1. [ἐκαθήμεθα] |
|  |  | 2. [κάθησθε] | 2. [ἐκάθησθε] |
|  |  | 3. κάθηνται | 3. ἐκάθηντο |
| SUBJ. | S. | 1. [καθῶμαι] |  |
|  |  | 2. [καθῇ] |  |
|  |  | 3. [καθῆται] |  |
|  | P. | 1. [καθώμεθα] |  |
|  |  | 2. καθῆσθε |  |
|  |  | 3. [καθῶνται] |  |
| IMP. | S. | 2. κάθου (as if from |  |
|  |  |     κάθομαι) |  |
|  |  | 3. ———— |  |
|  | P. | 2. ———— |  |
|  |  | 3. ———— |  |
| INF. |  | καθῆσθαι |  |
| PART. |  | καθήμενος, -η, -ον |  |

**§ 21.** κεῖμαι, *I lie, I am laid.*

STEM κει-

|  |  | *Present* | *Imperfect* |
|---|---|---|---|
| INDIC. | S. | 1. κεῖμαι | 1. [ἐκείμην] |
|  |  | 2. [κεῖσαι] | 2. [ἔκεισο] |
|  |  | 3. κεῖται | 3. ἔκειτο |

|  | | *Present* | *Imperfect* |
|--|--|-----------|-------------|
| P. | 1. | κείμεθα | 1. [ἐκείμεθα] |
|  | 2. | [κεῖσθε] | 2. [ἔκεισθε] |
|  | 3. | κεῖνται | 3. ἔκειντο |

INF.    κεῖσθαι

PART.    κείμενος, -η, -ον

§ 22. εἶμι, *I am going*, occurs only in compounds in the New Testament.

### STEM ἰ-, εἰ-

|  | | *Present* | *Imperfect* |
|--|--|-----------|-------------|
| INDIC. S. | 1. | ——— | 1. ——— |
|  | 2. | ——— | 2. ——— |
|  | 3. | ——— | 3. -ῄει |
| P. | 1. | ——— | 1. ——— |
|  | 2. | ——— | 2. ——— |
|  | 3. | -ίασι | 3. -ῄεσαν |

INF.    -ιέναι

PART.    -ιών, -ιοῦσα, -ιόν.

## E. Classes of Verbs

**§ 23.** The various tenses are built on the verb-stem or root with certain modifications of the verb-stem and with additions of suffixes.

In Greek verbs are classified according to the method of forming the present stem from the verb-stem or root. From the verb-stem the present stem is formed in several ways.

**§ 24.** FIRST CLASS. *The non-thematic root class.* Here the verb-stem or root without the thematic vowel appears as the present stem.

| Present | Fut. | Aorist | Perf. act. | Perf. pass. | Aor. pass. |
|---|---|---|---|---|---|
| 1. δύναμαι, *I am able* | δυνήσομαι | | | | ἠδυνήθην |
| 2. κάθ-ημαι, *I sit* | καθήσομαι | | | | |
| 3. κεῖμαι, *I lie* | | | | | |
| 4. φημί, *I say* | | | | | |

**§ 25.** SECOND CLASS. *The non-thematic reduplicated present.*

The reduplicated verb-stem without the thematic vowel appears as the present.

| Present | Fut. | Aorist | Perf. act. | Perf. pass. | Aor. pass. |
|---|---|---|---|---|---|
| 1. δίδωμι, I give | δώσω | ἔδωκα | δέδωκα | δέδομαι | ἐδόθην |
| 2. ἀφίημι, I forgive | ἀφήσω | ἀφῆκα | | ἀφέωνται | ἀφέθην |
| 3. ἵστημι, I stand | στήσω | ἔστην, ἔστησα | ἔστηκα, -ἑστώς (ptc.) | | ἐστάθην |
| 4. τίθημι, I place | θήσω | ἔθηκα | τέθεικα | τέθειμαι | ἐτέθην |

## § 26. THIRD CLASS. *The non-thematic present with -να- and -νυ-.*

| Present | Fut. | Aorist | Perf. act. | Perf. pass. | Aor. pass. |
|---|---|---|---|---|---|
| 1. δείκνυμι, I show | δείξω | ἔδειξα | | δέδειγμαι | ἐδείχθην |
| 2. ἀπόλλυμι, I destroy | ἀπολέσω | ἀπώλεσα | ἀπόλωλα | | |

## § 27. FOURTH CLASS. *The simple thematic present.*

*a.* The thematic vowel °/ε is added to the verb-stem or root to form the present stem.

| Present | Fut. | Aorist | Perf. act. | Perf. pass. | Aor. pass. |
|---|---|---|---|---|---|
| 1. ἄγω (αγ-), I lead | ἄξω | ἤγαγον, ἦξα | | ἦγμαι | ἤχθην |
| 2. ἀγαπάω (ἀγαπα-), I love | ἀγαπήσω | ἠγάπησα | ἠγάπηκα | | |
| 3. ἀκούω (ἀκου-), I hear | ἀκούσω, ἀκούσομαι | ἤκουσα | ἀκήκοα | | ἠκούσθην |

| Present | Fut. | Aorist | Perf. act. | Perf. pass. | Aor. pass. |
|---|---|---|---|---|---|
| 4. ἀνοίγω (ἀνοιγ-), I open | ἀνοίξω | ἀνέῳξα ἤνοιξα ἠνέῳξα | ἀνέῳγα | ἀνέῳγμαι ἠνέῳγμαι ἤνοιγμαι | ἀνεῴχθην ἠνεῴχθην ἠνοίχθην |
| 5. ἄρχομαι (ἀρχ-), I begin | ἄρξομαι | ἠρξάμην | | | |
| 6. γράφω (γραφ-), I write | γράψω | ἔγραψα | γέγραφα | γέγραμμαι | ἐγράφην |
| 7. δέχομαι (δεχ-), I receive | δέξομαι | ἐδεξάμην | | δέδεγμαι | -ἐδέχθην |
| 8. δοκέω (δοκε-), I seem | | ἔδοξα (δοκ-) | | | |
| 9. ζάω (ζη-), I live | ζήσω | ἔζησα | | | |
| 10. καλέω (καλε-), I call | καλέσω | ἐκάλεσα | κέκληκα | κέκλημαι | ἐκλήθην |
| 11. πιστεύω (πιστευ-), I believe | πιστεύσω | ἐπίστευσα | πεπίστευκα | πεπίστευμαι | ἐπιστεύθην |

b. The thematic vowel $^o/_\epsilon$ is added to the strong verb-stem to form the present stem. Weak verb-stems in α, ι, υ, have the strong verb-stems in η, ει, ευ.

| Present | Fut. | Aorist | Perf. act. | Perf. pass. | Aor. pass. |
|---|---|---|---|---|---|
| 1. πείθω (πιθ-), I persuade | πείσω | ἔπεισα | πέποιθα | πέπεισμαι | ἐπείσθην |
| 2. λείπω (λιπ-), I leave | λείψω | ἔλιπον | | λέλειμμαι | ἐλείφθην |
| 3. [σήπω, (σαπ-)], I rot | | | σέσηπα | | |
| 4. φεύγω (φυγ-), I flee | φεύξομαι | ἔφυγον | πέφευγα | | |

## § 28. FIFTH CLASS. *The reduplicated thematic present.*

The thematic vowel $^o/_\epsilon$ is added to the reduplicated (ι in redupl.) verb-stem.

The verb-stem shows syncope of the stem vowel.

| Present | Fut. | Aorist | Perf. act. | Perf. pass. | Aor. pass. |
|---|---|---|---|---|---|
| 1. γίνομαι (γεν-), *I become* | γενήσομαι | ἐγενόμην | γέγονα | γεγένημαι | ἐγενήθην |
| ( *γίγνομαι γιγένομαι) | | | | | |
| 2. πίπτω (πετ-), *I fall* | πεσοῦμαι | ἔπεσον ἔπεσα | πέπτωκα | | |
| 3. τίκτω (τεκ-), *I bear* | τέξομαι | ἔτεκον | | | ἐτέχθην |

## § 29. SIXTH CLASS. *The thematic present with a suffix.*

A suffix (-ι, -ν, -σκ, -τ, -θ) and the thematic vowel $^o/_\epsilon$ are added to the verb-stem to form the present stem.

*a.* With the suffix -ι.

(1) With stems in δ (sometimes γ). δι (sometimes γι) form **ζ.**

| Present | Fut. | Aorist | Perf. act. | Perf. pass. | Aor. pass. |
|---|---|---|---|---|---|
| 1. βαπτίζω (βαπτιδ-), I baptize | βαπτίσω | ἐβάπτισα | | βεβάπτισμαι | ἐβαπτίσθην |
| 2. ἐλπίζω (ἐλπιδ-), I hope | ἐλπιῶ | ἤλπισα | ἤλπικα | | |
| 3. κράζω (κραγ-), I cry | κράξω | ἔκραξα (ἐκέκραξα) ἔκραγον | κέκραγα | | |
| 4. σῴζω (σωδ-), I save | σώσω | ἔσωσα | σέσωκα | σέσωσμαι | ἐσώθην |

(2) With stems in κ, χ, and sometimes γ. κ, χ, or γ unites with ι to form σσ (ττ).

| Present | Fut. | Aorist | Perf. act. | Perf. pass. | Aor. pass. |
|---|---|---|---|---|---|
| 1. κηρύσσω (κηρυκ-), I announce | κηρύξω | ἐκήρυξα | κεκήρυχα | κεκήρυγμαι | ἐκηρύχθην |
| 2. τάσσω (ταγ-), I arrange | τάξομαι | ἔταξα | τέταχα | τέταγμαι | -ετάγην ἐτάχθην |

(3) With stems in λ, ν, ρ (liquids and nasals). λι forms λλ. -αν and -αρ form -αιν and -αιρ, respectively. -ενι, -ερι, -ινι, -ιρι, -υνι, -υρι form -ειν, -ειρ, -ῑν, -ῑρ, -ῡν, -ῡρ, respectively.

| Present | Fut. | Aorist | Perf. act. | Perf. pass. | Aor. pass. |
|---|---|---|---|---|---|
| 1. ἀγγέλλω (ἀγγελ-), I announce | ἀγγελῶ | ἤγγειλα | ἤγγελκα | ἤγγελμαι | ἠγγέλην |
| 2. αἴρω (ἀρ-), I raise | ἀρῶ | ἦρα | ἦρκα | ἦρμαι | ἤρθην |
| 3. ἀποκτείνω (ἀπο-κτεν-), I kill | ἀποκτενῶ | ἀπέκτεινα | | | ἀπεκτάνθην |

| Present | Fut. | Aorist | Perf. act. | Perf. pass. | Aor. pass. |
|---|---|---|---|---|---|
| 4. βάλλω (βαλ-), I throw | βαλῶ | ἔβαλον | βέβληκα | βέβλημαι | ἐβλήθην |
| 5. ἐγείρω (ἐγερ-), I raise up | ἐγερῶ | ἤγειρα | ἐγήγερκα | ἐγήγερμαι | ἠγέρθην |
| 6. κρίνω (κριν-),¹ I judge | κρινῶ | ἔκρινα | κέκρικα | κέκριμαι | ἐκρίθην |
| 7. σπείρω (σπερ-), I sow | σπερῶ | ἔσπειρα | | ἔσπαρμαι | ἐσπάρην |
| 8. φαίνω (φαν-), I show | φανοῦμαι | (ἔφανα) | | | ἐφάνην |
| 9. χαίρω (χαρ-), I rejoice | | | | | ἐχάρην |

b. With a suffix containing ν. Sometimes a sympathetic nasal is inserted in the root.

| Present | Fut. | Aorist | Perf. act. | Perf. pass. | Aor. pass. |
|---|---|---|---|---|---|
| 1. ἁμαρτάνω (ἁμαρτ-), I sin | ἁμαρτήσω | ἡμάρτησα ἥμαρτον | ἡμάρτηκα | | |
| 2. βαίνω (βα-),² I go | βήσομαι | ἔβην | βέβηκα | | |
| 3. λαμβάνω (λαβ-), I take | λήμψομαι | ἔλαβον | εἴληφα | εἴλημμαι | ἐλήμφθην |
| 4. μανθάνω (μαθ-), I learn | | ἔμαθον | μεμάθηκα | | |
| 5. πίνω (πι-), I drink | πίομαι | ἔπιον | πέπωκα | | ἐπόθην |
| 6. τυγχάνω (τυχ-), I happen | | ἔτυχον | τέτυχα | | |

¹ κρίνω has also stem κρι-.
² Suffix ι also has been added.

*c.* With the suffix τ. The verb-stem is always a labial mute (π, β, φ). β or φ changes to π before τ.

| Present | Fut. | Aorist | Perf. act. | Perf. pass. | Aor. pass. |
|---|---|---|---|---|---|
| 1. ἅπτω (ἁφ-), I fasten | | ἥψα | | | ἥφθην |
| 2. καλύπτω (καλυβ-), I cover | καλύψω | ἐκάλυψα | | κεκάλυμμαι | ἐκαλύφθην |
| 3. κόπτω (κοπ-), I cut | κόψω | ἔκοψα | | | ἐκόπην |

*d.* With the suffix σκ or ισκ. Sometimes the verb-stem is reduplicated. σκ is added if verb-stem ends in a vowel; ισκ is added if verb-stem ends in a consonant.

| Present | Fut. | Aorist | Perf. act. | Perf. pass. | Aor. pass. |
|---|---|---|---|---|---|
| 1. ἀποθνήσκω (ἀπο-θαν-), I am dying | ἀποθανοῦμαι | ἀπέθανον | (τέθνηκα) | | |
| 2. γινώσκω (γνο-), I know | γνώσομαι | ἔγνων | ἔγνωκα | ἔγνωσμαι | ἐγνώσθην |
| 3. διδάσκω (διδαχ-), I teach | διδάξω | ἐδίδαξα | | | ἐδιδάχθην |
| 4. εὑρίσκω (εὑρ-), I find | εὑρήσω | εὗρον, εὗρα | εὕρηκα | | εὑρέθην |

*e.* With the suffix θ. Only a few verbs in this division.

1. ἐσθω (εσ-), I am eating
2. νήθω (να-), I spin

§ 30.  SEVENTH CLASS.  This group of verbs is not properly a class as the other classes. This class consists of verbs containing in one or more tenses a verb-stem essentially different from the verb-stem of the present tense.

| Present | Fut. | Aorist | Perf. act. | Perf. pass. | Aor. pass. |
|---------|------|--------|------------|-------------|------------|
| 1. ἐσθίω (ἐσ‑), *I eat* | φάγομαι | ἔφαγον | | | ὤφθην |
| 2. ὁράω (ὁρα‑), *I see* | ὄψομαι | εἶδον | ἑώρακα | | |
| | | | ἑόρακα | | |
| 3. τρέχω (τρεχ‑), *I run* | | ἔδραμον | ἐδραμον | | |
| 4. φέρω (φερ‑), *I bear* | οἴσω | ἤνεγκα (‑ον) | ἐνήνοχα | | ἠνέχθην |

Many other verbs may be included in this class.

§ 31.  Perfect stems that end in a mute (**217**) suffer euphonic changes in the perfect and pluperfect middle (and passive) before the personal endings:

    1. A labial mute (π β φ) before μ becomes μ.

    2. A palatal mute (κ γ χ) before μ becomes γ.

    3. A lingual mute (τ δ θ) before μ becomes σ.

    4. A lingual mute before a lingual mute becomes σ.

    **5.** A mute of the stem before a mute of the personal ending becomes coordinate, as βτ > πτ, φτ > πτ, γτ > κτ, χτ > κτ, πθ > φθ, βθ > φθ, κθ > χθ, γθ > χθ.

6. σ coming between two consonants is dropped.

Perfect indicative middle (and passive) of

| τάσσω | γράφω | πείθω |
|---|---|---|
| Stem τεταγ | γεγραφ | πεπειθ |
| τέταγμαι | γέγραμμαι | πέπεισμαι |
| τέταξαι | γέγραψαι | πέπεισαι |
| τέτακται | γέγραπται | πέπεισται |
| τετάγμεθα | γεγράμμεθα | πεπείσμεθα |
| τέταχθε | γέγραφθε | πέπεισθε |
| τεταγμένοι εἰσί | γεγραμμένοι εἰσί | πεπεισμένοι εἰσί |

Likewise the same changes of the stem occur in the pluperfect, as (ἐ)γεγράμμην, (ἐ)γέγραψο, (ἐ)γέγραπτο, (ἐ)γεγράμμεθα, (ἐ)γέγραφθε, γεγραμμένοι ἦσαν.

The third person plural of the perfect ind. middle (and passive) of mute stems is a periphrastic form made up of the perfect participle and εἰσί (perfect) or ἦσαν (pluperfect).

# ENGLISH INDEX

# ENGLISH INDEX [1]

## A

Ablative case: meaning, 29; many examples

Accent: kinds, 22; meaning, 22; where and why placed, 23 f.; recessive, 23; in declensions, 29; oxytones, 50; proclitics, 44, 50; enclitics, 63 f.; 2d Aorist Inf., 79; participles, 98; comparatives and superlatives, 179; contract verbs, 178 f.

Accusative case: meaning, 29; general reference, 132; many examples

Action: expression of, 24, 73; kind of, 25, 82, 158; durative, 25, 41, 78, etc.; linear, 25, 41, etc.; punctiliar, 78, etc.; Aorist, 78; participle, 99, 103, 104, 156 f.; imperfect, 41, 168; perfective, 152, 156; constative, ingressive, effective, 124

Active voice: meaning, 36; examples, 24–27, 62 f., 175, 73–5, 96–8, 167, 176; 41–3, 68; 77–81, 163, 81–3, 101–5; 86–93, 162 f.; 120–5, 125–7, 128–30, 169; 149–52, 154 f.; 152 f.; 153; 155

Acute accent, 22, 31, 32, 65; many examples

Adjectives: gender, number, case, 56; agree with substantive, 32, 57; attributive and predicate use, 57 f.; substituted by phrase and adverb, 59; 1st declension,— endings, 56, 59; ἀγαθός, 56; forms, 56; accent, 57; 3d declension,— πᾶς, 130; accent, 131; use, 131; stems in -ες, 133; ἀληθής, 133; forms, 134; irregulars,— πολύς, 134 f.; μέγας, 135 f.; comparison, 178–80, 182

Adverbs: formation, 180; comparison, 180 f., 184

Affirmation, 24, 74, 212

Agent, 48

Agreement: adjectives, 32; pronouns, 67

Aktionsart: 123 f., 125, 127, 130, 139 f., 152, 156, 169

Alphabet, 19 f.

Antecedent, 67, 112

Antepenult, 23; many examples

# VOCABULARIES

# GREEK–ENGLISH VOCABULARY

## A

ἀγαθός, -ή, -όν, good
ἀγαπάω, I love
ἀγάπη, -ης, ἡ, love
ἀγαπητός, -ή, -όν, beloved
ἄγγελος, -ου, ὁ, messenger, angel
ἀγιάζω, I sanctify
ἅγιος, -α, -ον, holy
ἀγοράζω, I buy
ἄγω, I lead, bring, go; sec. aor., ἤγαγον.
ἀδελφός, -οῦ, ὁ, brother
ἄδικος, -ον, unrighteous
ἀδύνατος, -ον, unable, impossible
αἷμα, -ατος, τό, blood
αἴρω, I take up, bear
αἰσθάνομαι, I perceive
αἰτέω, I ask for (something)
αἰών, -ῶνος, ὁ, age (space of time), world
αἰώνιος, -α, -ον, eternal
ἀκάθαρτος, -ον, unclean
ἀκολουθέω, I follow
ἀκούω, I hear.
ἀκριβῶς, adv., accurately
ἀλέκτωρ, -ορος, ὁ, cock
ἀλήθεια, -ας, ἡ, truth
ἀληθής, -ές, true
ἀληθινός, -ή, -όν, true
ἀληθῶς, adv., truly, surely
ἀλλά, adversative conj., but,

ἀλλήλων, (gen. masc. plu.), of one another
ἄλλος, -η, -ο, other
ἀλλότριος, -α, -ον, belonging to another (another's), strange
ἁμαρτάνω, I sin
ἁμαρτία, -ας, ἡ, sin
ἀμήν, adv., truly, verily
ἀμπελών, -ῶνος, ὁ, vineyard
ἄν, see page 157
ἀνά, prep., on, upon, along; only used with acc. in N. T.
ἀναβαίνω, I go up, come up, ascend
ἀναβλέπω, I look up, recover sight
ἀναγινώσκω, I read
ἀνάστασις, -εως, ἡ, resurrection
ἄνεμος, -ου, ὁ, wind
ἀνήρ, ἀνδρός, ὁ, man
ἀνθίστημι,. I set against, withstand
ἄνθρωπος, -ου, ὁ, man
ἀνίστημι, I raise up, rise, arise
ἀνοίγω, I open
ἀντί, prep., with gen., opposite, against; instead of, in place of, for
ἄνω, adv., up, above
ἄνωθεν, adv., from above, again
ἄξιος, -α, -ον, fitting, worthy

255

ἀπαγγέλλω, I announce, declare

ἀπαρνέομαι,, I deny

ἅπας, ἅπασα, ἅπαν, all, altogether

ἀπέρχομαι, I go away

ἀπέχω, I keep off, have in full (of receipts); midd., I keep myself from, abstain

ἀπό, prep., from off, used only with the abl. in the N. T.

ἀποδίδωμι, I give up, give back, restore; pay; midd., sell

ἀποθνήσκω, I die

ἀποκρίνομαι, I answer

ἀποκτείνω, I kill, slay

ἀπολύω, I release

ἀποστέλλω, I send forth

ἀπόστολος, -ου, ὁ, apostle

ἅπτω, I fasten to; midd., ἅπτομαι, I touch

ἀρνέομαι, I deny

ἄρτι, adv., now, just now, this moment

ἄρτος, -ου, ὁ, bread

ἀρχή, -ῆς, ἡ, beginning

ἀρχιερεύς, -έως, ὁ, chief priest

ἄρχομαι, I begin

ἄρχων, -οντος, ὁ, ruler, prince

ἀσθένεια, -ας, ἡ, weakness

ἀσθενής, -ές, weak, sick

αὔριον, adv., tomorrow

αὐτός, -ή, -ό, self, very, same; he, she, it

ἄφεσις, -εως, ἡ, remission, forgiveness

ἀφίημι, I send away, forgive, leave, let

ἀφίστημι, I put away, depart from

ἄφρων, -ον, foolish

## B

βαίνω, I go

βάλλω, I throw, cast

βαπτίζω, I baptize

βασιλεία, -ας, ἡ, kingdom

βασιλεύς, -έως, ὁ, king

βασιλεύω, I am king, I reign

βιβλίον, -ου, τό, book, a written document

βίος, -ου, ὁ, life, manner of life

βλέπω, I see, look at, behold

βούλομαι, I will, wish

## Γ

γάμος, -ου, ὁ, marriage

γάρ, coördinating conj., for.

γέ, enclitic, postpositive particle giving especial prominence to a word, indeed, at last

γεννάω, I beget

γένος, -ους, τό, race, kind

γῆ, γῆς, ἡ, earth

γίνομαι, I become, be

γινώσκω, I know

γλῶσσα, -ης, ἡ, tongue

γνῶσις, -εως, ἡ, knowledge

γόνυ, -νατος, τό, knee

γράμμα, -ατος, τό, letter (of alphabet), writing

γραμματεύς, -έως, ὁ, scribe, town-clerk

γραφή, -ῆς, ἡ, writing, scripture

γράφω, I write

γυνή, -ναικός, ἡ, woman, wife

## Δ

δαιμόνιον, -ου, τό, demon, evil-spirit

δέ, copulative and adversative (milder than ἀλλά) conj., postpositive, *in the next place, and; but, on the other hand*

δεῖ, *it is necessary*

δεύτερος, -α, -ον, *second*

διά, prep., with gen., *through, by;* with acc., *because of, on account of, for the sake of*

διάβολος, -ου, ὁ, *devil*

διαθήκη, -ης, ἡ, *covenant, testament*

διακονέω, *I serve, minister*

διακονία, -ας, ἡ, *service, ministry*

διάκονος, -ου, ὁ, *servant, minister, deacon*

διαλογίζομαι, *I reason with, discuss, consider*

διάνοια, -ας, ἡ, *mind, understanding*

διδάσκαλος, -ου, ὁ, *teacher*

διδάσκω, *I teach*

δίδωμι, *I give, deliver*

διέρχομαι, *I go through*

δίκαιος, -α, -ον, *righteous*

δικαιοσύνη, -ης, ἡ, *righteousness*

δικαιόω, *I declare righteous, justify*

διψάω, *I thirst*

διώκω, *I follow after, pursue, persecute*

δοκέω, *I think, suppose;* δοκεῖ, *it seems good*

δόξα, -ης, ἡ, *glory*

δοξάζω, *I glorify*

δουλεύω, *I am a servant, I serve*

δοῦλος, -ου, ὁ, *servant*

δύναμαι, *I am able, can*

δύναμις, -εως, ἡ, *power*

δυνατός, -ή, -όν, *able*

δύο, *two*

δώδεκα, *twelve*

δῶρον, -ου, τό, *gift*

## E

ἐάν, conditional particle, *if*

ἐὰν μή, with a substantive = *except, unless*

ἑαυτοῦ, -ῆς, -οῦ, (rarely αὐτοῦ, -ῆς, -οῦ), reflexive, *himself, herself, itself*

ἔβαλον, *I threw, cast;* sec. aor. of βάλλω.

ἔβην, *I went;* μι- aorist of βαίνω.

ἐγενόμην, *I became;* sec. aor. of γίνομαι.

ἔγνων, *I knew;* μι- aorist of γινώσκω.

ἐγράφην, sec. aor. passive of γράφω.

ἐγγύς, adv., *near*

ἐγείρω, *I raise up*

ἐγώ, *I*

ἔθνος, -ους, τό, *race, nation*

ἔθος, -ους, τό, *custom*

εἰ, conditional particle, *if*

εἰ μή, with a substantive = *except, unless*

εἶδον, *I saw;* sec. aor.; ὁράω used in present

εἰμί, *I am*

εἶπον, εἶπα, *I said;* sec. aor.; λέγω used in present

εἰρήνη, -ης, ἡ, *peace*

εἰς, prep., *into,* used only with the acc.

εἷς, μία, ἕν, *one*

εἰσάγω, *I bring in*

εἰσέρχομαι *I enter*

ἐκ (ἐξ), prep., *out, out of, from within,* used only with the abl.

ἐκβάλλω, *I throw out, cast out*

ἐκεῖ, adv., *there*

ἐκεῖνος, -η, -ο, demons. pron., *that (one)*

ἐκκλησία, -ας, ἡ, *assembly, church*

ἐκπορεύομαι, *I go out*

ἐκτείνω, *I stretch out*

ἔλαβον, *I took;* sec. aor. of λαμβάνω.

ἔλεος, -ους, τό, *pity, mercy*

ἐλεύθερος, -α, -ον, *free*

ἐλπίζω, *I hope*

ἐλπίς, -ίδος, ἡ, *hope*

ἔλιπον, *I left;* sec. aor. of λείπω.

ἐμαυτοῦ, -ῆς, reflexive pron., *myself*

ἐμβαίνω, *I go into, embark*

ἐμός, -ή, όν, poss. pron., *my, mine*

ἐν, prep., *in;* used only with the loc.

ἐντολή, -ῆς, ἡ, *commandment*

ἐνώπιον, prep. with gen., *before, in the presence of*

ἐξέρχομαι, *I go out;* sec. aor. ἐξῆλθον.

ἔξεστιν, *it is lawful, is possible*

ἐξίστημι, *I am amazed, am beside myself*

ἐξουσία, -ας, ἡ, *authority, power*

ἔξω, adv., *without, outside;* used with abl., *without, outside*

ἑορτή, -ῆς, ἡ, *feast*

ἐπαγγελία, -ας, ἡ, *promise*

ἐπαύριον, adv., *on the morrow*

ἐπερωτάω, *I question, ask* (a question)

ἐπιγινώσκω, *I recognize, discover*

ἐπιδίδωμι, *I give over*

ἐπιθυμία, -ας, ἡ, *desire*

ἐπιθυμέω, *I desire*

ἐπιμένω, *I remain, abide*

ἐπιτίθημι, *I lay upon, place upon*

ἐργασία, -ας, ἡ, *work, business*

ἔργον, -ου, τό, *work*

ἔρημος, -ου, ἡ, *wilderness, desert*

ἔρχομαι, *I go, come*

ἐρωτάω, *I ask* (question)

ἐσθίω, *I eat;* ἔφαγον, *I ate*

ἔσχατος, -η, -ον, *last*

ἔσχον, *I got;* sec. aor. of ἔχω.

ἕτερος, -α, -ον, *another*

ἔτος, -ους, τό, *year*

εὖ, adv., *well*

εὐαγγελίζομαι, *I proclaim glad tidings* (preach the gospel)

εὐθέως, adv., *straightway, at once*

εὑρίσκω, *I find*

εὗρον, *I found;* sec. aor. of εὑρίσκω.

ἔφαγον, *I ate;* sec. aor.; ἐσθίω used in present

Ἐφέσιος, -α, -ον, *Ephesian*

ἐφίστημι, *I stand upon or by, come upon*

ἔφυγον, sec. aor. of φεύγω.

ἔχω, *I have, hold, get*

## Z

ζάω, *I live*

ζηλόω, *I am jealous, desire eagerly*

ζητέω, *I seek*

ζωή, -ῆς, ἡ, *life*

## H

ἤ, conj., *or*

ἡγεμών, -όνος, ὁ, *leader, governor*

ᾔδειν, old pluperf. (with pres. meaning) of οἶδα.

ἦλθον, *I went, came;* sec. aor.; ἔρχομαι used in present

ἥλιος, -ου, ὁ, *sun*

ἡμέρα, -ας, ἡ, *day*

ἡμέτερος, -α, -ον, poss. pron., *our*

## Θ

θάλασσα, -ης, ἡ, *sea*

θάνατος, -ου, ὁ, *death*

θανατόω, *I put to death*

θαυμάζω, *I wonder, marvel*

θεάομαι, *I behold, see, look at*

θέλημα, -ατος, τό, *will*

θέλω, *I wish, will*

θεός, -οῦ, ὁ, *God*

θεραπεύω, *I heal, doctor*

θεωρέω, *I look at, gaze, see*

θλῖψις, -εως, ἡ, *tribulation, distress*

θρίξ, τριχός, ἡ, *hair*

θρόνος, -ου, ὁ, *throne*

θυγάτηρ, -τρός, ἡ, *daughter*

## I

ἰάομαι, *I heal*

ἴδιος, -α, -ον, *one's own*

ἱερόν, -οῦ, τό, *temple*

ἱερεύς, -έως, ὁ, *priest*

ἵημι, *I send*

ἵνα, conj. generally with subjunctive, *in order that, that*

ἱμάτιον, -ου, τό, *garment*

ἵστημι, *I make to stand, place, stand*

ἰσχυρός, -ά, -όν, *strong*

## K

καθαρίζω, *I purify*

καθίστημι, *I set down, appoint*

καί, conj., *and; also; even;* καὶ ... καὶ, *both ... and*

κακός, -ή, -όν, *evil, bad*

καλέω, *I call*

καλός, -ή, -όν, *good, beautiful*

καλῶς, adv., *well, finely*

καρδία, -ας, ἡ, *heart*

καρπός, -οῦ, ὁ, *fruit*

κατά, prep., with gen., *down (upon), against;* with abl., *down (from);* with acc., *down (along), through, according to*

καταβαίνω, *I am going down*

καταλύω, *I destroy*

κατεσθίω, *I eat up*

κεῖμαι, *I lie (am laid)*

κεφαλή, -ῆς, ἡ, *head*

κηρύσσω, *I announce, proclaim*

κοινός, -ή, -όν, *common, unclean*

κοινόω, *I make common, unclean*

κόπτω, *I beat, strike*

κόσμος, -ου, ὁ, *world*

κράβαττος, -ου, ὁ, *pallet, bed*

κράζω, *I cry out*

κρίμα, -ατος, τό, *judgment*

κρίνω, *I judge*
κρίσις, -εως, ἡ, *judgment*
κρύπτω, *I hide*
κτίσις, -εως, ἡ, *creation*
κυριεύω, *I am lord of, rule (over)* with gen.
κύριος, -ου, ὁ, *Lord*
κύων, κυνός, ὁ, *dog*
κωλύω, *I hinder*
κώμη, -ης, ἡ, *village*

## Λ

λαλέω, *I speak*
λαμβάνω, *I take, receive;* sec. aor., ἔλαβον.
λαός, -οῦ, ὁ, *people*
λέγω, *I say, speak*
λείπω, *I leave, abandon;* sec. aor., ἔλιπον.
λῃστής, -οῦ, ὁ, *robber*
λίθος, -ου, ὁ, *stone*
λίψ, λιβός, ὁ, *the S. W. wind*
λόγος, -ου, ὁ, *word*
λούω, *I wash*
λυπέω, *I grieve*
λύω, *I loose*

## M

μαθητής, -οῦ, ὁ, *disciple*
μακάριος, -α, -ον, *happy, blessed*
μᾶλλον, adv., *more, rather*
μανθάνω, *I learn;* sec. aor., ἔμαθον.
μαρτυρέω, *I bear witness, testify*
μάστιξ, -ιγος, ἡ, *whip, scourge, plague*
μάχαιρα, -ας, ἡ, *sword*
μέγας, μεγάλη, μέγα, *great*

μέλει, *it concerns, is a care,* with dat.
μέλλω, *I am about* (or *going*) *to do* something
μέλος, -ους, τό, *member*
μένω, *I remain*
μέρος, -ους, τό, *part*
μετά, prep., with gen., *with;* with acc., *after;* μετὰ ταῦτα, *after these things, after this*
μεταβαίνω, *I pass over, depart*
μετανοέω, *I repent*
μή, *not*
μηδείς, μηδεμία, μηδέν, *no one, nothing*
μήτε . . . μήτε, *neither . . . nor*
μήτηρ, -τρός, ἡ, *mother*
μικρός, -ά, -όν, *small, little*
μισέω, *I hate*
μισθός, -οῦ, ὁ, *pay, wages, reward*
μνᾶ, μνᾶς, ἡ, *mina* (a weight and a sum of money)
μνημεῖον, -ου, τό, *sepulchre, tomb*
μνημονεύω, *I remember,* with gen.
μονογενής, -ές, *only begotten*
μόνον, adv., *only*
μόνος, -η, -ον, *only, alone*
μυστήριον, -ου, τό, *mystery*

## N

ναός, -οῦ, ὁ, *temple*
νεανίας, -ου, ὁ, *youth*
νεκρός, -ά, -όν, *dead*
νέος, -α, -ον, *young, new*
νεφέλη, -ης, ἡ, *cloud*

νεωκόρος, -ου, ὁ or ἡ, temple-keeper

νηστεύω, I fast

νικάω, I conquer

νίπτω, I wash

νομίζω, I think, suppose

νόμος, -ου, ὁ, law

νῦν, adv., now

νύξ, νυκτός, ἡ, night

## O

ὁ, ἡ, τό, the definite article the

ὁδός, -οῦ, ἡ, way, road

οἶδα, I know

οἰκία, -ας, ἡ, house

οἰκοδομέω, I build

οἶκος, -ου, ὁ, house

οἶνος, -ου, ὁ, wine

ὀλίγος, -η, -ον, few, little, small

ὅλος, -η, -ον, whole

ὁμοιόω, I make like

ὁμολογέω, I agree with, confess

ὄνομα, -ατος, τό, name

ὅπου, rel. adv., where

ὅπτομαι, I see

ὁράω, I see; fut., ὄψομαι; sec. aor., εἶδον

ὅς, ἥ, ὅ, rel. pron., who, which, that, what

ὅστις, ἥτις, ὅτι, indef. rel. pron., who, which, that, what

ὅταν, rel. temporal adv. used with the subj. and ind., whenever, when

ὅτε, rel. temporal adv. used with the ind., when

ὅτι, conj., because, that

οὐ, not; οὐκ before vowels; οὐχ before rough breathing

οὐ μή, see page 173

οὐδείς, οὐδεμία, οὐδέν, no one (nobody), nothing

οὐκέτι, no longer, no more

οὐρανός, -οῦ, ὁ, heaven

οὖς, ὠτός, τό, ear

οὔτε ... οὔτε, neither ... nor

οὗτος, αὕτη, τοῦτο, demons. pron., this (one)

ὀφείλω, I owe, ought; sec. aor. without augment, ὄφελον

ὀφθαλμός, -οῦ, ὁ, eye

ὄχλος, -ου, ὁ, crowd

ὄψομαι, fut. midd., I shall see; ὁράω used in present

## Π

παιδίον, -ου, τό, little child

παλαιός, -ά, -όν, old, ancient

πάλιν, adv., again

παρά, prep., with the loc., by or at (the side of); with the abl., from (the side of); with the acc., along (side of)

παραβολή, -ῆς, ἡ, parable

παραδίδωμι, I give over (to another), deliver up, betray

παρακαλέω, I beseech, exhort, encourage

παράκλησις, -εως, ἡ, exhortation

παραλαμβάνω, I take, receive; sec. aor., παρέλαβον

παρατίθημι, I set before, commit

παρέχω, I provide, supply

παρίστημι, I place beside, stand by

παρουσία, -ας, ἡ, coming, presence

πᾶς, πᾶσα, πᾶν, all, every

πάσχα, (indeclinable), τό, *the Passover*

πάσχω, *I suffer;* sec. aor., ἔπαθον

πατήρ, -τρός, ὁ, *father*

παύω, *I stop;* midd., παύομαι, *I cease*

πείθω, *I persuade*

πεινάω, *I hunger, am hungry*

πειράζω, *I test, tempt*

πέμπω, *I send*

περί, prep., with gen., *about, concerning;* with abl., *from around;* with acc., *round about, about, concerning*

περιάγω, *I go about, carry about*

περιπατέω, *I walk, live*

περισσός, -ή, -όν, *abundant*

πιστεύω, *I believe*

πίστις, -εως, ἡ, *faith*

πιστός, -ή, -όν, *faithful*

πλανάω, *I cause to wander* (to err), *lead astray*

πλῆθος, -ους, τό, *crowd, multitude*

πληρόω, *I make full, fill*

πλησίον, adv., *near;* ὁ πλησίον, *neighbor*

πλοῖον, -ου, τό, *boat*

πλούσιος, -α, -ον, *rich*

πνεῦμα, -ατος, τό, *spirit*

πόθεν, interrog. adv., *whence*

ποιέω, *I do, make*

ποιμήν, -ένος, ὁ, *shepherd*

πόλις, -εως, ἡ, *city*

πολύ, adv., *much*

πολύς, πολλή, πολύ, *much, many*

πονηρός, -ά, -όν, *evil*

πορεύομαι, *I go, proceed*

ποτήριον, -ου, τό, *cup*

ποῦ, interrog. adv., *where*

πούς, ποδός, ὁ, *foot*

πρεσβύτερος, -ου, ὁ, *elder*

πρίν (ἤ), *before;* see page 190

πρό, prep. with abl., *before*

προάγω, *I lead forth, go before*

πρόβατον, -ου, τό, *sheep*

πρός, prep., with loc., *near, by;* with acc., *towards, to;* with abl. (once), *"from the point of view of"*

προσέρχομαι, *I go to, come to*

προσευχή, -ῆς, ἡ, *prayer*

προστίθημι, *I add, give in addition*

πρόσωπον, -ου, τό, *face*

προφητεύω, *I prophesy*

προφήτης, -ου, ὁ, *prophet*

πρῶτος, -η, -ον, *first*

πώποτε, adv., *ever yet*

πῶς, adv., *how*

## Ρ

ῥῆμα, -ατος, τό, *word*

## Σ

σάββατον, -ου, τό, *Sabbath*

σαλεύω, *I shake*

σάλπιγξ, -ιγγος, ἡ, *trumpet*

σάρξ, σαρκός, ἡ, *flesh*

σεαυτοῦ, -ῆς, reflexive, *thyself*

σημεῖον, -ου, τό, *sign*

σήμερον, adv., *to-day, this day*

σιγάω, *I am silent, keep silence*

σιωπάω, *I am silent, keep silence*

σκανδαλίζω, *I cause to stumble, offend*

σκηνόω, *I dwell* (as in a tent)

σκόλοψ, -οπος, ὁ *stake, thorn*
σκοτία, -ας, ἡ, *darkness*
σκότος, -ους, τό, *darkness*
σός, σή, σόν, poss. pron., *thy, thine*
σοφία, -ας, ἡ, *wisdom*
σοφός, -ή, -όν, *wise*
σπείρω, *I sow*
σπέρμα, -ατος, τό, *seed*
σταυρός, -οῦ, ὁ, *cross*
σταυρόω, *I crucify*
στέλλω, *I send*
στενάζω, *I groan*
στόμα, -ατος, τό, *mouth*
στρέφω, *I turn, change*
σύ, *thou (you)*
σύν, prep., *with*, used only with the instrumental
συνάγω, *I gather together*
συναγωγή, -ῆς, ἡ, *synagogue*
συνεσθίω, *I eat with* (someone)
συνίημι, *I perceive*
συνίστημι, *I commend, establish*
σύρω, *I drag, draw*
σώζω, *I save*
σῶμα, -ατος, τό, *body*
σωτήρ, -ῆρος, ὁ, *Saviour*
σωτηρία, -ας, ἡ, *salvation*
σώφρων, -ον, *of sound mind, sober-minded*

# Τ

ταπεινόω, *I make low, humble*
ταχέως, adv., *quickly*
ταχύ, adv., *quickly*
τὲ ... καὶ, *both ... and*
τέκνον, -ου, τό, *child*
τέλειος, -α, -ον, *finished, complete*
τελειόω, *I end, complete, fulfill*

τελευτάω, (*I finish*), *I die*
τελέω, *I finish, end, complete*
τέλος, -ους, τό, *end*
τέσσαρες, τέσσαρα, *four*
τέταρτος, -η, -ον, *fourth*
τηρέω, *I keep*
τίθημι, *I place, lay, put down*
τιμάω, *I honor*
τίς, τί, interrog. pron., *who, which, what*
τις, τι, indef. pron., *one, a certain one, a certain thing; some one, something*
τολμάω, *I dare*
τόπος, -ου, ὁ, *place*
τότε, adv., *then*
τοῦτο, see οὗτος
τρεῖς, τρία, *three*
τρίτος, -η, -ον, *third*
τυφλός, -ή, -όν, *blind*
τυφλόω, *I make blind, blind*

# Υ

ὑγιής, -ές, *whole, healthy*
ὕδωρ, ὕδατος, τό, *water*
υἱός, -οῦ, ὁ, *son*
ὑμέτερος, -α, -ον, poss. pron., *your*
ὑπάγω, *I go away, depart*
ὑπέρ, prep., with abl., *in behalf of, in the interest of; instead of; in place of; for the sake of; about, concerning;* with acc., *over, above, beyond*
ὑπό, prep., with abl., *by;* with acc., *under*
ὑποκριτής, -οῦ, ὁ, *pretender, hypocrite*

## Φ

φαίνω, I shine, appear
φανερός, -ά, -όν, manifest
φανερόω, I make manifest
φέρω, I bear, carry
φεύγω, I flee, take flight; sec.
  aor., ἔφυγον
φιλέω, I love
φίλος, -ου, ὁ, friend
φοβέομαι, I am afraid, I fear
φόβος, -ου, ὁ, fear
φυλάσσω, I guard, keep
φωνέω, I call, speak aloud
φωνή, -ῆς, ἡ, voice
φῶς, φωτός, τό, light

## X

χαίρω, I rejoice
χαρά, -ᾶς, ἡ, joy
χάρις, -ιτος, ἡ, grace

χάρισμα, -ατος, τό, gift, free
  gift
χείρ, χειρός, ἡ, hand
χρεία, -ας, ἡ, need
χρονίζω, I spend time, tarry
χρόνος, -ου, ὁ, time

## Ψ

ψεύστης, -ου, ὁ, liar
ψυχή, -ῆς, ἡ, soul

## Ω

ὧδε, adv., here, hither
ὥρα, -ας, ἡ, hour
ὡς, rel., comp., and temporal
  adv., as, when
ὥστε, consecutive particle, so
  that
ὥστε, inferential conj., and so,
  therefore

# ENGLISH–GREEK VOCABULARY

## A

Abide, μένω, ἐπιμένω
After these things, μετὰ ταῦτα
Am, εἰμί
Am able, δύναμαι
Am about (to do something).
  μέλλω
And, καί
Angel, ἄγγελος
All, πᾶς, ὅλος
Announce, κηρύσσω
Answer, ἀποκρίνομαι
Apostle, ἀπόστολος
Appoint, καθίστημι
Ask (a question), ἐρωτάω

## B

Bad, κακός
Baptize, βαπτίζω
Bear witness, μαρτυρέω
Because (conj.), ὅτι
Become, γίνομαι
Before, πρό with abl.
Beget, γεννάω
Beginning, ἀρχή
Behold, βλέπω
Believe, πιστεύω
Blind (adj.), τυφλός
Blind (verb), τυφλόω
Boat, πλοῖον
Bread, ἄρτος
Brother, ἀδελφός

But, ἀλλά
Buy, ἀγοράζω
By (denoting agent), ὑπό with
  abl.

## C

Call, καλέω
Came to pass, ἐγένετο
Care, it is a, μέλει
Cast out, ἐκβάλλω
Cease, παύομαι
Certain (indef.), τις, τι
Child, τέκνον; little child,
  παιδίον
Christ, Χριστός
Church, ἐκκλησία
Come, ἔρχομαι
Commandment, ἐντολή
Commend, συνίστημι
Concerning, περί with gen.
Covenant, διαθήκη
Crowd, ὄχλος
Crucify, σταυρόω

## D

Darkness, σκοτία, σκότος
Daughter, θυγάτηρ
Day, ἡμέρα
Dead, νεκρός
Defile, κοινόω
Demon, δαιμόνιον
Depart, ἀπέρχομαι
Destroy, καταλύω

Devil, διάβολος
Die, ἀποθνήσκω
Disciple, μαθητής
Do, ποιέω

## E

Eat, ἐσθίω
Eat up, κατεσθίω
Enter, εἰσέρχομαι
Eternal, αἰώνιος
Every, πᾶς
Evil, κακός
Eye, ὀφθαλμός

## F

Face, πρόσωπον
Faith, πίστις
Faithful, πιστός
Father, πατήρ
Fear, φοβέομαι
Find, εὑρίσκω
First, πρῶτος
Follow, ἀκολουθέω
Foot, πούς
For (conj.), γάρ
Forever, εἰς τὸν αἰῶνα, εἰς
    τοὺς αἰῶνας
Forgive, ἀφίημι
Friend, φίλος
From, ἀπό with abl., παρά with
    abl.
Fulfill, πληρόω

## G

Garment, ἱμάτιον
Give, δίδωμι
Glorify, δοξάζω
Glory, δόξα

Go, βαίνω, ἔρχομαι
Go away, ἀπέρχομαι
Go to, προσέρχομαι
God, Θεός
Good, ἀγαθός, καλός
Gospel, εὐαγγέλιον
Grace, χάρις
Great, μέγας
Guard, φυλάσσω

## H

Hand, χείρ
Hate, μισέω
Have, ἔχω
He (in the oblique cases), αὐτός
He himself (intensive), αὐτός
Heal, θεραπεύω
Hear, ἀκούω
Heart, καρδία
Heaven, οὐρανός
Himself, herself (reflexive),
    ἑαυτοῦ, ἑαυτῆς
Holy, ἅγιος
Hope, ἐλπίς
Hope (verb), ἐλπίζω
Hour, ὥρα
House, οἶκος, οἰκία
How, πῶς

## I

I, ἐγώ
If, εἰ with the ind., ἐάν with the
    subj.
In, ἐν with loc.
In order that, ἵνα with subj.
Into, εἰς with acc.
It (in oblique cases), αὐτό
It itself (intensive), αὐτό
Itself (reflexive), ἑαυτοῦ

## J

Joy, χαρά
Judge, κρίνω
Judgment, κρίσις
Justify, δικαιόω

## K

Keep, τηρέω
Kill, ἀποκτείνω
King, βασιλεύς
Kingdom, βασιλεία
Know, γινώσκω, οἶδα

## L

Last, ἔσχατος
Law, νόμος
Lawful, is, ἔξεστι
Lay, τίθημι
Lay down, τίθημι
Lead, ἄγω
Life, ζωή
Light, φῶς
Look, βλέπω
Look up, ἀναβλέπω
Lord, κύριος
Love, ἀγάπη
Love (verb), ἀγαπάω

## M

Make, ποιέω
Man, ἄνθρωπος
Manifest, make, φανερόω
Many, πολύς
Marvel, θαυμάζω
Master, κύριος
Mercy, ἔλεος
Month, στόμα

Mother, μήτηρ
Multitude, πλῆθος
Myself (reflexive, in oblique cases), ἐμαυτοῦ, -ῆς.
Mystery, μυστήριον

## N

Name, ὄνομα
Nation, ἔθνος
Necessary, is, δεῖ
New, καινός, νέος
Night, νύξ
No one, οὐδείς
Not, οὐ, οὐκ, οὐχ; μή with subj., inf., and partic.
Nothing, οὐδέν
Now, νῦν

## O

Obtain, ἔχω
On, ἐν with loc., ἐπί with loc.
One another, ἀλλήλων
Only begotten, μονογενής
Other, ἄλλος
Out of, ἐκ with abl.

## P

Parable, παραβολή
Part, μέρος
Paul, Παῦλος
Peace, εἰρήνη
People, λαός
Persuade, πείθω
Place, τόπος
Place upon, ἐπιτίθημι
Power (authority), ἐξουσία
Power, δύναμις
Preach, κηρύσσω, εὐαγγελίζω

Priest, ἱερεύς
Proclaim, κηρύσσω
Promise, ἐπαγγελία
Prophet, προφήτης
Pursue, διώκω

## Q

Quickly, ταχέως, τάχα

## R

Raise, ἐγείρω
Rather, μᾶλλον
Receive, λαμβάνω
Remain, μένω
Righteous, δίκαιος
Righteousness, δικαιοσύνη
Ruler, ἄρχων

## S

Sabbath, σάββατον
Salute, ἀσπάζομαι
Same, αὐτός *with the article*
Sanctify, ἁγιάζω
Save, σώζω
Saviour, σωτήρ
Scribe, γραμματεύς
Scripture, γραφή
Sea, θάλασσα
See, βλέπω
Seed, σπέρμα
Seek, ζητέω
Send, πέμπω, στέλλω
Send forth, ἀποστέλλω
Servant, δοῦλος
Serve, διακονέω, δουλεύω
Shake, σαλεύω
She (*in the oblique cases*), αὐτός

She herself (*intensive*), αὐτός
Sheep, πρόβατον
Shepherd, ποιμήν
Sin, ἁμαρτία
So that, ὥστε
Son, υἱός
Soul, ψυχή
Sow, σπείρω
Speak, λέγω, λαλέω
Spirit, πνεῦμα
Stand, ἵστημι
Stone, λίθος
Strong, ἰσχυρός
Sword, μάχαιρα
Synagogue, συναγωγή

## T

Take, λαμβάνω
Take away, αἴρω, ἀπαίρω
Take up, αἴρω
Teach, διδάσκω
Teacher, διδάσκαλος
Temple, ἱερόν
Testament, διαθήκη
Than, ἤ
That, ἐκεῖνος
The, ὁ, ἡ, τό
Thief, λῃστής
Third, τρίτος
This, οὗτος, αὕτη, τοῦτο
Thou, σύ
Throne, θρόνος
Through, διά *with genitive*
Throw, βάλλω
Thyself (*reflexive*), σεαυτοῦ, -ῆς
Touch, ἅπτομαι
Tribulation, θλῖψις
Truth, ἀλήθεια
Two, δύο

## U

Under, ὑπό *with acc.*

## V

Village, κώμη
Voice, φωνή

## W

Walk, περιπατέω
Wash, λούω, νίπτω
Way, ὁδός
We, ἡμεῖς
Well, καλῶς, εὖ
What, *see* Who
When, ὅταν, ὅτε
Where, ποῦ

Who, which, that, what (*relative*), ὅς, ἥ, ὅ
Who, which, what? (*interrog.*), τίς, τί
Whole, ὅλος
Why, τί
Will, θέλημα
Wisdom, σοφία
Wish, θέλω
Word, λόγος, ῥῆμα
Work, ἔργον
World, κόσμος
Worthy, ἄξιος
Write, γράφω

## Y

You (*sing.*), σύ
You (*plu.*), ὑμεῖς